SHOTGUNNING
TRENDS IN TRANSITION

SHOTGUNNING
TRENDS IN TRANSITION

Don Zutz

Wolfe Publishing Company
6471 Airpark Drive
Prescott, Arizona 86301

All rights reserved. No part of this book may be used or reproduced in any manner whatsoever without prior written permission from the publisher except by a reviewer who wishes to quote brief passages in connection with a review.

Queries regarding rights and permissions should be addressed to Wolfe Publishing Co., 6471 Airpark Drive, Prescott, AZ 86301

ISBN: 0-935632-86-7
Zutz, Don
Shotgunning Trends in Transition
Copyright © by Wolfe Publishing Company, 1989

Manufactured in the United States of America

Book Design: Mark Harris
Editor: Holly McLean-Aldis

Contents

Preface v

Part 1 THE GUNS 1

  1 The Short Barrel Syndrome: Several Inches Too Far 3
  2 Does the Side-by-Side Deserve Another Day? 17
  3 The Over/Under Revolution: Diamonds in the Rough 29
  4 The Outmoded Pumpgun 47
  5 Modern Autoloaders: The Closest Thing to Perfection 63
  6 Gun Collecting Facts and Fallacies: A Personal View 83
  7 Modified Choke — Myth and Confusion 99

Part 2 THE LOADS 111

  8 Our Sophisticated Shotshells 113
  9 Exploding Some Ballistics Myths 135
 10 A Flame Still Flickering: The 16 Gauge 149
 11 Barrels of Fun 155
 12 The Steel Shot Solution: The "Rule of Two" 175

Part 3 THE GAMES 191

 13 Sporting Clays: Is It Really a Hunter's Game? 193
 14 Registered Skeet: Some Call It "Modern" 207
 15 Trapshooting: The Old Grey Mare 225
 16 The International Games Get Tougher 243
 17 The Best Game of All: Hunters' Skeet 249

Part 4 THE GUNNER 253

 18 Advanced Concepts in Sports Vision and Sports Optics 255
 19 Sports Psychology Comes to Shotgunning 267
 20 Can We Cure a Flinch with Amino Acids? 277
 21 Changes and Refinements in Wingshooting Techniques 287
 22 New Traditions: The Changing Nature of Hunting
     and Gunmaking 305

Preface

IT IS ironic that the late Bob Nichols' rambling and disjointed opus, *The Shotgunner*, appeared at a time when transitional forces were about to explode. The year was 1949, and practically everything going on in the decision-making board rooms and engineering offices of American gunmakers was to usher in changes that would create a totally new shotgunner. With the exceptions that shot charges still scatter and moving targets still must be led, we have little in common with the equipment and concepts of Nichols' book. That book can be viewed as a period piece, a sharp line delineating one era from another.

For example, as Nichols' *Shotgunner* was leaving the bindery, post-World War II inflation was escalating. Remington, ahead of the game, was busy introducing the ultra-streamline Model 11-48 autoloader, with the famous Model 870 only one year away. This pair of repeaters from Ilion not only had a lasting impact on the cosmetics of modern shotgun designs, but they symbolized another era in gunmaking, one that sought to hold down production and assembly costs while still providing a reliable, reasonably priced gun with mass appeal.

Moreover, while Nichols typed his manuscript, the great names in American doubles were fading rapidly. He could write of Parkers, L. C. Smiths, A. H. Foxes and the like, but another decade would find those side-by-sides missing from dealers' racks. However, the buying public didn't complain; they bought pumpguns and autoloaders, along with some bolt-actioned smoothbores.

Although Nichols still could praise the game of skeet as a place to learn gun-handling skills, the National Skeet Shooting Association soon thereafter made the game terribly easy by instituting a rule change which permitted a fully mounted gun in close-range skeet, as in trapshooting. Thus, Nichols' writing left off where the new age and vast majority of current shotgunners began.

With this book, I hope to update American shotgunning from those post-World War II transitional years to the high-tech present. There is much to discuss, not only in the way of guns and loads, but also in concepts, techniques, engineering,

SHOTGUNNING TRENDS IN TRANSITION

and both personal and equipment performance. Indeed, the whole fabric of shotgunning has been altered, in some instances radically so. We now shoot steel pellets, whereas Nichols and his predecessors knew only lead shot in less-than-magnum loads. The nature of hunting has changed drastically in many areas and subtly in others. Commercial hunting preserves, once frowned upon, have become respected institutions. Ballistics theories and shotgun performance notions concocted by old-time "experts" have been put to scientific tests and knocked into the proverbial cocked hat. New powders and the plastic revolution in shotshells have made shotshells much more efficient than any Nichols ever fired. That efficiency has made shorter barrels more effective. Likewise, the clay target games have changed and expanded. Games such as Starshot and Sporting Clays are upon us. And, finally, shooting techniques have been refined by the application of sports psychology and sports vision principles.

In short, then, the wingshot's world has not only changed since Bob Nichols penned *The Shotgunner* in 1949 (a time when I was just out of grade school and beginning to take the smoothbore seriously), but it has become significantly more sophisticated. Therefore, if you'll tramp through these chapters with me, we will attempt to hunt up the major changes and apply some reason to the last 40 years or so of shotgunning progress.

D. Z.
Sheboygan, Wisconsin
1988

The title page from Bob Nichols' *The Shotgunner*, which appropriately summarized shotgunning during the first half of the twentieth century.

PART 1
THE GUNS

Chapter 1

The Short Barrel Syndrome: Several Inches Too Far

WE LIKE TO think of the twentieth century as a modern era, but established concepts do not change as quickly as one can take down last year's calendar to hang another. Notions linger. And when the twentieth century arrived, it was still commonly maintained that a shotgun's barrel length should be 40 times its bore diameter. For a 12 gauge with its nominal .729-inch bore diameter, that meant 29.16 inches. That helps to explain why the British, who conjured up the rule of thumb, were obsessed with barrels of 30 inches or so for their famous handmade game guns and waterfowling pieces, plus the live pigeon guns that were becoming fashionable among competitive wingshots. It also explains why so many early American-made shotguns invariably had long barrels, because most, if not all, American shotgun makers imported their Damascus barrels from Belgium and England, while fluid steel tubes came from Germany. Thus, despite the transition from black powder to semi-smokeless and smokeless powders that was then occurring, the European and British barrelsmiths were locked into a carry-over concept which had taken on the proportions of a staunch tradition.

In reality, of course, the 29 or 30-inch barrel isn't all bad. With the slow burning properties of black powder, said length was a good compromise between ballistics efficiency and overall gun balance for responsive handling. The classic British game guns actually are delightful pieces, despite barrels of 29 to 30 inches, because they invariably were made very light.

In *The Gun and Its Development*, W. W. Greener espoused another rule of thumb which set the shotgun's weight at 96 times the shot charge. With the one-ounce load often favored by the British, this rule suggested a 6-pound gun, and many British doubles do scale 6 to 6½ pounds although being 12 gauge with 30-inch barrels. For 1⅛-ounce shot charges, the rule indicates a 6¾-pound gun weight, which is actually about as heavy as a bona fide game gun will get in 12 gauge.

SHOTGUNNING TRENDS IN TRANSITION

To create the dynamic responsiveness of a true game gun, the gun's basic halfweight is located between the shooter's hands, and the barrels are contoured so that their weight balances with that of the buttstock. Thus, there is equal weight fore and aft of the gripping positions. This allows the gun to pivot easily about its midpoint for fast, smooth, almost effortless handling, accurate pointing and controllable swing. Indeed, although a hurried glance at a 30-inch-barreled British game gun might not indicate it, such a lengthy gun has better handling qualities than repeating guns and thicker-walled doubles with shorter barrels.

But traditions and traditionalists gradually loosen up, and the fundamental trend has been toward constantly shorter shotgun barrels. Even Greener backed off a little, writing that, "In practice, as good results are obtained with sporting loads if the length of the barrel is slightly less than the theoretic maximum..." and that, "barrels of 28 inches seldom fail to give complete satisfaction...."

Greener's acceptance of *slightly* shorter barrels didn't cause a revolution, of course, but it did justify the building of what I believe to be the most responsive yet disciplined shotgun of all time, the British 12-gauge game gun with 28-inch barrels. Were it not for the mandated use of steel shot, I believe I would be using that type of sporting arm for everything from geese to woodcock, skeet, Sporting Clays and hand trap behind Uncle Gus' barn. But, alas, the thin-barreled game gun isn't made for steel shot. Even if the bore pressures were safe, there always would be the potential for barrel separation as steel shot charges ram into the choke constrictions and produce ring bulging and/or choke migration to the outside barrel diameter. Isn't it sad that just as a man can afford one of the true niceties of his life, the fates conspire against him!

An interesting thing about the steady abbreviation of shotgun barrels is that in order to reach the gunmakers' stated purpose of greasing an uplander's gun handling speed, the center of balance was brought backward on formerly muzzle-heavy repeaters and heavily barreled doubles. This retraction of the balance point merely apes the between-the-hands weight condition of a British game gun. In other words, we've gone full cycle, thus subtly admitting that the British game gun concept wasn't so wrong after all. Perhaps British influence on American shotgunning really isn't over despite our venture into pumpguns, autoloaders and muzzle-heavy doubles.

The main reason why radically short shotgun barrels of 21 to 22 inches are considered relatively new these days is because they are being put on the most popular repeaters for sporting use, and, suddenly being accepted as legitimate novelties, have extensive sales appeal. The stumpy shotgun's time has come.

It wasn't always thus, of course, although the utility of short-barreled scatterguns was noted most enthusiastically by Bob Nichols in 1949 when he opined in *The Shotgunner* that, "Possibly the deadliest weapon we could have in our hands today, for short-range thicket and woodland gunning on woodcock, quail, and grouse,

THE SHORT BARREL SYNDROME: SEVERAL INCHES TOO FAR

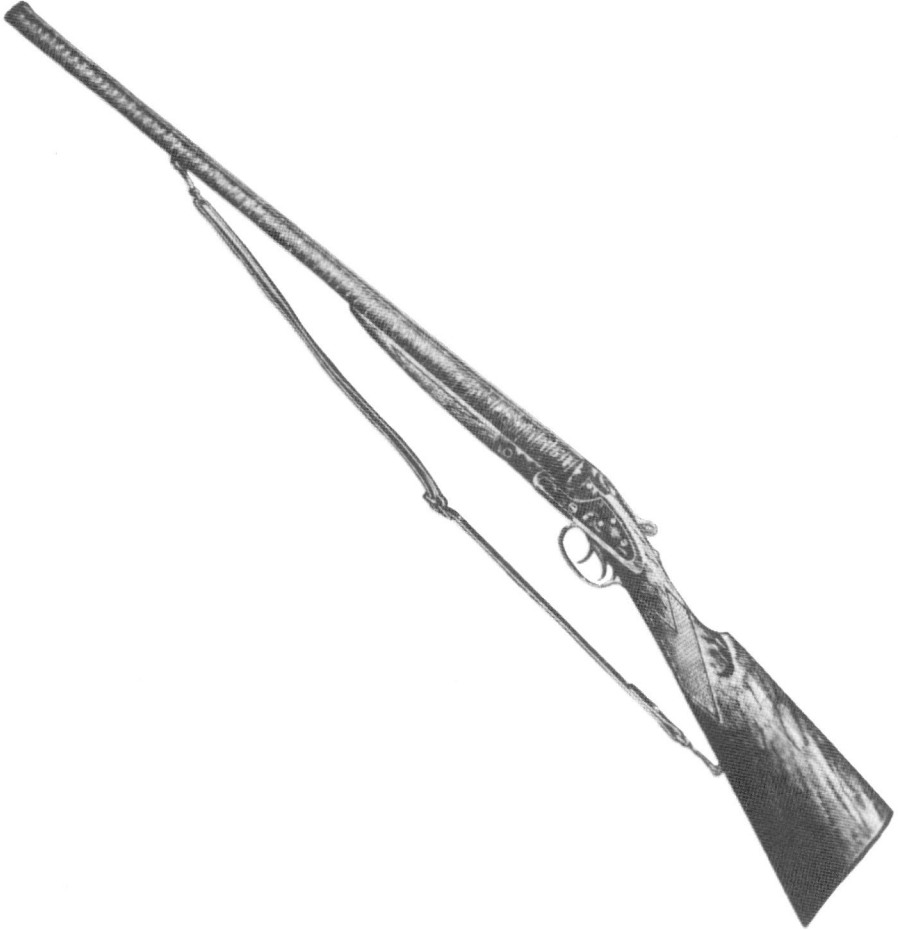

Americans have always had an interest in short-barreled brush guns like the old Baker brush gun shown above. The author believes the recent trend toward ultra-short barrels of 20 to 22 inches may have gone several inches too far.

would be the old Model 97 Winchester pumpgun with 20-inch 'riot' barrel...." Obviously, not many bird hunters followed Nichols' advice at the time, undoubtedly because the Model 97 was being outdated by smoother, more streamlined repeaters, and because it looked ugly and was equated with the Capone gangsterism that ran rampant barely a decade earlier. Moreover, sportsmen who were brought up to respect the supposed hard-hitting power of a Long Tom invariably questioned the ballistics of such diminished barrels. Thus, social, streamlining and traditional factors retarded the concept.

I must confess that, as an embryonic teenage gun nut in the 1940s, I saw only one Model 97 riot gun afield, and that was in the hands of a grand old hound man and cottontail rabbit hunter. The gun had lost most of its finish and reputedly had tumbled "more cottontails than you'll ever see." Still I sneered, not at the potential utility of the gun but at its lack of a sporting air. Gunmakers of the 1980s have vastly improved the appearance of such repeaters so that even staunch critics of the stumpy repeater are hard-pressed to declare them outright unsightly. They may lack the lean elegance of a classic game gun, but they no longer look like something out of the Prohibition era or a jailer's office. Guns like the Remington Model 1100 and Model 870 in their "Special Field" mode, along with the Browning B-80 and BPS in the "Upland Special" category, actually can be eye-catching and appealing as bobbed repeaters go. On an overall basis, this gives them a length of 41 to 42 inches, which is just a tad shorter than most 26-inch-barreled doubles and roughly the equivalent of Robert Churchill's once-controversial 25-inch-barreled side-by-side, the XXV.

Unfortunately, some makers of double-barreled shotguns have followed suit and fitted their designs into this stumpy category by lopping barrels back to 24 inches. The amputations may generate some added sales, but in my opinion it is carrying things too far. Not only does a 24-inch-barreled double lose some of its aesthetics, but it also sacrifices discipline, smoothness of swing, and follow-through momentum. Churchill's XXV is as short as a double need be bobbed. Anything shorter in a double almost automatically becomes whippy and doesn't contribute anything to the swing. Such guns are mainly fast-starting "poke" guns, leaving much to be desired when it comes to properly executed swings as the range lengthens. And this, again in my opinion, is not only a weakness in the breed, but is a syndrome in American wingshooting. For whatever reason, American upland hunters have become unduly obsessed with fast-starting guns that emphasize the beginning of action to the occlusion of swing smoothness and positive follow-through. Time and again we hear hunters croon over the way a certain sawed-off, lightweight 20 gauge comes up like lightning. "Man, what a grouse gun!" they exclaim. "You can really get on 'em with a gun like that!"

If one thinks in terms of a total swing technique rather than a simple poke or snap shot, however, there's more to it than just the starting thrust. I can't help wondering if, in our sudden acceptance of radically short shotgun barrels and in

THE SHORT BARREL SYNDROME: SEVERAL INCHES TOO FAR

An 870 "Special Field" pokes at a rising woodcock. For that type of snap shooting, they work out nicely for some hunters, but you'll never see them in the hands of serious tournament skeetmen!

SHOTGUNNING TRENDS IN TRANSITION

our manufacturers' attempts to be novel, we haven't gone a few inches too far! The gun that starts quickly doesn't always finish like a winner. Back in the 1960s, for example, I bought a Franchi over/under that had 24-inch barrels bored cylinder below and improved cylinder on top. The gun had an alloy receiver and started like an Olympic sprinter. When a bird flushed, that Franchi popped up like finished toast; and if the shot were at a close-flushing woodcock or ruffed grouse in thick cover, where I tried a snap shot rather than a full swing, it worked nicely. But when that same gun was put to the test on more distant crossing birds and skeet, it died. There wasn't enough barrel inertia to convert into momentum for smoothness and follow-through. If the shooter's technique was not perfect, missing was inevitable. At the time I was a serious skeet shooter and could break 100 straight, and with other guns I managed to win International style events. But with the Franchi 24-inch O/U, I had difficulty breaking more than 90 percent. All the gun contributed was an explosive start, which in overall wing-gunning isn't enough.

If you take a close look at the clay target games of skeet and Sporting Clays, you'll find no serious competitor using the ultra-short barrels. Even Olympic skeet shooters who must start from a low-gun position on targets emerging at roughly 100 mph employ longer, smoother-stroking barrels. On an over/under, the typical winning skeetman uses 28-inch barrels. The British, who are far ahead of us in their understanding of Sporting Clays, opt for O/Us with barrels of 27 to 28 inches, and some deadly serious shots have been trying 30-inch-barreled over/unders for Sporting. On autoloaders, a 26-inch barrel is the shortest that is truly popular for 12-gauge skeet or Sporting. Why don't these clay target shooters, whose birds spring off the trap faster than any upland bird has ever flushed, switch to the ultra-short barrels of 21 to 24 inches? Because the stubby tubes don't deliver. Moreover, advanced shotgunners have learned the fallacy of overemphasizing the start in wingshooting, and instead they concentrate on guns that finish smoothly by lending momentum to the final part of the equation. Thus, the American obsession with "getting on 'em quickly" may be fine under certain field conditions, but it isn't accepted broadly by knowledgeable all-around shots. The stumpy smoothbore is mainly a poke-and-hope piece for highly specialized use.

Within its specialty, the ultra-short-barreled shotgun can be magic. When Remington introduced the Special Field guns, I had a 12-gauge with improved cylinder choke for two seasons. With it, I shot a lot of woodcock and never missed one, and I never threw in a second shot. That Special Field raced to the target and had it centered as briskly as any side-by-side or over/under I've ever owned, including a peppy 24-gauge Belgium double that I periodically toted through the alders when I could get ammunition for it.

But the stubby stuff can lose its magic, too. Although I gave the same Special Field ample opportunity on grouse, pheasants and skeet, it never scored the same. This is not a rap against the Model 1100 as my favorite skeet gun is a Model 1100 with 26-inch skeet barrel. I happened to tie a club's Sporting Clays course record

THE SHORT BARREL SYNDROME: SEVERAL INCHES TOO FAR

The 20-gauge Remington "Special Field" snaps off a quick pattern in cover. Although fast-starting, guns this short contribute little, if anything, to a smooth swing and positive follow-through.

SHOTGUNNING TRENDS IN TRANSITION

Remington's straight-gripped Model 1100 Special Field with its 21-inch barrel ran two perfect seasons for the author on woodcock, but it left something to be desired on grouse and skeet.

with the Model 11-87 and 26-inch barrel, which is closely akin to the original Model 1100. Indeed, if I don't use a good double, I almost invariably pick a Model 1100 or Model 11-87 these days; therefore, I'm certainly not out to criticize the Model 1100. The simple, undisputed fact is that the 21-inch barrel doesn't swing like a 26 to 30-incher. True, the ultra-short repeater may be nearly as long as a 26-inch-barreled double, but, as noted previously, 26-inch-barreled doubles are also somewhat freakish in sophisticated skeet and Sporting Clays circles. Sophisticated wingshots find they like a bit more gun out front to help things along by glossing over human failures to be smooth and to follow through.

For the snap-shooting hunter of woodcock and cottontails, a riot-type of repeating shotgun may work out just fine. If a hunter isn't going to make a full swing anyway, why bother about gun dynamics that contribute to the middle and final segments of the move. I must not leave this subject without pointing out that hunters who let themselves become obsessed with the promise of blazing starts with short, lightweight guns are only deluding themselves into believing that the start of a shotgunning move is overpoweringly important. There's a lot more to sound, all-around wingshooting than a jumpy gun mount and a hastily launched pattern.

My feeling is that just a few more inches of barrel length would add to the versatility of short-barreled repeaters. Rather than the 21 to 22-inch novelties, a 24-inch barrel should enhance the swing. At one time, I had a 24-inch Poly-Choke-equipped barrel for the Remington 12-gauge Model 1100, and I *know* I used it more effectively for all-around upland shooting than I did the 21-inch Special Field. Just a little extra barrel length steadies the swing. Moreover, I can't agree with the idea that the shortest barrels handle better in the brush. My Merkel has $28^{5}/_{8}$-inch barrels, and in all the seasons I've used it for Wisconsin woodcock and ruffed grouse I can't remember more than a couple of instances when the muzzles got hung up. More often, vines or branches grab onto one's hands or arms, which has nothing to do with gun length. Nor do I believe I ever missed a chance at a grouse while hunting with that 24-inch Model 1100 barrel. Thus, if I were pressing computer buttons at a gun shop, I would punch up some 24-inch repeater barrels to bring the pumps and autoloaders closer to the overall length of 28-inch over/unders. In double shotgun designs, I would program the machinery for some 27-inch barrels instead of lopping them shorter than 26 inches. I've always felt that, because American-inspired doubles had heavier barrels than classic British game guns, 27 inches would be a compromise between steadiness and snappiness. The doubles with 24 to 26-inch tubes, on the other hand, can be flighty.

Ballistically speaking, the radically short shotgun barrels now in vogue can be used in the uplands without any fear of weak hits with most, but *not* all, modern shotshells. The main caveat involves the more recent "lite" target loads that have come along to lower the recoil level of 12-gauge skeet and trap guns. These loads tend to have powder charges below the $2^{3}/_{4}$ drams equivalent level for reduced chamber pressures and, in turn, variously lower velocities. Some also employ slower burning powders than normal for factory target loads in an effort to generate

SHOTGUNNING TRENDS IN TRANSITION

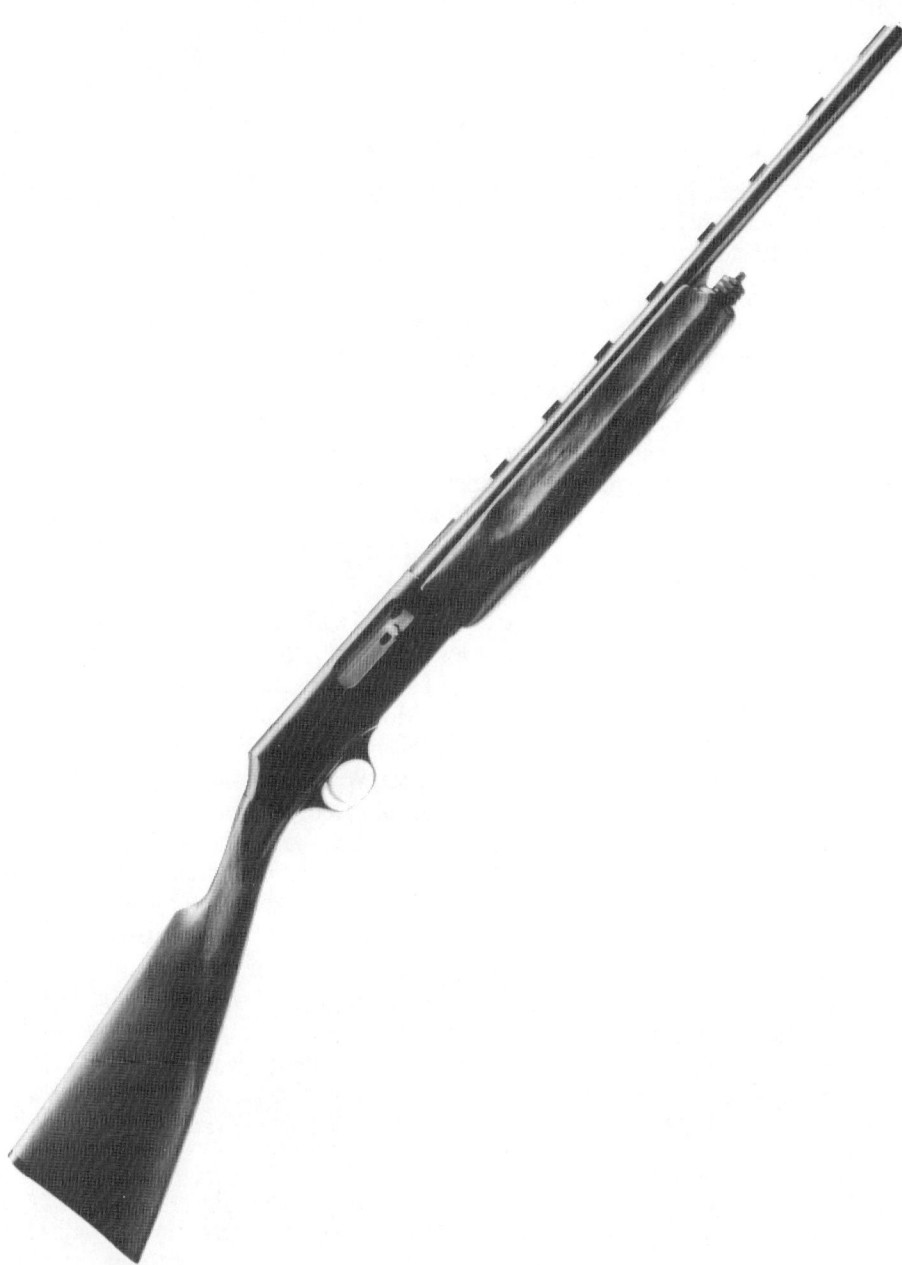

Browning's stumpy Model B-80 Upland Special competes with Remington's Special Field, but it tends to die from lack of forward weight. It is a good poke gun, however, if you prefer poking to swinging. *Dropped from 1990 catalog.*

THE SHORT BARREL SYNDROME: SEVERAL INCHES TOO FAR

The author favors more barrel length to smooth the swing and help with a positive follow-through. The Merkel has 28⅝-inch barrels, scales a tad under 6¾ pounds and seems to have done just fine in this covert.

a push-type recoil rather than a quicker, sharper "kick" sensation. Specifically, these are Federal's Extra-Lite® target loads, Winchester's Super-Lite® skeet and trap ammo, and ACTIV Industry's Ultra-Lite® concept, all of which are made in 12 gauge only with 1 1/8 ounces of Nos. 7 1/2, 8, 8 1/2 and 9 shot.

My chronographing of these lite loads through 30-inch barrels has produced velocities from 1,110 to 1,135 fps, and in 26-inch barrels they have dropped below 1,100 fps. With a combination of low chamber pressures and slower-rate powders, the lite target loads drop to pedestrian speeds from 21 to 24-inch barrels, and they may not cycle autoloading actions reliably. Thus, the new category of lite target loads can't be recommended for stumpy bird guns, mainly because they can be light hitters that don't possess the necessary shocking and penetrating power for clean kills.

Another dubious factory load for the radically short 12 gauge is the one-ounce target round. This is regulated for about 1,185 fps from a 30-inch test barrel, but it wilts as the barrel length shrinks and may turn out to be a crippler.

The lightest load advisable for the 12 gauge with 21 to 24-inch barrel is the three drams equivalent trap or skeet load with 1 1/8 ounces of shot. The industry standard for it is 1,200 fps from a 30-inch barrel, but many ammo makers increase that to 1,220 to 1,250 fps. I've chronographed them as high as 1,265 fps, which is why so many trapshooters get beat up by recoil. In a sawed-off kind of shotgun, however, the three drams equivalent target load tends to provide adequate impact on close to moderate-range upland game. I prefer No. 7 1/2 shot because it retains energy better than the smaller 8s, 8 1/2s and 9s.

I would steer clear of the 2 3/4 drams equivalent "light" (as opposed to "lite") target loads, as they are regulated for about 1,145 fps and, in my experience, shed too much velocity when launched from the radically short barrel.

In the 20-gauge shorties, my load selection would begin with the one-ounce and a minimum powder charge of 2 1/2 drams equivalent of powder. This is a mediocre round, capable of just 1,165 fps from a 26-inch barrel, but it handles close-range quail and woodcock. Far better is the one-ounce load with 2 3/4 drams equivalent of powder for 1,220 fps in a 26-inch test barrel, which generates more speed even from a 21 to 22-inch tube than does the 2 1/4 drams equivalent round. Again 7 1/2s are a good selection in the 2 3/4-drammers.

Of all the loads I have tested in the short shotguns (especially the 12 gauges), my favorite upland loading is the 3 1/4 dram equivalent field load with 1 1/8 ounces of shot for something like 1,255 fps from a 30-inch test barrel. It still records 1,200 fps or a bit better over my chronograph screens for good upland performances from the 21-inch Remington Special Field. The Remington "Premier" field loading of this type with copper-plated 7 1/2s cleanly dropped woodcock, grouse and pheasants.

THE SHORT BARREL SYNDROME: SEVERAL INCHES TOO FAR

Handloaders who use ultra-short bird guns will need to know which powders and concepts produce the best velocities. At one time, it was commonly held that powders with a fast burning rate were the best for short barrels, although most handloaders arrived at that assumption purely by logic. The faster a powder releases its energy, they reasoned, the better it will work in short barrels. After serious work with a chronograph, all sorts of powders and stubby shotguns, however, I find that popular logic and science don't always agree. Logic aside, experiments indicate that the fastest velocities come from short-barreled shotguns when handloads are given maximum or near-maximum charges of powders with intermediate or slow burning rates. This will be explained more thoroughly in Chapter 9. Suffice it to say here that heavy charges of intermediate or slow-rate shotshell powders stoked to maximum chamber pressures produce more gas than lighter charges of fast-rate powders. The more massive gas thrusts simply transfer more energy to the ejecta in a short travel than do the quicker-dropping gas levels of fast-rate propellants. The only problem with this finding, of course, is that heavy powder charges intensify the muzzle blast, and short-barreled shotguns can knock the appendages off the proverbial brass monkey. This, in fact, is one of my personal objections to radically short-barreled smoothbores: The muzzle blast is practically deafening!

Thus, between the concussion and inherently poke-type handling qualities of radically short bird guns, I must repeat that, in an attempt to market novel guns and to emphasize the fast-starting qualities of a fowling piece, we have probably gone a couple of inches too far. A pumpgun or semiautomatic with a 21 to 22-inch barrel may have the overall length of a 26-inch-barreled double, but the repeater's tube is still so short that annoying blast occurs. In all my years of using barrels of 25 inches or longer, I never once was aware of muzzle blast afield; however, when I began using 21 to 22-inchers I became cognizant of it from shot number one. Anything that would move the blast forward would be helpful, thank you.

Moreover, I have never seen a "typical" hunter shoot well with a stumpy shotgun. They score some birds, to be sure, but they miss copiously, too. Why? Because typical hunters have poorly developed techniques — most of them being jerky rather than smooth. Few of them have a positive follow-through, and the radically short shotguns don't assist one iota in smoothing out the stroke or lengthening it into a follow-through. Therefore, while the short shotguns sell and I don't blame any manufacturer for supplying them, let the wingshot beware! What catches one's eye as a novelty may not harbor all the qualities of a bird gun. Buy one if you must, to poke at woodcock, cottontails or bobwhite; there are niches which the short guns fit and in which I have used them with deadly results. But as range lengthens and the wingshot must use a complete swing rather than merely relying on a reflexive jab, a bit more gun would again be helpful, thank you.

Chapter 2

Does the Side-by-Side Deserve Another Day?

THERE HAVE always been American sportsmen whose allegiance lay with side-by-side shotguns, but, like the ocean's tide, the double's popularity passed through a major ebb and only now is it rising toward a high water mark. Using the turn of the century as a historic peg for the time when the stateside double's popularity began to run low, we can trace their rejection to two major factors: At the turn of the century pumpgun designs were being refined to deliver improved smoothness, and John M. Browning had harnessed the shotshell's energies, resulting in reliable autoloading performance.

By the 1930s, despite the Great Depression, repeaters were rapidly replacing side-by-sides, and the grand old names among American builders of break-action shotguns were financial failures. Through the entire first half of the twentieth century, gunmakers who specialized only in doubles either fell by the wayside or were absorbed by those who switched to repeaters. Ithaca Gun Company bought the Lefever outfit as early as 1915, Savage Arms Company acquired the A. H. Fox Gun Company in 1930, and Remington found itself with the prestigious-to-be Parker concern in 1934. Immediately following World War II, Marlin Firearms Company picked up the old L. C. Smith (Hunter Arms) business. But even those moves didn't bolster the double's popularity or ensure its longevity. By 1950, catalogs were practically devoid of side-by-sides. The names and guns that had been so prevalent 30 years earlier were dead and, for most practical purposes, buried, except for some collector appeal. Interestingly enough, even collectors didn't scurry after the foremost old Yankee doubles. Late in the 1960s I bought L. C. Smiths for less than $100 and some excellent Parkers for $200 apiece.

For at least a 20-year stretch after World War II, virtually no one sat on the beach to wait for the side-by-side's tide to rise. With the exception of a faithful few who bought Winchester Model 21s or British or European masterpieces, American hunters and clay target shooters remained quite content with pumpguns,

SHOTGUNNING TRENDS IN TRANSITION

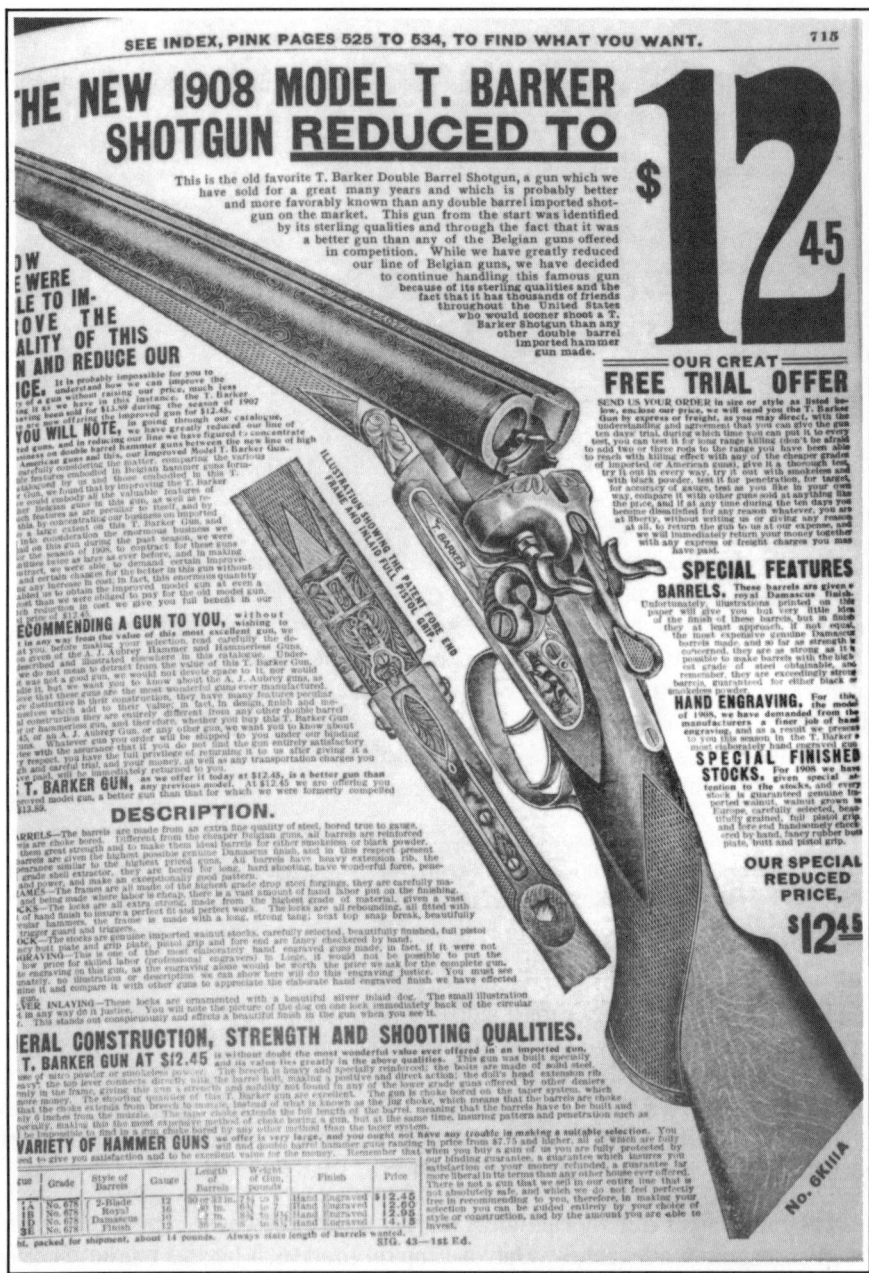

Despite twinges of nostalgia and currently high collectors' prices on old American doubles, a savvy shotgunner realizes that most Yankee-made doubles were less than equal to the British game guns. As illustrated by this page from an early Sears, Roebuck catalog, a tremendously high percentage of early American doubles were cheap, clubby and poorly balanced.

autoloaders and even some bolt-action smoothbores. They bagged game and, in skeet and trap, won tournaments and set long-run records without the side-by-sides. If shooters of that time had one collective question to ask, it might have been: "Who really needs a side-by-side?" Other than tradition-bound Britons and conservative box pigeon competitors, the answer seems to have been: No one! As Bob Nichols' *Shotgunner* reflects at midcentury: "there seem[ed] to be a steadily accelerating exodus from the field of first-grade double-gun manufacturers here in the United States...."

With the demise of side-by-sides as profitable items, American gunmakers switched their advertising heavily to repeaters. The deepest ebb in the dearth of publicity for doubles ran from about the mid-1930s to the late 1960s, during which time advertisements for side-by-sides virtually dried up in the pages of sporting journals. This lack of publicity may have accounted for much of the side-by-side's plight, for it is well-known today that extensive publicity and effective advertising are needed to impact a market and retain consumer interest. Suffice it to say here that when the public forgets something, it does a thorough job!

The tide began rising again for side-by-sides late in the 1960s when new products from, of all places, Japan received publicity. As another historic peg, the year 1966 marks Ithaca Gun Company's introduction of SKB side-by-sides. Almost immediately the sporting press ran articles about the return of the double. The reviews of Ithaca-SKB models 100 and 200 were excellent, as well they should have been, because the guns were exceptionally well-made for their price ranges.

Two years later, in 1968, Charles Daly announced a Japanese-made side-by-side known as the Empire Grade, which was a throwback to the former European guns that Daly once imported. This, too, was a nice gun in its price range, and again there were peppy magazine articles proclaiming better days ahead for the doubles.

That same year, Marlin surprised everyone by coming on-line with an upgraded model of the L. C. (Elsie) Smith sidelock field gun in both standard and deluxe grades. From what I have seen of those re-introduced Smiths, they gave more attention to fit and finish than any other American-made double at the time with the exception of Winchester's Model 21. Thus, in just two years, several new doubles were in the news — all of them greeted enthusiastically. Sportsmen began to talk about a return of the side-by-side.

The time wasn't exactly ripe for a roaring return, however. The public hadn't been conditioned adequately. Daly's Empire Grade fell off the market in 1971. Marlin's resurrected Elsie disappeared in 1973 after 2,539 had been manufactured. However, the SKB line continued steadily and eventually was expanded to include a Model 280 English-style gun with straight grip, 25-inch barrels, and semi-beavertail forend. At one point, SKB guns fell from the American market because of the company's poor marketing tactics, but they re-appeared in the late 1980s.

SHOTGUNNING TRENDS IN TRANSITION

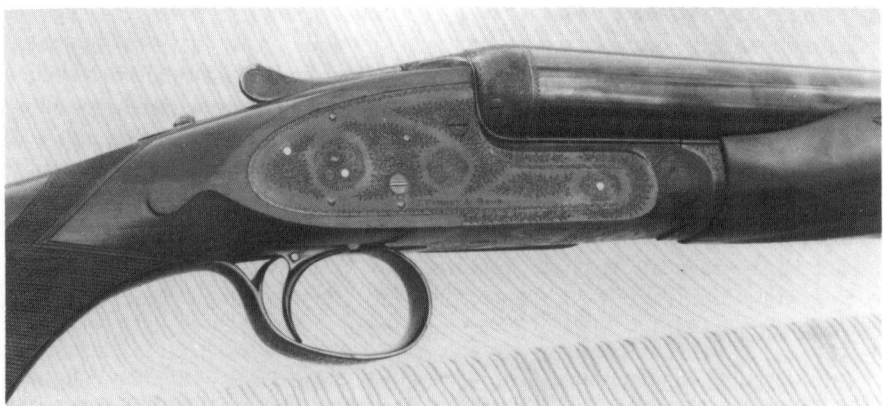

Considered the epitome of British game guns, this Purdey possesses the traditional engraving for its genus and species.

DOES THE SIDE-BY-SIDE DESERVE ANOTHER DAY?

What seems to have sparked the popularity of the side-by-sides was the introduction of Winchester's Model 23 and Browning's B-SS. Not only were these excellent guns within the lower price range, but more importantly they received considerable publicity. Once again the double was back in print; the public couldn't help but notice them. And as the 1980s rolled in, various books and new magazines for shotgunners solidified the side-by-side's role in wingshooting. Instead of looking askance at the side-by-side and shrugging it off as an "old double," people began to read about them and to understand their attributes. Gradually, it dawned on hunters that there was more to a shotgun than the number of shells it carried; books and magazine articles informed them about handling qualities, balance, dynamics and simplicity. Slowly, the side-by-side gained a fresh, new image. Its tide may still not be at flood stage, but the market has become brisk and interesting once more.

All of this activity causes a meditative sort of wingshot to wonder if the side-by-side deserves another day. After we've bagged so many ducks, geese, partridge, pheasants and quail with repeaters; after we've won so many clay target championships and set so many world records with pumps, autoloaders and over/unders — do we *really* need the side-by-side again? Didn't we give it a fair chance only to find it lacking? Why turn back the clock?

After having spent considerable time studying the history and development of shotguns and shotgunning, I tend to believe that the side-by-side does *indeed* deserve another day in America for one important reason: On an overall basis, our Yankee gunmakers didn't do it justice the first time around! As a secondary reason, most American hunters never used the technique perfected for the lively game gun by British wingshots. Perhaps this time we'll not only learn how to make a better double, but also how to use it!

Although we don't have to sell our souls to British shotgunning precepts, it is unfortunate that some stateside schools of thought are hostile toward any and all British approaches. For example, when Bob Hinman, author of *The Golden Age of Shotgunning*, writes that this early twentieth century period of repeater development was significant because "the dominant British influence in American shotgunning *at last* was at an end," [italics mine] one should ask whether that was for the better or the worse. The British weren't (and aren't) all wrong, especially insofar as field shooting is concerned. Their slender, straight-gripped game guns are lethal when used with the technique devised for them. Both the British game gun and the so-called "Churchill" technique are far more dynamic than the long, heavy-barreled guns and the draggy, "aim 'em" method employed by so many stateside hunters and Sporting Clays shooters.

From my point of view, the tragic thing about America's switch to pumpguns at the turn of the century is that it detracted from the development of finer stateside doubles. For although many American-made doubles are now cherished collectors' items, they gained those values primarily because of scarcity and rarity, *not*

SHOTGUNNING TRENDS IN TRANSITION

One of the best bargains ever offered to American hunters, and one that came close to the British concept, was the Browning B-SS Sidelock.

Two industry giants who attempted to upgrade the artistry in American shotguns were the late John Pachmayr (left) and Frank Pachmayr (right) (sons of the famous August Pachmayr). But decor alone doesn't make a double great, and American-designed and manufactured side-by-sides have not yet caught up with the dynamics of the fine British game guns.

because of their shooting qualities. I have hunted with three Parkers, a pair of Foxes, a trio of L. C. Smiths and a Lefever or two and not one of them handled like a true British game gun or Belgian copy thereof. American 12-gauge side-by-sides always have been heavier, topping 7 pounds with any conventional barrel length and tending noticeably toward a weight-forward condition. Doubles of this sort are simply not the ultimate as responsiveness goes; thus, a lot of America's most collectible doubles have draggy handling and swinging characteristics akin to those of repeaters.

My own discovery through the years has been that the only way one can approach the delightful handling qualities of a British double in an early American-made side-by-side is to select the 16 gauges. The 16s are not perfect replicas of classic game guns, of course, but at least they lop a pound or more off the gun's overall weight and, with 28-inch barrels, are reasonably responsive without being whippy. To heap unstinting praise upon the early American side-by-sides, then, is to display a total lack of savvy and discretion.

If American makers of side-by-sides hadn't been forced to switch into pump-guns for profits, it is possible that one or more of them eventually would have picked up on British sophistication. Perhaps more attention would have been given to weight distribution for enhanced dynamics; perhaps somebody would have incorporated the cast-off stock into an American double; perhaps our 12 gauges wouldn't have scaled a short ton; perhaps there would have been articulated front triggers; perhaps there would have been higher combs rather than the dogleg buttstock configurations that predominated; perhaps....

The point is that such refinements were never worked into early American doubles. Therefore, the supposedly "fine ol' American doubles" were sadly lacking in all those features which made the British game gun so great, so responsive, so natural pointing, and so extremely effective and efficient. While British wingshots stroked lithe 6¼ to 6½-pound 12 bores with delightful between-the-hands weight distribution, the Yankees cranked up muzzle-heavy 7½ to 8-pounders not realizing what they were missing, for those clubby, low-combed, weight-forward 7½ to 8-pounders are hardly akin to the snappy classics regardless of what early American name may be stamped on them! Nor are all doubles truly great just because, like the various editions of L. C. Smiths, Parkers, Foxes or Lefevers, they have engraving and gold splattered all over them. Artwork has never grassed a single bird or broken a clay target. Thus, what the stateside side-by-side needs is time to catch up, to be refined with features and qualities that jibe with and enhance a wingshot's natural pointing abilities.

And if the American double's qualities are to improve, so must the typical hunter's knowledge of technique. For the classic British doubles, which can be used so effectively for everything from pass shooting to rough (flushing bird) shooting and running hares, evolved through a process that matches form with function, and the function blends in with a very definite handling technique. It is based upon

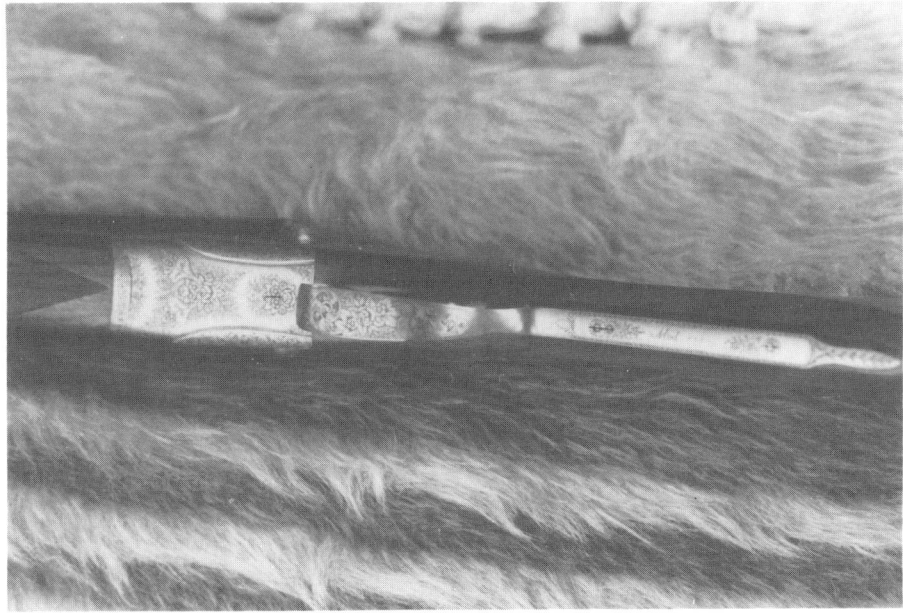

One of the niceties of a true, finely made game gun is the long, lower tang and cast-off. American gunmakers may have used the long tang on their side-by-sides, but cast was seldom, if ever, a feature.

the fast swing (overthrow) and optimum eye-hand coordination, whereas, unfortunately, the typical American hunters employ a self-taught, deliberate mounting move and a long, sustained, tracking swing that results in equally deliberate firing.

To get the most from a side-by-side, people who believe they love the horizontal gun must make an attempt to understand the wingshooting system upon which the gun is modeled. Using the dawdling, deliberate, tracking move with a gun styling that oozes speed and responsiveness is like hitching the winner of the Kentucky Derby to a buckboard: You simply don't make use of its full potential or specialized nature. Indeed, unless the correct technique is applied with responsive side-by-sides, hunters might as well lug 8-pound pumpguns with 30-inch barrels! The exact technique is popularly known as the British or the Churchill method, and it is detailed in Chapter 21. However, we may conclude that, although horizontal doubles are again in vogue among stateside shotgunners *and* manufacturers, much work remains to be done in refining the guns and the American hunters' use of them.

Hopefully, this time around both gunmakers and gunners will get their acts together. Despite their mystiques, overly inflated collectors' prices, and auld lang syne — no American gunmaker yet has turned out anything equivalent to the British classics or the leading Belgian copies thereof.

DOES THE SIDE-BY-SIDE DESERVE ANOTHER DAY?

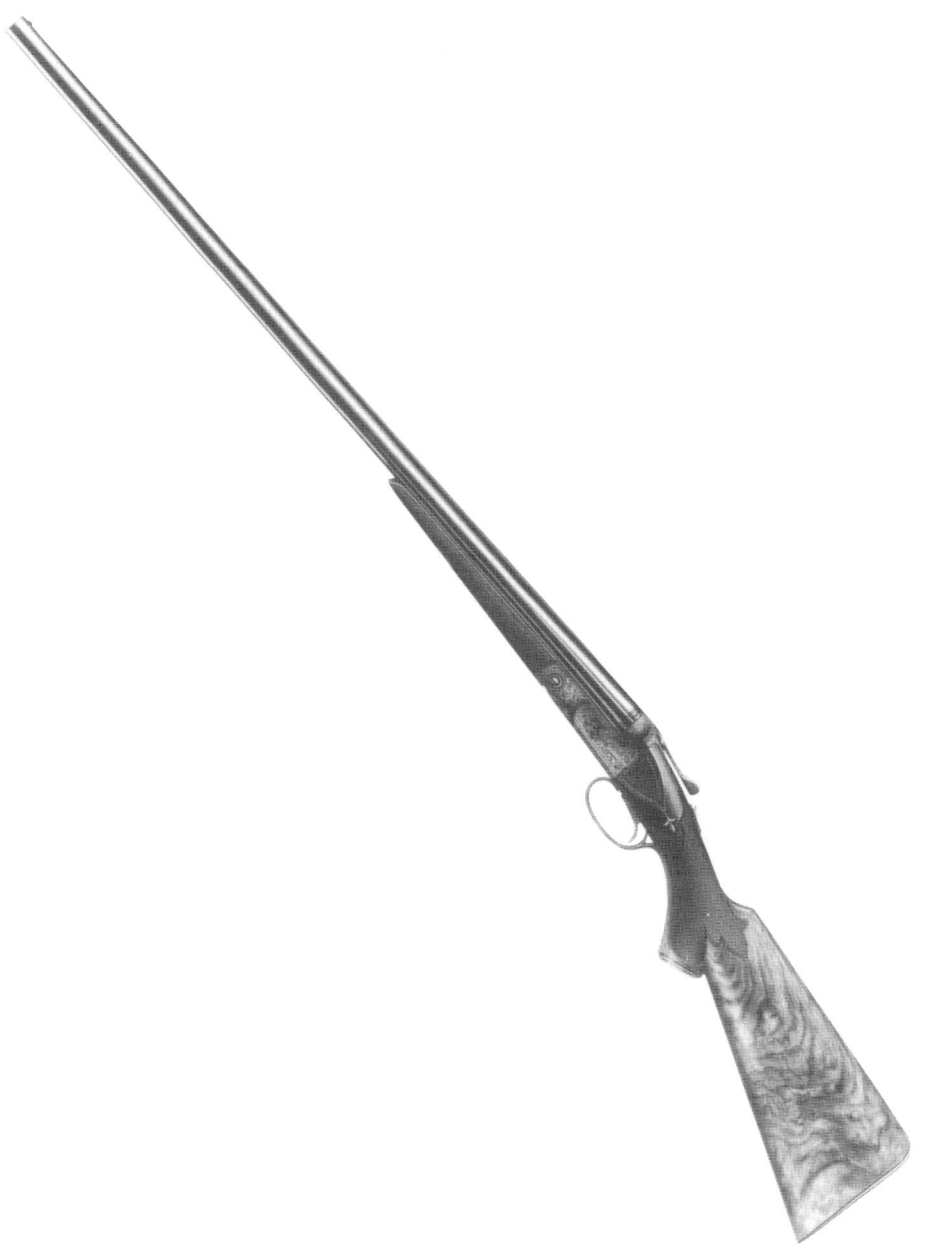

Remington's re-introduction of the Parker gun as a custom shop offering rekindles one's hopes that a truly fine stateside double may still be possible.

SHOTGUNNING TRENDS IN TRANSITION

Many American uplanders opt for the 20 gauge side-by-side (as did this quail hunter) simply because so many 12-gauge horizontal doubles marketed stateside have outrageously heavy barrel hang.

Chapter 3

The Over/Under Revolution: Diamonds in the Rough

WHEN I graduated from college in the mid-1950s, one of my first paychecks went into a Browning Belgian-made Superposed. The retail price was then about $265, but the stackbarrel had sat on the dealer's shelf too long and he gave it to me for $235. At the time, it was a deal. Nobody discounted Brownings in those days. (They still don't discount them. In fact, not even the Japanese-made Citoris are discounted. What manufacturers do is publish ridiculously high retail figures, then set up behind-the-scenes pricing so dealers continue to make profits despite actual selling prices at published dealer or distributor prices.)

Besides the fact that typical hunters had difficulty coming up with a spare $265 in those days, when many jobs still paid less than $2 an hour and post-war inflation was present, there were other reasons why the Superposed and other over/unders languished on local dealers' racks. One of the foremost reasons was that the United States had become a nation of pumpgunners, and those guns were still available for a mere pittance. Why would a weekend hunter spend $265 on an over/under when he could get as much game with a $75 trombone gun? No way!

Moreover, in many respects the over/under was still considered a relatively newfangled, unproved entity in the 1950s. Aside from some skeet and trap aficionados who had witnessed its brilliant performance on clays, few shotgunners saw any real advantages in it. To them, it was just another break-action double, and so what if it had a single sighting plane? Didn't their pumps and autoloaders also have that? Finally, it took the world a long time to accept the over/under's depth, which was hardly becoming in a world accustomed to seeing superbly trim Purdeys, Bosses, Holland & Hollands, Powells, and even L. C. Smiths and Parkers. Thus, the over/under had its share of obstacles to overcome.

Manufacturers who entered the over/under market in the first half of the twentieth century met with hunter indifference or disfavor. Both Savage and Marlin made less expensive O/Us prior to World War II, and both lines barely survived.

SHOTGUNNING TRENDS IN TRANSITION

The Savage Model 430 was a neat looking stackbarrel, in fact, and the Marlin Model 90 handled well, especially in 16 gauge. Remington's Model 32 won considerable silverware in skeet, along with some money in trap, but in the long run, hunters didn't go for any of them. As stated earlier, when hunters ignore a product concept, sales volume remains very low, thus the Savage line folded and didn't return after World War II. When Remington took a hard look at past sales volumes and future projections based on consumer demand, they unceremoniously dropped the Model 32. Eventually its manufacturing rights were sold to Krieghoff of West Germany, where it became known as the Krieghoff Model 32 and, more recently with a few minor changes, the K-80. The Marlin Model 90 hung on as the only stackbarrel stateside entry until it also floundered in 1958. Although the great Brownings definitely were considered prestigious guns, they didn't sell very briskly. Thus, as I was graduating from college just after midcentury, the over/under not only hadn't been "discovered" by typical hunters and weekend shooters, but it actually was hurting. Time was needed before the over/under would have an impact on the mass market.

The over/under's struggle is not well-documented. It must be interpolated because enthusiastic mention of the over/under often is conspicuous by its absence. Some writers were prejudiced against them; others, though of a more open mind, treated them in passing rather than in detail. The British especially rejected the "under-and-over" concept, as they termed it because the lower barrel of an over/under normally is fired first. Robert Churchill, whose book (*Game Shooting*) has had such a marked influence on wingshooting style, left the subject untouched in said tome.

Major Sir Gerald Burrard, writing *The Modern Shotgun* in the late 1950s for a 1960's publication, admitted the existence of over/unders, but he opined that they were mainly sales gimmicks and that the trade's "primary object [in the development of the under-and-over] was the search for something new." After a reasonable in-depth discussion of the under-and-over's mechanical and shooting advantages, Burrard concluded that he "doubt[ed] whether the benefit conferred by the narrow line of aim is so generally great as some enthusiastic admirers of the over and under gun would have us believe."

Another British torpedo was launched at the stackbarrel by respected gunmaker Charles Lancaster, whose book, *The Art of Shooting*, sold heavily from 1889 into the post-World War II era. I quote from the 11th edition as published in 1945: "For technical reasons these guns [over/unders] are more expensive to make than the side by side variety and have certainly suffered in popularity from the clumsy appearance and handling of certain makes, notably from abroad." Remarks like that hardly encouraged wingshots to try over/unders.

It remained for some American writers, but not all, to champion the over/under. In all my research, I find that the first enthusiastic mention of the over/under was made in 1939 by Bob Nichols' *Skeet and How to Shoot It*. Nichols prophesied that,

THE OVER/UNDER REVOLUTION: DIAMONDS IN THE ROUGH

"any type of shotgun which offers the sporting equivalent of the standard side-by-side double — and which also makes it possible for us to utilize the principle of single alignment with which we are so familiar — such a gun is bound to advance tremendously in popular acceptance."

Nichols was sticking his neck out a bit when he wrote those words, of course, for at that time the O/U was rock bottom in popularity. As he himself reported in *Skeet*, only 4.2 percent of the shooters at the 1938 National Skeet Championships used over/unders, whereas 67.1 percent shot autoloaders, 18.1 percent had pumpguns and the remaining 10.6 percent swung side-by-sides.

Another peppy endorsement of the over/under didn't arise until the 1950s when Colonel Charles Askins Jr., called it "The most exciting shotgun today..." in *The Shotgunner's Book*. Contrary to the British view, which continually was critical of the over/under's qualities, Askins found the stackbarrels "a joy to handle; a beautiful, vibrant over/under is truly a glamor piece!"

However, even at that date well into the second half of the twentieth century, Askins accurately observed that the over/under was still "virtually unknown to the average wingshot." I tend to agree. When I showed up at a local skeet field with that first Superposed, it was the only over/under in sight. Everyone wanted to paw it. How did it feel? How did it handle? How did it swing and point? How much did it cost? How could a mere teacher (albeit a gun-nut) afford it? Did it get game?

For roughly two years it was the only over/under fired on that field, but people did sit up and take notice when, in my first-ever round of skeet, I broke 22x25 from the old low-gun starting position.

It wasn't until the prosperity of the Soaring Sixties got under way that other over/unders began to appear at our skeet club. I mark that decade as the jumping-off point for the over/under's vault to fame and unbelievably widespread acceptance. In fact, my interpretation of the over/under's history suggests that it was economics, not shooting qualities, that triggered its rise. And Browning's constant advertising finally paid off, for the company had been running full-page ads religiously since the production of sporting arms began again after World War II. They stressed the Superposed as "the Aristocrat of shotguns," and following a prolonged bombardment of that salesmanship many hunters and shooters probably began to believe it. I guess I did, or why else would I lay down a month's teaching pay for a Grade I Superposed? It is another example of a company succeeding because it had the finances for staying power until a product caught on.

Thus, Burrard may well have been correct: Part of the over/under's attraction may have been its new and/or novel design, which shotgunners were willing to try once they had some discretionary coin.

SHOTGUNNING TRENDS IN TRANSITION

It seems likely that the over/under's vaunted shooting and scoring qualities weren't fully discovered until after the gun became popular in the 1960s. Except for Colonel Askins' in-depth chapter in *The Shotgunner's Book*, writers seldom elaborated on the over/under's strength. One of America's most popular gun writers was Jack O'Connor of *Outdoor Life*, and he basically ignored the over/under in favor of Winchester Model 21s. Moreover, O'Connor never was knowledgeable about tournament shooting, and he totally missed the features of a winning skeet, trap or box pigeon gun. If O'Connor had taken up the cause of the over/under, it might have caught on much sooner. Likewise, Bob Nichols' *Shotgunner* didn't pick up where his skeet shooting tome left off, and his emphasis on pumps and autoloaders certainly didn't advance the over/under's cause. Warren Page at *Field & Stream* was an astute shotgun man with an appreciation of the over/under's qualities, but by midcentury he was wrapped up in benchrest shooting, big game hunting, and the development of the 6mm rifle so that scatterguns tended to get short shrift in his columns. Thus, for want of expert publicity, the over/under struggled alone. To many hunters and shooters, it was just another double stood on its side with nothing special to recommend it. Except for stressing the single sighting plane, the gun media didn't educate the public about shotgun subtleties.

Over/under shotguns were helped along considerably by two events in the 1960s. First, the Charles Daly import business (Sloan's Hardware) began importing Japanese-made over/under that strongly resembled the Brownings but sold for a significantly lower price. This put a solid O/U in the price range of anyone who really wanted one. Moreover, the Daly proved to be a good value and it was mechanically innovative. Instead of utilizing a bottom-pivoted tumbler for the lower barrel, which can be inefficient, the Daly guns were designed with a top-pivoting hammer that swung downward to impact the lower striker, thereby increasing tumbler energy via a less restricted arc. It's unfortunate that current designers haven't picked up the concept. To my knowledge, the only weakness that appeared regularly in Daly O/Us was in the lower lock's mainspring, and that was easily exchanged for a more powerful coil. Thus, my interpretation of the over/under's history argues that the Charles Daly line of 1963 to about 1975 put the over/under front and center. Daly, like Browning, was willing to advertise broadly, but, alas, Daly apparently didn't have the staying power that Browning generated with its more extensive lines.

Winchester gave further impetus to the over/under by building a lower-priced line to compete with the Brownings and Dalys. Known as the Model 101, the Winchester guns were built in Japan through a joint venture called Olin-Kodensha. The 101 line had some problems initially. Triggers and inertia blocks gave timing problems, and ribs loosened, but eventually the line settled down. A major advantage was that it could put an over/under into one's hands for less than a Browning.

About the only other over/unders available in the sixties were the Krieghoff Model 32 (which wasn't being made nearly as well then as it is today under the

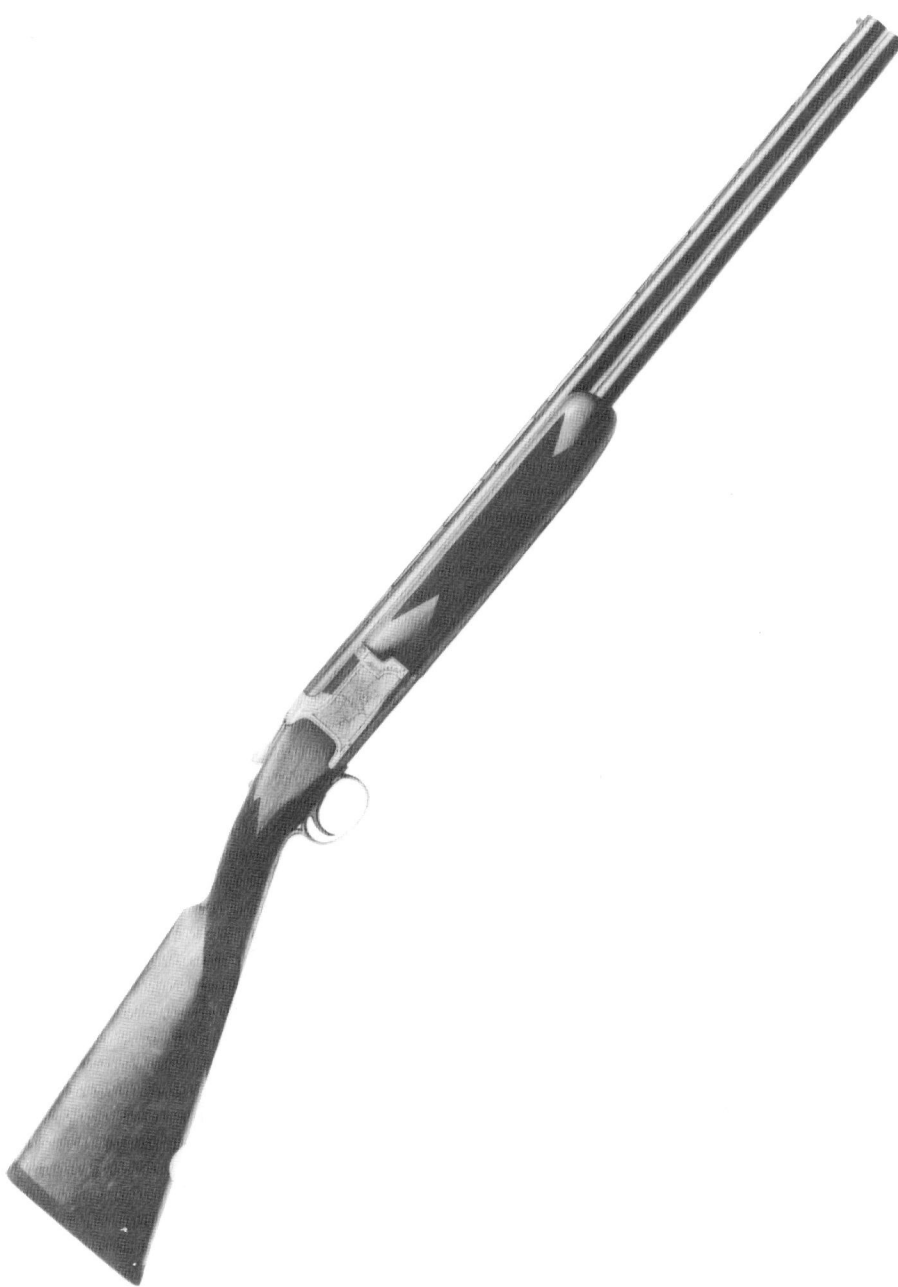

For a number of years, Winchester kept over/under fans happy with new commemorative versions of the Model 101. The 20-gauge Grand European Featherweight was a delightful piece compared to many muzzle-heavy American-style stackbarrels.

K-80 style) and a $150 Valmet from Finland which anyone could buy through the mail. For several seasons, I used such a Valmet as a back-up and knockabout. It handled quite well despite its reasonable price, but whenever it was shot with magnum loads, it invariably doubled! In general, neither of these guns had the impact that the Charles Daly Japanese-made guns had in winning typical shooters and hunters to the over/under fold.

Interestingly, the Daly and Winchester over/unders never found favor among champion skeet and trapshooters. The guns were apparently somewhat light for ultra-serious tournament shooting. The Krieghoff Model 32 did catch on, but very slowly. Through the 1960s, in fact, the Belgian Browning remained the most popular clay target over/under. It was this gun which received the most attention when Claude Purbaugh introduced full-length smallbore inserts at the 1960 World Skeet Shooting Championships, something that will be more fully discussed in Chapter 14.

The second major event in the over/under's stateside climb was Ithaca's 1969 introduction of Perazzi tournament guns. Made in Italy, this line not only won a lot of trophies in a very short time, but it captured the imagination of American competitors like no previous over/under. The world first heard of Perazzi over/unders in 1964 when Ennio Matarelli won the Olympic gold medal in trapshooting with a Perazzi Mirage. Although at that time the Perazzi's impact was slight, American registered trapshooters started to climb over each other to buy Perazzis in the 1970s when the Ithaca imports began sweeping tournaments. The bandwagon psychology set in and, despite their high prices, Perazzis sold like jellybeans. Thus, although the availability, publicity and reasonable prices of Charles Daly and Winchester 101 stackbarrels caught the attention of typical American hunters and shooters, it was the Perazzi Mirage and Competition I line that finally proved the over/under concept's position in the United States and Canada.

What happened in the 1970s, and especially in the 1980s, is nothing short of a revolution. The over/under has risen from the status of a novelty to that of a broadly established, totally accepted and unquestioned design. Beginners may continue to start with pumpguns, but as the clerk rings up the sale they frequently are heard to say, "Someday I'm going to get an over/under."

Finesse Points

Just what is there about an over/under that makes it so desirable today but failed to generate much interest in time past? Why were the British apparently so wrong about the over/under?

Bluntly stated, it is apparent that the over/under's strengths more than offset its theorized and oft-published weaknesses. The British, along with some American detractors, enjoyed harping about the over/under's lack of aesthetics and the way its cramped lower barrel made loading difficult. Too, critics of the O/U dismissed the need for a single sighting plane (something which I tend to agree with *for field shooting*), and there has always been a certain lament about over/unders having

THE OVER/UNDER REVOLUTION: DIAMONDS IN THE ROUGH

Perazzi over/unders are among the best-handling stackbarrels being made in field or target grades, thanks apparently to the use of thin-walled barrels and an action body that helps concentrate the weight between a shooter's hands. It's difficult to find another modern over/under that pivots like a Perazzi. This is a Sporting Clays gun with 28-inch barrels and interchangeable choke tubes.

high-shooting tendencies. But when you wrap all those criticisms and laments into one lump, you only have to look at the scoreboard at any trap, skeet or Sporting Clays tournament to see that over/unders racked up winning scores. I don't know what gun could have performed better on that day when I dropped five ruffed grouse with five first-barrel shots from my Merkel, or cleanly folded that pair of high honkers with a Winchester. There was another time when a Manitoba limit of five greenheads fell to the knockabout Valmet in minutes. And one fall an SKB 20-gauge whipped through a partridge purely by muscle memory. The bird was dead in the air before I realized what I had done. Events like that account for the over/under's current appeal.

Although I don't believe a hunter necessarily points more accurately with an over/under than he does, or can with a side-by-side, I do believe that the over/under improves one's scoring by presenting better target visibility. This is especially true on rising targets, where the broader SxS might blot out a low bird. Indeed, it is for such a reason that the side-by-side has practically disappeared from all forms of trapshooting, including American doubles. And when current manufacturers put a high-post rib on the over/under, it enhances target visibility even more. Unfortunately, however, some makers have taken the high rib to a nonsensical extreme, elevating the pointing plane well above the barrels and hands, thus detracting from the potential for optimum eye-hand coordination. The best use of natural eye-hand responses seems to occur when the twain are in reasonably close juxtaposition, not many inches from each other. Thus, there is a balancing of factors involved with rib heights and gun designers must consider them all before leaping to radical extremes. Suffice it to say, then, that the over/under can contribute to hitting by giving the shooter enhanced target visibility, but we should not get reckless with the feature and carry ribs to excessive extremes. Those guns with the architecture of the Golden Gate Bridge are dubious entities, often being sales attractions at best.

Assuming a sensible and efficient rib height, one of the over/under's important features is its hand-to-barrel relationship. On a theoretical basis (albeit a theory that works when practiced correctly and isn't a pipe dream), the most accurate shotgun pointing can be done when the bore axis(es) lies deeply in one's cupped leading hand; for it is the hands that go naturally to where the eyes are focusing, and the closer the bore(s) comes to the pointing hand, the closer it will come to the target without necessitating conscious gun manipulation (aiming). Over/unders provide this hand-to-barrel relationship beautifully, especially field-grade guns with trim forends. In this respect, we duplicate the side-by-side's excellent hand-to-barrel relationship but gain added target visibility with the over/under.

Another subtlety of the O/U is its ability to throw in the fastest second shot in wingshooting. It is this feature which endears itself to competitive shotgunners. Except for the successful Remington Model 1100s and 11-87s, the only type of gun seen in American trap doubles is the over/under. Whereas box pigeon shooting was once the uncontested domain of twin-triggered side-by-sides, the over/under is taking over. Applied to bird hunting, the same hasty follow-up shooting can add birds to the bag.

To what do over/unders owe this speedy second shot capability? Mainly to the under barrel's depressed location, which sends the tube's center line below the comb line to result in "straightline" recoil. The consequence is a more directly backward recoil thrust which reduces upward whip; hence, a shooter can recover more quickly because he doesn't have to pull the muzzle down and fight to regain alignment. There also is less of a tendency for the butt to slip around against the shouldering area. To a certain extent, the presence of a stiff upper barrel may thwart upward flexing (whip or vibration). Whatever the contributing factors, the point is that reduced recoil jump improves the potential for a fast follow-up with alignment and smoothness. The only thing that upsets straightline recoil is the heavy load. To utilize an over/under's quick second shot capability, ammunition must jibe with the gun's weight. The newly imported SKB 20-gauge over/under I tested was rat-tat swift with one-ounce field loads, but three-inch Magnums made it leap and slowed the second shot noticeably.

What about the criticism that over/unders throw their patterns high? There may be some potential truth to that judgment, but it isn't universally true. In general, the high-shooting tendency focuses more heavily on the top barrel than on the lower one, and the potential pivots on the top barrel's high perch which places its bore axis' center line above the comb and presents a different recoil dynamic. In turn, the recoil dynamic can be altered by various factors, including the shooter's hand position. Likewise, the stiff resistance of the lower barrel tends to deny an upper barrel of its normal initial downward flip (negative vibration) on firing, and that can result in a rapid rebound which pops the muzzle sharply upward before the shot charge emerges.

However, despite these potentials for high pattern placement with upper barrels, the point must be made that most modern gunmakers have designed and regulated their over/unders to negate said potentials. Most of the over/unders I've shot recently place their patterns either flush with or insignificantly above the intended center of impact.

In some cases, this high-shooting feature is helpful; for instance, it can blend into upland gunning or trapshooting perfectly as it provides a built-in vertical lead on rising targets. My own M200E Merkel delivers its top-barrel pattern rather high — to the dismay of more than a few steeply rising ruffed grouse and woodcock. When I gave that Merkel to my godson's younger brother for his first serious try at trapshooting, he tore 'em up while other beginners were shooting well below those upward-angled clays. So the phenomenon isn't all bad, although it certainly can't be tolerated *in extremis*. Just recently, for example, I had a new model Sporting Clays over/under from one of Italy's more aggressive gunmakers and it shot half a pattern high, which is to say the very bottom of the pattern hit where the bead was held. When I took it out to a Sporting Clays course, I made a fool of myself by shooting over so many targets that I scored just 12x21. After throwing that over/under into the car's trunk, I went back on the course and tied the record with 19x21 using a Remington Model 11-87 which shot dead-on. Thus, the top barrel's pattern placement *can* be high because of resulting factors inherent in the concept's design, but a vast majority of gunmakers have the problem under control. Nevertheless, it's always intelligent to pattern a new over/under for point of impact at 40 yards using your normal hunting/shooting grip.

Stackbarrel Dynamics

An unfortunate thing about over/unders is that, unlike the classic side-by-side game guns, they haven't been engineered for optimum dynamics. If there are exceptions to that statement, they are the early British unders-and-overs which were mainly low-profiled and built for elegance with a weight distribution similar to that of the vaunted game guns. In general, however, even British Woodwards, Holland & Hollands, Bosses and Purdeys (which are basically the Woodward creation) were a bit heavier than the side-by-side game guns. I would be remiss if I did not mention that my Merkel comes close to game gun weight, scaling $6\sfrac{3}{4}$ pounds with its original $28\sfrac{5}{8}$-inch barrels, which is why I enjoy it so much as opposed to the heavier, bulkier Yankee over/unders. Aside from a few noteworthy artifacts, a very high percentage of current 12-gauge O/Us don't possess exemplary balance, weight distribution or responsiveness.

The reason classic British and European doubles have such delightful qualities, such ability to pivot about their midsections, is because the barrels were individually contoured to match the weight of the butt section. This provided equal weights fore and aft of the middle, or "between-the-hands" section. Given that distribution of halfweights, any gun will move gracefully and responsively as long as it doesn't weigh too much overall. However, so many current over/unders are made with heavily walled barrels to handle magnum loads that inevitably they take on a muzzle-heavy hang.

A mass-produced, 30-inch-barreled over/under made for American waterfowling leaves much to be desired when measured against optimum responsiveness; their barrels start slowly and can drag. When the same guns, and even those with 28-inch barrels, are used in the uplands on flushing game, they can leave one well behind fast birds. Thus, although I think highly of the over/under concept, I see little advantage in it when the guns are poorly weighted and ill-conceived. I honestly believe the Remington Model 1100 Magnum 12 swings as well as, if not better than, many ponderous over/unders now on the market. The Model 3200 Remington was a difficult gun to get started, scaling 8 to 8½ pounds, and Ruger's Red Labels with their investment-cast components come nowhere near the great handling qualities of the Holland & Holland over/under they were designed to emulate. Trim lines aside, the Rugers weigh 7 to 7½ pounds in 20 gauge and about

THE OVER/UNDER REVOLUTION: DIAMONDS IN THE ROUGH

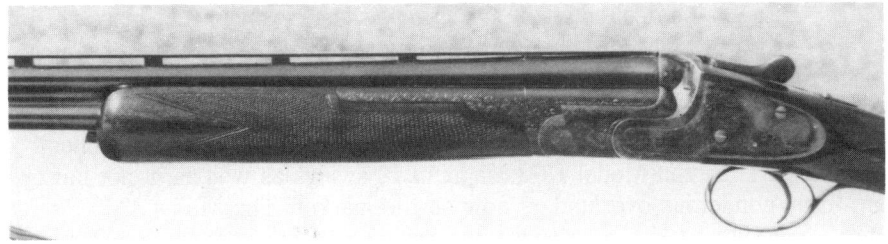

(Photo courtesy of Bill Jacqua)

One of the low-profiled classics, a Boss over/under in .410 bore.

SHOTGUNNING TRENDS IN TRANSITION

For many bird hunters and target shooters, the over/under combines the handling qualities of a side-by-side with the advantages of a narrower pointing plane. However, the author believes that gunmakers must still improve the weight distribution and handling qualities of the over/under before it can duplicate the ease of using a true side-by-side game gun.

THE OVER/UNDER REVOLUTION: DIAMONDS IN THE ROUGH

8 pounds in 12 gauge with 28-inch barrels, with much of that weight noticeably up front and sagging. A 30-inch barreled Citori or Superposed doesn't pivot like a prima ballerina, either.

In other words, just having an over/under doesn't automatically mean a hunter or shooter has the ultimate shotgun, one with the efficient combination of a side-by-side's quick-handling qualities coupled to a single sighting plane. Over/unders, like poorly conceived side-by-sides, can be clunkers. I have handled more than a few of each type, and I feel I can get on target faster with an old Remington Model 11 "Sportsman" skeet gun and its steel Cutts Compensator on a 25 to 26-inch barrel than I can with the long, heavy-walled, droopy-muzzled doubles of either sort! The long gun may be swung through the same geometric arc as the short one, but the shorter version swings through that arc faster. Thus, before purchasing an over/under, a hunter or shooter must use some discrimination when testing such things as overall weight and weight distribution, plus responsiveness and swing dynamics. Just because a shotgun has one barrel atop the other doesn't mean it's the ultimate. Note how many skeet shooters use the tubed over/unders in small gauges but return to the Remington Model 1100/11-87 for 12-gauge events. If the over/under is to outshoot repeaters, it must contribute something lively to the dynamics of wingshooting. It is mainly when an over/under has sophisticated design concepts predicated on responsive movement that it can excel beyond a repeater's ability.

In many respects, it is little wonder that pumpguns and single shots won handily over stackbarrels in early trap and skeet, because the initial over/unders didn't possess outstanding characteristics. The Browning Superposed kicked shooters unmercifully, and it was mainly the Remington Model 32 that attracted attention and did some winning. In Europe, the Merkel fared reasonably well, but in general, the over/unders built during the first half of the twentieth century offered little more than the Remington 31s, Winchester Model 12s and the various skeet-grade semiautos.

Although the British low-framed under-and-overs were lighter and more responsive than anything found stateside, few people bought them because they were very expensive and took years to build. Moreover, the British stackbarrels weren't intended for target shooting, but were instead created to emulate the famous side-by-side game gun.

When the Ithaca Gun Company began bringing in Perazzis during the late 1960s, however, American shooters at last got the feel of a dynamic over/under. Even in their heavier target grades, Perazzis were fast to the target; they were a revelation to the writer, in whose hands they were more responsive than any other match-grade over/under around, bar none. What do Perazzis have that other over/unders don't? Somewhat thinner barrels to eliminate muzzle hang and front-end inertia. The guns are made to pivot for crisp, positive action. Shooters who are slow, dawdling pointers and trackers won't appreciate Perazzi guns. In fact, they may

SHOTGUNNING TRENDS IN TRANSITION

The Perazzi MX-8/Mirage action body is built like the old Holland & Holland with side lugs and tremendous strength while still remaining very stylish. With thin-walled Perazzi barrels, it currently epitomizes O/U dynamics.

do quite poorly with them because the Perazzi is made to be swung NOW! But when guns like the Perazzi Mirage, MX-8 and Competition I are used with grace, dispatch and discipline, they can't be beat for responsiveness and smoothness.

To a surprising degree, Winchester Model 101s were equally responsive due to conservative barrel weights. A main difference seems to be that Perazzis pack a bit more weight between the shooter's hands. However, the Model 101 "American Flyer" was an underrated trap and live pigeon gun, while the various commemorative Model 101s — the Ruffed Grouse Society guns or Quail Specials, to name two — were extremely good bird guns. Why the line didn't have more success, especially among bird hunters, is beyond me. The British recognized the Model 101's qualities early on, and it remains one of their favorite Sporting Clays pieces in models 5500 and 6500.

Exactly to what extent the Winchester Model 101 design will figure in America's future is a moot question. In 1987, the Winchester Group of Olin Corporation sold its share of Olin-Kodensha, the Japanese gunmaking plant where models 101 and 23 were assembled. The line has since become known as Classic Doubles International. Prices almost doubled, but management justified that by explaining that overall quality has improved markedly, and that a hand engraving process is now in place. Initial comments from the new owners indicate that the guns' forcing cones have been lengthened to reduce recoil, and that higher-quality wood is being employed. All that remains is to determine if the new American shotgunner will buy Model 101s for $2,000 and up.

If any American maker of mass-produced over/unders is taking a hard look at improvements, it seems to be Remington, where a new design is in the works and nearing prototype as this book was being written. In the past, mass-production manufacturers merely came up with one gun and simply modified it to trap, skeet or field models by using different stocks and barrel lengths. However, Remington's manager of firearms marketing, E. O. "Bub" Fini, informed me that the forthcoming over/under will be weighted and balanced for the specific use. Target-grades will be heavier with some weight forward to provide the smoothness and positive follow-through fitted to tournaments, while the hunting grades will have different weight distribution for better responsiveness afield. To a large degree, this new Remington over/under field gun may have been influenced by the born-again Parker that Remington is turning out as a custom shop beauty. The new Parker has thinner barrel walls and has given the Remington people some experience with the concept. Apparently, this over/under will be based upon Italian low-profile styling. If the weight can be kept down and centered, it should be one of the best Yankee stackbarrels of all time. For now, we can only wait and see.

A great entry among over/unders was Browning's 16-gauge Citori. It was the first such gun since Marlin dropped its 16-gauge Model 90 a generation ago. Despite a loyal following among uplanders, the 16 gauge has lain dormant since the 1960s, mainly because the sporting arms industry wanted it that way. True, the volume wasn't that great and midcentury production methods couldn't handle tooling turnovers profitably, but with modern computerized machining, smaller runs of specialized products again can be made without the company sacrificing profits. This means the 16 gauge can come alive once more to split the difference between bulky, barrel-heavy 12s and whippy 20s. The 16s should also do well in Sporting Clays for those who can't get the most from an obese 12 bore, as 16s will pattern beautifully with one or $1^1/_8$-ounce loads. Except for the fact that my Merkel scales in at 6¾ pounds, I would already have a Citori 16 on the rack.

The Gun of the Future, but...

There can be no doubt that current trends project a grand future for over/under shotguns. Frankly, I believe that light-recoiling autoloaders can, and will, run them a good race. Entries like the Benelli, Remington Model 11-87 and Beretta Model 303 have adequate talent to match the over/unders in popularity and scoring potential. It may require some further weight reduction to keep the gas-operated models competitive if over/unders are upgraded for optimum dynamics. A gun like the Benelli is already a smart-swinging gun which points and moves as spiritedly as most over/unders (and better than many) while also providing a low recoil level, but over/unders currently have market momentum.

To reach its pinnacle as a classic bird gun providing every bit of its potential, the over/under concept must be taken closer to the dynamics and weight distribution of British game guns. This requires more attention to barrel and butt weights relative to the action/breech weight so that, as on the side-by-side game gun, the extremities represent an equal division of one halfweight while the action/breech nucleus comprises the remaining halfweight. Without additional crafting of over/under design and balance, the concept will remain a diamond in the rough.

An unfortunate over/under feature is that while its extremities may be in balance, there is a very slight, weight-forward feel. This exists because the over/under stacking concentrates barrel weight, whereas the side-by-side arrangement broadens weight distribution to provide a different sensation. Consequently, a hunter must approach the over/under with a sensitive pair of hands. Moreover, it is quite likely that modern designers who understand these niceties will not apply the tack, for reducing barrel thickness isn't a logical step while steel shot threatens to invade all aspects of shotgunning.

Were any gunmaker to take the over/under seriously, however, he could follow the Perazzi mode and incorporate the dynamics of a classy, responsive side-by-side into a vertical-breaking double that also offers the visibility of a single-barreled gun. At that point, the over/under revolution will have come of age and the diamond will have been polished. But it probably won't happen as long as gunmakers employ golf-playing engineers to design guns without consulting knowledgeable shooters and theoreticians.

THE OVER/UNDER REVOLUTION: DIAMONDS IN THE ROUGH

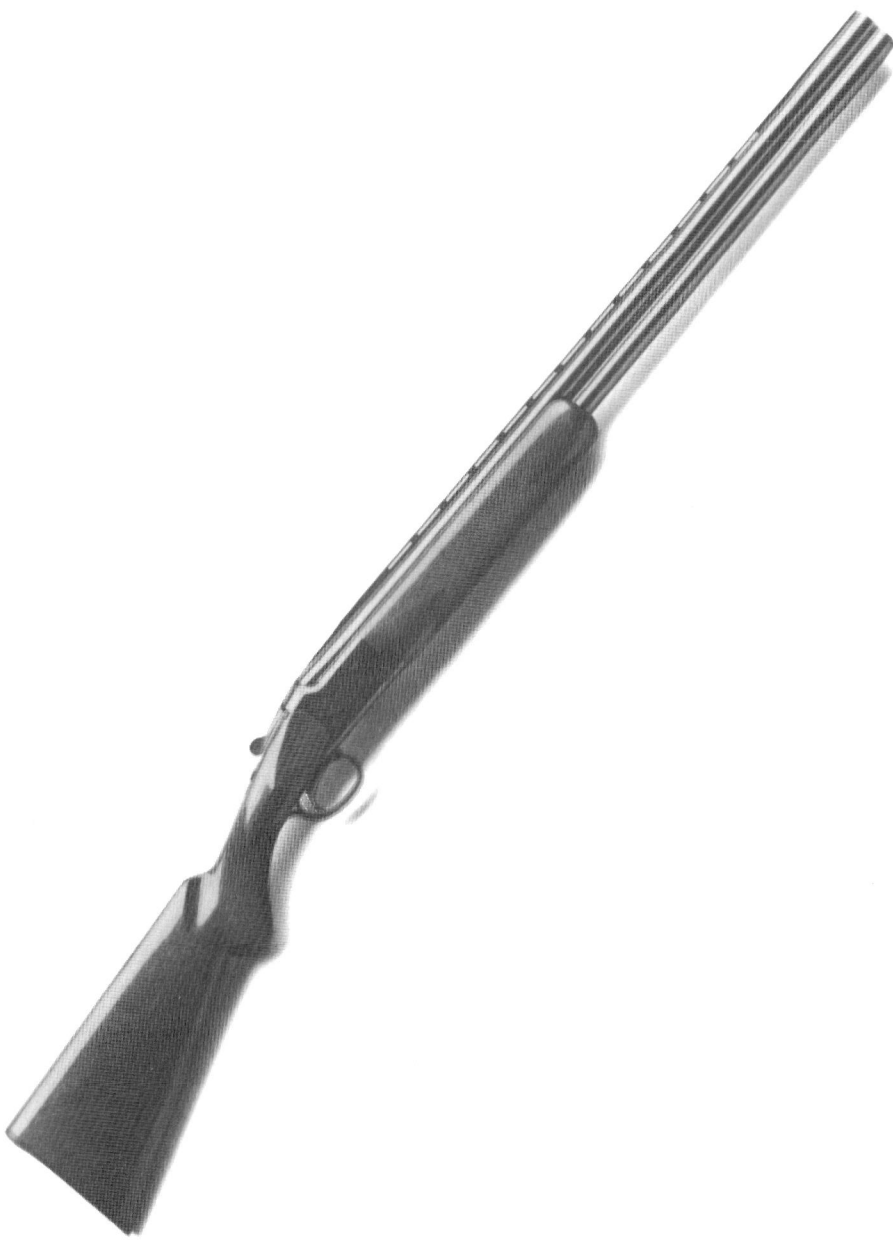

A great new entry on the American over/under market is Browning's 16-gauge Citori, which has a stock and forend duplicating the lines of the old Belgian-made Superposed Lightning model. Besides the Marlin Model 90 and the German-made Merkel, it is one of the few 16-gauge vertical doubles ever offered to American bird hunters, who should love it. *Dropped from 1990 catalog.*

An exceptionally well-made over/under is the Beretta SO line of true sidelocks. The above is an SO3EELL. Unfortunately, even this family has a tendency toward barrel weight.

Chapter 4

The Outmoded Pumpgun

PRIOR TO Bob Nichols' *Shotgunner* of 1949, and continuing thereafter, few writers waxed enthusiastically about pumpguns. The British tended to dominate shotgun literature, and they would sooner have cut off their tongues as to have said anything favorable about repeating smoothbores. The great W. W. Greener, whose thoughts reflected British sentiment around the turn of the century, opined in *The Gun and Its Development* that while "the repeating rifle is the best mechanism for sporting rifles ... it does not follow that a shot gun constructed on the same principle will fulfill the requirements of the wing shot."

Relative to the efficiency of a pumpgun, Greener further recorded nothing but abject failure for the outstanding American live pigeon competitor, Dr. W. F. Carver, when the latter tried to demonstrate the Spencer trombone gun in England. Of course, pumpgun design and development were barely in their infancies then, but the British attitude toward them was solidly established. In *Game Shooting*, a 1955 publication, British gunmaker Robert Churchill bluntly accused the repeater of being a "slow action, ill-balanced, and ugly weapon." In fact, British field gunning is such a tradition-laden institution predicated on side-by-side game guns that Churchill cautioned against the faux pas of showing up with one for an English hunt. "In the English shooting field," Churchill wrote, "the pump gun is not welcome."

It was not until after World War II that a contrary opinion arose from England, and then it was only a weak pronouncement, but it did accept and praise repeaters in varying degrees. The book was entitled *Automatic and Repeating Shotguns*, and it was written by Richard Arnold, who was an active British shooter as well as the founder of the Muzzle Loaders' Association of Great Britain. Arnold did not level the same heavy criticism against pumpguns that most British traditionalists did, but he still managed to find various faults with trombone guns. While narrating his personal development as a shooter, Arnold informed the reader that his

SHOTGUNNING TRENDS IN TRANSITION

grandfather encouraged him to become familiar with all guns, and that his early training included a Winchester Model 97 hammer pump. However, that episode with the Model 97 didn't enamor him with the breed. As he reminisced, "Looking back over the years I realize now what a cumbersome piece it was compared with the traditional British double...." Arnold concluded by finding that another "drawback to the pump-action weapon is its appearance. No matter how good the craftsmanship ... the great length of the receiver, and the large fore-end militate against its having the clean lines of a traditional double." Thus, although Arnold's book was generally favorable to repeaters, he did level some digs against pumpguns and their lack of aesthetics.

Technologically, slide-action shotguns were expedient, stopgap measures to enhance the American hunter's firepower while he awaited a successful autoloader. Charles Askins Sr., forecast that "an auto-loading mechanism is the ultimate fate of all pump repeaters," when he wrote his 1910 tome, *The American Shotgun*. In other words, the shooter's leading hand was going to supply the cycling energy only until inventors perfected the self-loading designs. Thereafter, why would anyone want to shuffle a scattergun's forearm to eject spent hulls and bring fresh ones from the magazine when an autoloading mechanism would accomplish that, leaving the shooter to concentrate on eye-hand coordination? Why, indeed? For on a purely scientific basis, the pumpgun was outmoded on December 17, 1901, when John M. Browning received a patent on his soon-to-be-famous Auto-5.

Despite the availability of successful autoloaders, such as the Browning A-5 and the Remington and Winchester Model 1911s, an amazing phenomenon grew out of the early twentieth century: Rather than fade into history as a defunct, obsolete, outmoded device, the pumpgun became deeply entrenched among hunters and, for a time, clay target shooters. Whereas a side-by-side with rabbit-eared hammers was once the symbol of shotgunning, the new symbol became that of a long-barreled pump with a barrel choked so tightly that "she won't take a dime." As the Roaring Twenties gave way to the Depression of the 1930s and the thirties slipped into the war-torn forties, the pumpgun market expanded. Conversely, the demand for traditional side-by-sides declined sharply. Companies that didn't convert to repeaters soon saw red ink flowing all over their ledgers. As discussed in Chapter 2, this period of transition in the early 1900s terminated the refinement of the American double and left it inferior to the British and European doubles for the remainder of the twentieth century. True, some new work is being done with the stateside doubles, but one cannot project any American builder matching or surpassing the fine, handmade overseas guns in the remainder of this century. If there is to be an American Boss, Purdey or Powell, it will perforce be an achievement of the twenty-first century. The point, however, is that research and development monies were spent on new pumpgun models during the early 1900s, and this brought the pumpgun to its peak prior to World War II while the American side-by-side still has a long row to hoe.

THE OUTMODED PUMPGUN

The old Winchester Model 97 didn't have a slickety-click stroke, but it was one of the best-pointing trombone guns ever designed. It had an extremely low profile and worked naturally to one's eye.

SHOTGUNNING TRENDS IN TRANSITION

Beginning with the Spencer contraptions in the mid-1880s and extending into the Marlin and Winchester hammer pumps of the 1890s, the sporting arms industry developed vastly improved hammerless designs which slicked up pumpgunning posthaste. Stevens introduced the first hammerless pumpgun in 1904, the Model 520, and it eventually was improved and designated the Model 620 in 1927. In many respects, Stevens pumps were a link with the past, for although they were hammerless, they still had a *chug-chug* action and, to my judgment, slow-action releases. Too, the Stevens line always was slanted toward the low-price range for hunters who wanted a repeater but didn't want to spend much. My diggings into the history of skeet and trap indicate that very few, if any, trap and skeet shooters used Stevens pumps for serious competition. Its forend stroke was always one of the longest, which, coupled with a slow-action release, was less than appealing to clay target gunners who had to shoot doubles.

The first truly great pumpgun design was Winchester's Model 12, which appeared in 1912. Eventually, the Model 12 became known as "the perfect repeater." It combined good old-fashioned craftsmanship, using machined parts carefully fitted and finished, with a streamlined profile that remains modern. The Model 12 was made in all popular gauges, including the 28 gauge starting in 1935. The scaled-down receiver used on the lesser gauges may very well have led American hunters into the smaller gauges. The first Model 12s ever made were 20 gauges with 25-inch barrels, and these proved to be delightful guns for upland hunters. It appears that the popularity of the 20-gauge Model 12 spurred Remington into building a competitive gun which, eventually, launched an entirely new repeater.

This was the Remington Model 17, a John M. Browning invention that was scaled down to 20-gauge proportions. Introduced in 1921, the Model 17 scaled roughly 5¾ pounds with a 28-inch barrel, which made it decidedly lighter than the 6½ to 6¾-pound Winchester Model 12 in 20 gauge. In keeping with Remington's then-current line of 12-gauge pumps, the Model 10, the Model 17 was a bottom-ejecting design similar to the current Ithaca Model 37/87. In fact, it was exactly like the Model 37 Ithaca, because Ithaca Gun Company under Lou Smith (the brother of L. C. Smith) picked up the Model 37 concept after Remington tired of it and the patents ran out in the early 1930s. Ithaca merely scaled up the Model 17 for 12 and 16-gauge shells as well and brought it out in 1937 as the new Model 37 family of pumpguns.

The way Remington made Model 17s from 1921 to 1933 was classic. Parts were machined and fitted for a swift action release and slide handle throw. Even today, a Model 17 can race with any other 20-gauge pump and win. It was relative to the Remington Model 17 that Nichols wrote in *The Shotgunner*: "We believe we killed more game with this little 5½-pound, 2¾-inch-chambered 20-gauge during the three years we shot it exclusively in the field than we killed with any other single gun we ever owned and shot over an equal period of time. It was a wonderful carrying gun. . . ." About the only fault Nichols found with the Model 17 was its humped top grip, which he felt could contribute to high patterning, and he quickly worked that down with a piece of glass. Otherwise, in a book filled with discussions of the other repeaters then available, the Model 17 received his highest endorsements.

Between 1913 and 1930, Marlin made a series of hammerless pumpguns known as the models 28, 31, 43, 44, 53 and 63. Some criticized them as ugly because of the way their receiver geometry angled steeply into the top tang on a slant that gave an awkward profile. Nevertheless, photos of trapshooting from that era show a considerable number of Marlin pumpguns in the hands of recognized shooters, so the Marlin hammerless pumps must have possessed positive qualities their profiles didn't indicate.

In 1929, Remington introduced an upgraded version of the Model 10, calling it the Model 29. However, the Model 29 and its bottom-ejection still failed to appeal to clay target shooters. From all indications, the Winchester Model 12 and side-ejecting Marlins dominated trapshooting. Remington quietly developed a competitive product with the same side-positioned loading-ejection port. Introduced in 1931, the new Remington was tagged the Model 31. At that point in time, it was the fastest, shortest-stroking pumpgun around, and it was soon advertised as "the gun with the ball bearing action." Both skeet and trap shooters employed it for major tournament wins, but overall the Model 31 didn't reach the Winchester Model 12's popularity among competitive shooters — maybe because the Model 31's trigger had a "lift" characteristic to it, whereas the Model 12 had the straightback pull favored by serious gunners. To a hunter, the difference between a Model 31's fire control group and that of a Model 12 is insignificant.

After World War II, Remington brought out a lightweight version of the Model 31, cataloging it as the Model 31-L. This gun had an alloy receiver (not aluminum) and was at least one pound lighter than the standard, steel-receivered Model 31. The blue wore off this number's edges quickly, but it was a good hunting gun. However, by the time the Model 31-L came along, the design was already in its last years.

Shortly after Remington introduced the Model 31, Winchester practiced a bit of one-upmanship and, in 1933, introduced the Model 42 .410-bore slide action. This obviously played well with the skeet shooting crowd. For many years, the Model 42 invariably won the national .410-bore (sub-small) skeet championship because it was the only gun with which skeeters could score well using the ½-ounce shot charge.

Although today's gun collectors consider the side-by-side Parker and L. C. Smith .410s to be the ultimate, especially in skeet grades, it actually was the Model 42 that improved .410 skeet scoring. The side-by-sides were too whippy and did not lend themselves to modification, but the Model 42s were weighted down for smoothness and follow-through. Many serious skeetmen put lead slugs in the

SHOTGUNNING TRENDS IN TRANSITION

One of the best pumpguns ever produced, in the author's opinion, was the Remington Model 31.

Model 42's tubular magazine and additional lead shot in the butt cavity. Those who selected the 26-inch barrel length, rather than the more popular 28-inch, normally had a steel Cutts Compensator added for more muzzle weight. Moreover, a lot of Model 42 skeet guns were chambered for the 2½-inch shotshell, rather than the three-incher, because it was believed that the shorter load would pattern better from its own chamber length. Whatever its chamber length or grade, however, the Model 42 was a scaled-down Model 12 and was a very high quality production gun with machined parts plus excellent American walnut.

Despite the Great Depression of the 1930s, the pumpgun enjoyed a heyday of sorts. Ironically, it reached its zenith in mechanical design and quality production just as America was experiencing its economic nadir. Perhaps that tells us something about the American pumpgun phenomenon: They have mass appeal because, compared to doubles and autoloaders, they are cheaper. The rank and file hunter considers himself to be anything but a rich man, and he will usually opt for the least expensive repeater shotgun. Since the pumpgun fills those requirements, it will continue to sell as long as casual hunters pinch pennies and fail to develop an appreciation for the finer aspects of wingshooting and bird guns.

Shortly after World War II, the pumpgun's quality began to slip. Years of price regulations and shortages led to inflation and it became obvious to gunmakers that changes had to be made to keep pumpguns in the popular price range. Increased labor costs had nearly driven American-made doubles from the scene. Guns like the Parkers, Smiths and Foxes were advertised in catalogs immediately after World War II, but few were ever delivered. To keep their businesses profitable, gunmakers either had to increase retail prices or lower production expenses and, knowing that the American hunter would balk at higher prices, the gunmakers embarked on a new path of reducing labor and other production costs. The pumpgun was a focal point for this project because it attracted the most cost-conscious hunters.[1]

The first hint of things to come occurred in 1950 when Remington dropped the excellent Model 31 and introduced the new Model 870 Wingmaster. Initially, the Model 870 was criticized as a "punch press" gun, because it had stamped rather than machined parts. What wasn't realized at the time, of course, was that the Model 870 actually had tremendous strength and longevity for a model lacking machined components, and it has sold over three million copies since its introduction. The better grades actually come from the box with immediately smooth operation, although the economy grade, known as the Model 870 "Express," needs considerable work to smooth it out. In due course, the Model 870 was absorbed into skeet and trap and has become a winner at both.

The change from machined to stamped parts and from the Model 31 to the Model 870 may have helped save Remington from financial difficulties in mid-century. By engineering ways to provide a truly substantial pumpgun at somewhat lower prices, the company remained profitable. There was no doubt that continued

SHOTGUNNING TRENDS IN TRANSITION

Although sportsmen who enjoy doubles and autoloaders continually request better guns, those who favor pumpguns are more frugal and constantly demand cheaper models. Such a market has caused Remington to downgrade the Model 870 Wingmaster concept and release it with a stained hardwood stock and forend, and a less lustrous metal finish under the name of "Express" Magnum. Although it is a very serviceable gun, it illustrates the differences in tastes and interests.

, or, at best, marginal
,m for several seasons
extant Winchester Model
pre-war machined parts),
the game. The other com-
.ty guns and remain profitable.

.ctance to surrender the Model
. of the Olin Corporation, which
ighest-quality guns possible. He
in favor of quality with the assump-
.eant the company would balance out
ce Olin was both an enthusiastic sports-
er, he didn't have to answer to anyone.
his business making sizeable profits, who
a paltry few stockholders who showed up

ally oblivious to the problem of pumpgun sales.
, costs and hunters' apparent refusal to pay higher
er brought out a cheapened version of the Model
ated the Model 25, and except for a slightly shorter
me profile and handling qualities as the Model 12.
25's parts were machined with Model 12 tooling. To
owever, the Model 25 was not given the Model 12's
a solid-framed gun. And to reduce the price even more,
e great finish as the Model 12. The public wasn't recep-
e only, the Model 25 sold less than 88,000 pieces and was
jarently its price, which was less than $15 below that of the
nough of an incentive. Besides that, the Model 870 always
el 25's price. As the seasons progressed, the Model 870 began
tion as a sturdy, reliable pump despite its cheaper components.

1960s, however, Winchester saw what lay ahead. The Model 12
ing a living, and with John Olin in retirement, the company accepted
it could no longer turn out high-quality repeaters at low retail prices
the black. Either the hunter would have to pay more, or the producer
ve to lower his quality. Since many pumpgun purchasers either had little
onary money or didn't choose to spend much on guns, there was only
ute for Winchester in the 1960s — an entire new line of guns (rifles included)
n reduced manufacturing costs. The result was the Model 1200 pumpgun,
ch subsequently has become the Model 1300, and the low-grade Ranger series.
iese guns have aluminum alloy receivers for fast machining and minor tool wear.
Hunters found cutting chips and dust that jammed the actions on many of the
early examples.) The gun's bolting was steel-on-steel, with a rotary bolt

SHOTGUNNING TRENDS IN TRANSITION

The famous Remington Model 870 changed the nature of pumpgun manufacturing from that of totally machined parts to the use of stampings and castings. It has stood the test of time, but pumpgunners want still-cheaper models.

engaging cavities in the barrel extension, and the fire control unit was a study in stampings. Eventually, the models 1200/1300 and the Ranger guns were accepted by hunters, but clay target marksmen generally have had nothing to do with them.

In actuality, Winchester didn't halt production of the Model 12 entirely in 1964. The gun continued to be available in the so-called Y-series, which employed some changes and castings rather than machined parts. From 1964 to 1972, Y-series Model 12s had a retail price of $875. Their sales were low because few hunters would pay that much for a pumpgun. The Y-series guns were mainly popular in trap grades. By 1976 the Y-series line again hit the skids except for trap grades, and the final Y-series guns were manufactured from remaining parts in 1985 to 1986 as factory-engraved models in trap, skeet and field persuasions bearing factory letters of engraving authenticity. The trap guns sold swiftly, but field and skeet grades languished; few people wanted a $1,000 hunting pump, and skeeters have given up entirely on the slide action.

By the time Winchester switched to the Model 1200 in 1964, other gunmakers also were flooding the marketplace with cheap pumpguns. Mossberg began in 1962 with its Model 500, which continues as a competitive gun being made in myriad grades. Discount gun shops push plenty of Mossbergs each season, mainly to hunters, as the Mossberg does not have an adequately sophisticated fire control unit for good trapshooting. Its safety lies atop the receiver's rear somewhat like the sliding safety of a double barrel. Some hunters prefer that arrangement to the conventional cross-bolt button in most other pumpguns' trigger guard. The Model 500s are made with an aluminum alloy receiver and copious stampings and castings.

Immediately after World War II, a company known as the Nobel Manufacturing Company brought out several stylings of cheap pumpguns. These were all solid-frame, non-takedown designs, and they were in the lower price ranges for repeaters. They sold for a time, but then the post-war expansion began to fold, and so did Noble in 1970. Whatever came out of the Savage-Stevens combine also deteriorated. The former Model 620 Stevens, although not the slickest pump ever designed, had machined parts. But the revamped Stevens, known as the Model 820, was a solid-framed eyesore with gooseneck stock and, on the "SC" model, a bulbous Savage "Super-Choke" which hung like a rock in the toe of a sock making it terribly muzzle-heavy. Stevens further degraded its pumpgun line in the 1950s with a downgraded gun tagged the Model 77. That gun had a stained hardwood stock and one of the worst triggers ever made. Under the Savage name, the Model 30 was another play to the hunter who was snug with a buck. It was available in solid-frame and takedown models, beginning in 1958, but ran into hard times in the late 1970s. Savage Arms eventually went bankrupt, but at the time of this writing was attempting to regain a foothold.

Finally, there is the High Standard Manufacturing Corporation which, between 1962 and the mid-1970s, sold a series of relatively inexpensive pumps under its

SHOTGUNNING TRENDS IN TRANSITION

When the pumpgun market could no longer support the Winchester Model 12, Winchester turned to the Model 1200/1300 series of slide actions which had rapidly machined receivers of high-strength aluminum and castings plus punch-press parts. It was another example of deteriorating quality in pumpguns.

own name. Prior to that, High Standard hammered out thousands of equally inexpensive pumps for Sears, Roebuck & Company under the once-famous J. C. Higgins tradename. The Higgins and High Standard pumps were solid-framed, but in my opinion could well have been the best of a relatively sorry bunch.

None of these less-expensive pumps could cozy up to the old Remington models 29, 17 and 31 or the Winchester Model 12 and Ithaca Model 37. The bargain basement guns sold, and while the market was expanding they produced profits because production costs were held down, but when the gun market slowed down in the 1980s, many firms experienced severe economic traumas. The marginal manufacturers dropped out: High Standard is gone; Noble dropped out; Winchester changed hands and is now U.S. Repeating Arms, Inc; Savage Arms suffered under Chapter 11; Ithaca folded but was resurrected by new money. The demand for a low-priced pumpgun persists, however, and after lo these many decades Remington has been dragged into the economy market with a gun which, for all practical purposes, may well be the best low-priced pumpgun ever — the Model 870 "Express." Basically this is the same gun as the higher-priced Wingmaster, but it has less attention to finish and bears a hardwood-stained stock and forend. The Express' barrel is equipped with the versatile "Rem" Choke feature, and its dull finish plays right into the hands of waterfowl and turkey hunters. The action of the Model 870 Express is tighter than the higher-priced Model 870s as it comes from the box, but some stroking smooths it out. Jeweler's rouge also will help to hasten a slicker action. Indeed, the presence of a long-proven action and a machined steel receiver makes the Model 870 Express one of the leading economy-grade repeaters of all time.

Weatherby, the famous designer of big game cartridges and rifles, has also learned that it isn't easy to market a higher-priced pumpgun these days. In 1982, Weatherby began importing a Japanese-made slide action called the Model 92. Like all Weatherby guns, it was fashionable. The wood was claro walnut, often of fancy grain, and the grip was a long, full pistol grip *a la* Weatherby tradition. Interestingly, the Model 92 had a semi-humpbacked receiver which, although different, was not unattractive. The gun has a relatively short stroke and can be obtained with solid choke barrels or a screw-in choke system. Despite the catchy styling, however, the 92s haven't set the sales world afire. To attract attention, Weatherby has taken a radical step by starting to sell through chain stores. Whereas once the Weatherby name was a prestige item, it is now on a rack in the corner selling for a discount. The reason doesn't lie with Weatherby, but rather with the fact that pumpgunners won't pay for fancy guns.

After seasons of steady slippage, Ithaca Gun Company went bankrupt in the mid-1980s. Model 37s simply didn't sell, and the company's line of autoloaders wasn't competitive. Remington bought manufacturing rights to the Ithaca MAG-10 autoloader, and some fresh money entered the scene to re-introduce the Model 37 pumpgun as the Model 87 (after the year of its return). This Model 87, we are told, will be made the old-fashioned way with machined parts, not castings or stampings. It will be interesting to see if hunters will pay the prices needed to keep the new Ithaca in business. My bet is that they won't and there will be a gradual cheapening of the gun or a final bankruptcy as long as the pump remains the company's bread and butter.

Browning's BPS pumpgun has had some appeal among hunters, and it will gain added impetus because the company has been innovative enough to make it in 10-gauge Magnum for more effectiveness with steel shot goose loads of BBBs, Ts and Fs. In reality, the BPS is a well-made Asian pump with a noticeably high rib ramp which acts as a customer-catcher as well as an eye-catcher. Current BPS guns are quite smooth as they come from the box, although the first shipments had some problems and were gritty. The top-mounted safety slide is easily accessible and something a lot of hunters will enjoy, but when it comes to skeet, trap and Sporting Clays, the bottom-ejecting feature turns off serious shooters. And the BPS wasn't able to get its foot in the door as a winning clay target piece. The trap-grade BPS has been dropped due to lack of sales.

The fact is that no modern tournament shooters are interested in any pumpguns, with the sole exception of trap singles where the models 870 and 12 are still in use. However, one must remember that this is *singles* shooting where fast firing doesn't come into play. When it comes to trap doubles or rapid action in skeet and Sporting Clays, over/unders and autoloaders get the nod. Skeet clubs were once flooded by Cutts-equipped Model 12s, Model 42s and Model 31s, but the presence of a slide-action smoothbore on skeet is now something of an oddity. The demand for skeet-grade pumps has fallen to such an all-time low that Remington has dropped all Model 870 skeet grades. About the only time one sees a pumpgun in skeet or Sporting Clays is when a hunter shows up for his first go-rounds.

It is well documented that anyone who enjoys clay target games involving multiple targets (doubles) doesn't stick with a pumpgun. Slide actions are entirely outmoded in the new game of skeet doubles from all stations, and they fail entirely on the fast-starting targets in International (Olympic) skeet. Few people still use a pump on ATA trap doubles, and those who do seldom win against over/unders and soft-shooting autoloaders. I have never heard of an important Sporting Clays match being copped by a pumpgunner, and International trapshooting (alias Olympic trap, trench or bunker) turns pumpgunners inside out. Although a shooter is allowed two shots at each target in International trap, the targets start at roughly 100 mph, and if the shooter misses with his first shot, the pumping stroke tends to give the clay time to outfly the second effort. One's timing simply isn't fast enough, nor is recovery swift enough, to throw in an accurate second pattern. This was more than proved in the 1960 Olympics.

At the time, the hottest American trapshooter was Arnold Riegger from the state of Washington, a truly magnificent champion in American ATA trapshooting.

He averaged over 99 percent and won broadly in ATA trap doubles despite the fact that he used only one gun, a Winchester Model 12. Riegger qualified for the U.S. Olympic team, but when he arrived in Rome he found the high-speed International clays overwhelming. When he missed the first shot, his second shot was normally a wasted effort, too. He broke only 168x200, a dismal showing when compared to the winning 198x200 posted by Italian Ennio Mattarelli or the bronze medal tally of 194x200 shot by America's second entry, William C. Morris III (both of whom shot over/unders). Thus, when it boils down to the finer points of fast shotgunning, pumpguns simply don't have it.

It is a widespread belief among many American hunters that a pumpgun can be made to fire as fast as, or faster than, an autoloader. On a purely theoretical basis, the belief has merit. While one must wait for the recoil or gas energy of a shotshell to operate the autoloader's mechanisms, he can potentially shuck a slide action's handle a mite faster. There is no waiting.

But there is a catch to it: The hunter must, in fact, develop the timing and hand speed which outrace the autoloader. If a hunter pauses for a split instant after his first shot, the autoloader is ahead and can't be caught by any pump; and if the pumpgunner hears any part of his stroke after the muzzle blast, he's too slow. An expert pumpgunner has that gun open and closed so rapidly that one's eye can't follow it; he appears to be shooting an autoloader. Most hunters I've seen can't come close to this pumping velocity.

I must confess that I am prejudiced against pumpguns and rarely use them. This is not because of a British influence or snobbish attitude. It's because there are far better shotgun types, ones which leave the shooter to concentrate solely on the target. Moreover, pumpguns always have the potential for error. Slow-shucking, short-shucking, jams, malfunctions, difficulties in loading the bottom-ejecting models — all occur to complicate something that should be done with grace and dispatch. While I can tolerate pumpguns for waterfowling more than I do for uplanding, I can think of nothing I enjoy less in wingshooting than having to manipulate a slide action for high-angle firing. For me, getting that forend back into battery takes a lot out of the overall smoothness. Be it with an autoloader, a side-by-side or an over/under, it is so much nicer to establish one's grip, keep one's eyes on the target, and swing without the necessity of making a stutter-stroke with one's leading hand. Indeed, we no longer hand-crank automobiles, so why should we hand-crank shotguns?

Chapter Notes

1. Holding the line on gun prices is not an easy thing to manage. While it can be done simply enough in the factory, it involves the onus of reducing obvious quality to the extent that the buying public soon complains that "They aren't making 'em like they used to!"

SHOTGUNNING TRENDS IN TRANSITION

Depending on the amount of budgeting a gunmaker does, he always runs the risk of losing sales. Perhaps the only thing that helps the pumpguns' prestige at this time, is that practically all of them have been cheapened as compared to their quality in the 1930s, when they were carefully fitted with machined parts and good walnut. Today, the hottest selling pumpguns have stained hardwood stocks and forends, hastily finished metallic exteriors, castings and stampings, and non-stylish profiles. In large measure, such shoddy work is necessary to keep pumpguns within range of the typical hunter's willingness to pay. Unfortunately, if a certain market segment of pumpguns aren't made like they used to be, it is largely the hunter's fault. People who are willing to spend more money on doubles are not complaining because the doubles continue to be made better for a more sophisticated shooter.

Chapter 5

Modern Autoloaders: The Closest Thing to Perfection

SPORTSMEN and collectors who are devout worshipers of trim, racy doubles will view this as heresy heaped upon blasphemy, but Charles Askins Sr., had a point when he wrote in the 1928 edition of *The American Shotgun* that, "it is true beyond question or dispute that there is more gun, better gun value for the money, in an American repeater than in any other shotgun in the world." For although the grand old names in American doubles were still around in 1928, a definite change was taking place in the sporting arms business. As already discussed in the previous chapters on side-by-sides and pumpguns, the industry was gradually shifting from break-action guns to repeaters, and the repeaters were being improved and held to high manufacturing standards. All personal prejudices aside, it seems obvious that the evolving repeaters were simply becoming better guns than the old splinter-gripped, twin-triggered, low-combed doubles.

(I must note here that my interest in double-barreled shotguns goes back a long way. I always have argued that they have certain features which, when properly applied by the gunmaker and utilized by the wingshot, enhance natural pointing, smoothness and speed afield. But I also must make a qualifying statement that the doubles' enhancements are a matter of degree and application. In many instances, they are mainly something that a sophisticated wingshot or theorist can appreciate and use to his advantage when he splits fine hairs and develops a technique suited to the guns. By stressing the finer points of a double, one simply can't assume that autoloaders aren't any good. Indeed, if classic side-by-sides are such effective guns, why aren't they in greater demand among serious skeet, trap and Sporting Clays competitors?)

As noted in Chapter 4, I have little personal regard for pumpguns, but autoloaders — they're another story. If the British game gun can be regarded as the optimum side-by-side, and if the various specialized over/unders have reached the nth degree of performance on game and clays, then *some* modern autoloaders are the closest

SHOTGUNNING TRENDS IN TRANSITION

thing to perfection! Unlike the pump repeaters which reached their pinnacle in the 1930s and 1940s only to backslide, the autoloading concept didn't come close to mechanical perfection until the 1980s.

The history of autoloading shotguns dates back to the late nineteenth century. Inventors knew that the recoil and powder gas energies of shotshells could operate a gun's mechanism for semiautomatic and full automatic firing, but they had difficulty perfecting mechanisms which would function reliably with the myriad loads and powders then on the market. Remember, this was a transitional period, a time when black powder tarried, semi-smokeless was in use and smokeless powders were just becoming popular. Each powder had its own pressure-building characteristics, and getting one self-shucking mechanism to operate with all of them interchangeably proved impossible. Indeed, reviewing the history and development of autoloading scatterguns, we learn that it has taken about 100 years to reach the final goal, namely autoloaders which handle all legitimate commercial loads interchangeably *without* the need for any mechanical adjustments or barrel changes.

The first technological breakthrough came when John M. Browning devised the friction ring concept for his Auto-5, which became famous for its high-sterned receiver. By the expedient of changing ring locations on the magazine tube vis-a-vis the recoil spring, a shooter could adjust the Auto-5 for light or heavy rounds and anticipate reasonably reliable operation even though that gun was patented in 1901. The Remington Model 11 and Savage Model 720 were exact copies of the Browning Auto-5 and also did yeoman service during the first half of the twentieth century.

Although the Browning Auto-5 enabled hunters and clay target shooters to use different loads, it did not approach the ideal of complete interchangeability. Ammunition was limited to one potency per ring setting; a hunter who wanted to go from light to heavy loads had to remove the forend, slip off the barrel and alter the position of the ring. That's a lot of fiddling when a surprise flock of geese appears overhead! Moreover, when three-inch Magnum loads became available, neither the 12 nor 20-gauge Auto-5s could accommodate the full range of loads — target and light upland through the three-inchers. The company had to build special three-inch guns, and these wouldn't function with light loads. For all that lack of versatility, however, the Browning Auto-5 and its so-called "long-recoil" system rated huzzas over many other mechanical contraptions, such as the German-made Walther and the Scandinavian Sjogren, which were based on toggle and inertia block systems. In fact, it is still going strong for many hunters and continues to be made in Japan by Browning. Some people simply like the ol' "humpback," and modern manufacturing technologies have helped resurrect the "Sweet Sixteen." Many skeet championships were won with the Remington Model 11 "Sportsman," too. The point is that hunters were left without the final degree of versatility.

Even the technologies of World War II didn't advance the autoloader's cause immediately. The first bit of improvement came when Remington dropped the Model 11 and introduced the streamlined Model 11-48 in the 1948 to 1949 period. This sleek design used Browning's long-recoil system, but it was given an advanced friction ring device that let hunters interchange between light and heavy loads without requiring any mechanical adjustment. I did considerable grouse and pheasant hunting with a 20-gauge Model 11-48 Sportsman during the early 1950s and it was a pleasant gun to carry and point. I do not recall any malfunction incidents due to load changing. That was a step in the right direction by Remington, but it was 1956 before any other significant developments occurred in autoloading smoothbores.

In 1956, the first commercial gas-operated autoloader was offered to shotgunners. Known as the J. C. Higgins Model 60, it was developed and built for Sears, Roebuck & Company by the High Standard Manufacturing Corporation following the design concepts of the famed M-1 Garand rifle. This involved a bulky piston-and-spring assembly wrapped around the magazine tube, and it required a deep, protruding beavertail forearm which critics found unsightly and even humorous. Gun-writing Colonel Charles Askins Jr., writing in *The Shotgunner's Book* (1958) opined that the "J. C." in J. C. Higgins did not stand for John Clarence at all, but rather, "Those initials stand for Josephine Clementine; for you see J. C. Higgins is a female. I know this to be a fact, for the gal is in a family way."

After High Standard finished putting a steel rib and bold compensator-type choke device on the barrel, the Model 60 became rather ponderous, too. Some folks objected to the gun's action bar, which was openly exposed along the receiver's right side, running just below the ejection port.

The Model 60 did have one interesting early feature: the ability to handle all standard-length 12-gauge loads with no need for mechanical adjustments or barrel switching. Excess powder gases from heavy loads were bled off through a gas orifice. Thus, although the Model 60 never did catch on with skeet and trap shooters or advanced bird hunters because it was heavy, bulbous and possessed an indifferent trigger, a number of years would pass before another manufacturer made load interchangeability as simple as High Standard had on the pregnant-appearing "Josephine Clementine."

The problem in reaching the ideal with autoloading shotguns designed for gas operation was the gas pressure remaining at the bleeder valve location down the bore (normally at the location of the barrel loop). Light loads generate less powder gas than high-velocity and magnum loads and if the bleeder valve or valves are generously sized to conduct ample volumes of gas from light loads, they will invariably permit too much of the more robust gases from the heavier and magnum loads to enter the piston chamber. As a result the action will be battered when magnum loads slam into the piston and ram it backward. On the other hand, bleeder valves made smaller to control the amount of powder gas from magnum loads

SHOTGUNNING TRENDS IN TRANSITION

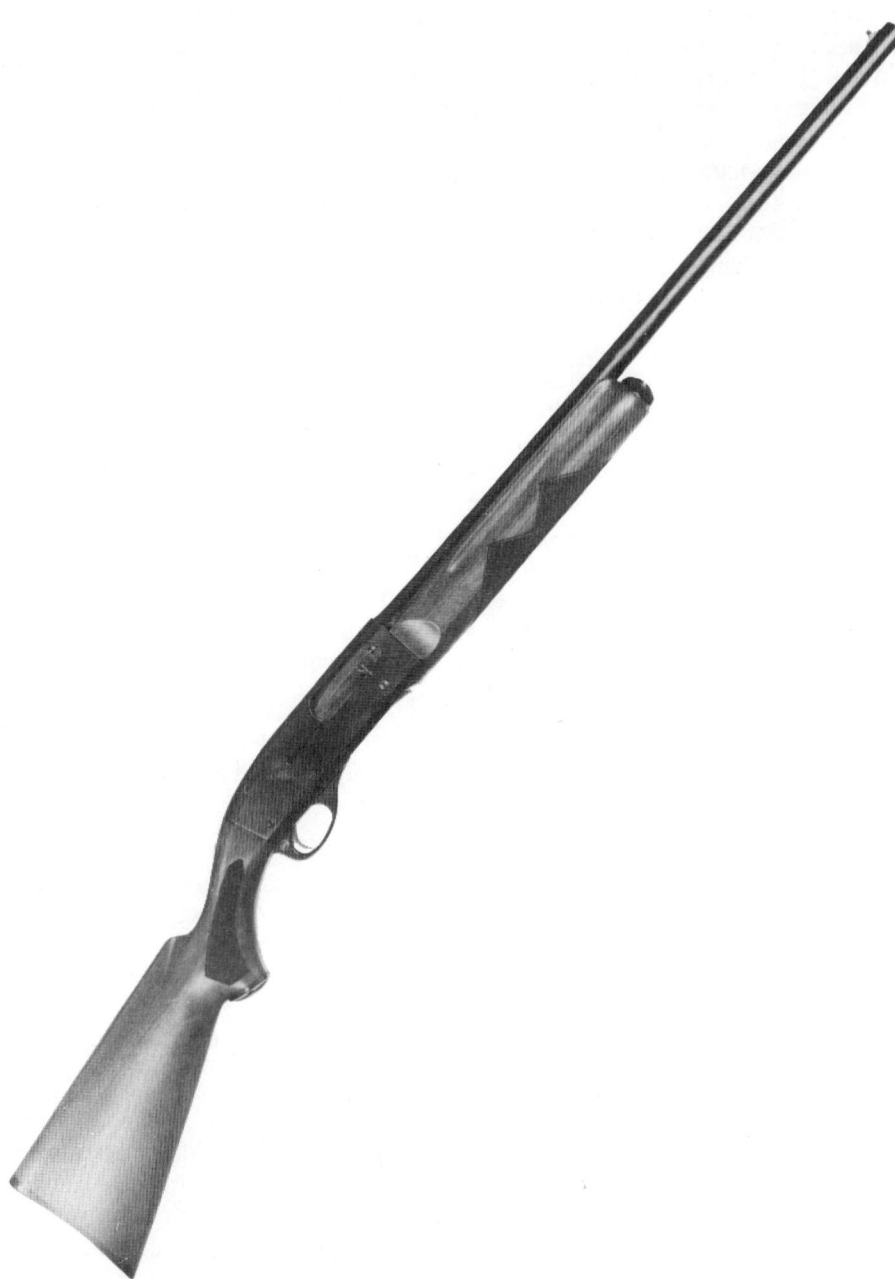

The Remington Model 11-48, introduced near mid-century, was the first commercially successful streamlined autoloader. Although it still used the Browning long-recoil mechanism, it did away with the Browning "humpbacked" receiver.

MODERN AUTOLOADERS: THE CLOSEST THING TO PERFECTION

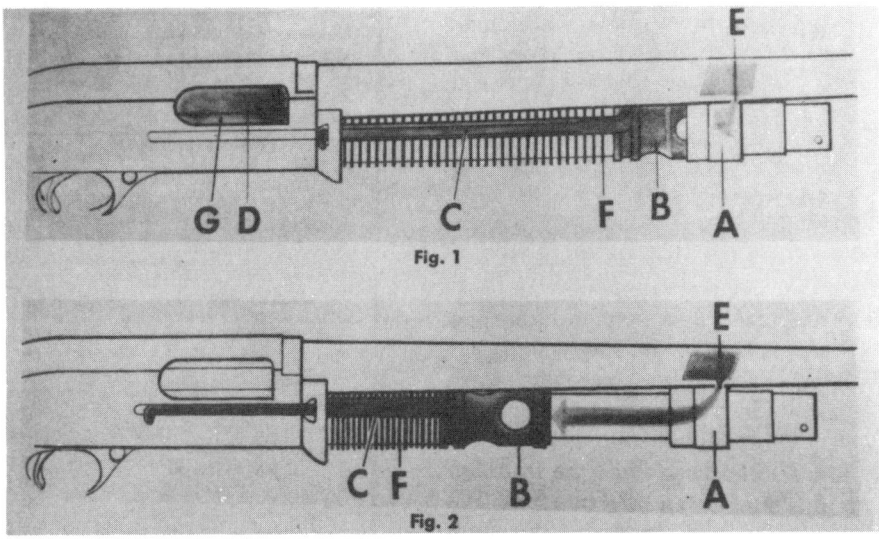

The mechanism of the first commercially offered semiauto shotgun, the J. C. Higgins Model 60, utilized a bleeder valve at Point E. Powder gases were diverted from the bore to the piston at Point A, and the piston and action bar (points B and C, respectively) were driven back to open the ejection port and bring up a fresh load. The massive coil spring wrapped around the magazine tube (Point F) controlled the piston's rearward force and supplied the energy which brought the bolt back into battery.

don't conduct enough gas from the lighter rounds to open the action. Thus, for a time, compromises had to be made in gas-operated guns; the gas ports had to be designed for standard or magnum-length loads, and the extremes in load potencies could not be interchanged without altering the mechanism or changing barrels for the appropriate valve diameter.

Remington's Model 58 gas-operated auto came along at roughly the same time as the J. C. Higgins Model 60, but it didn't solve the gas-venting problem without a mechanical feature in the magazine cap. With a standard-chambered Model 58, one could not switch from light to heavy loads without indexing the magazine cap for the anticipated amount of powder gas. This cap was indexed with "H" and "L" settings, the "H" obviously standing for heavy loads and the "L" for light ones. By positioning the cap at "H," the shooter opened more holes in the cap to exhaust excess powder gas so that the action wouldn't be hammered; by dialing the cap to "L," he closed off the multiple holes so that the lower gas pressure from light loads would be utilized efficiently. While this was no major inconvenience, it was not yet perfection in autoloader design. And when the three-inch 12-gauge Magnum Model 58 came along, it normally wouldn't function with the lighter loads — again depriving hunters of optimum versatility.

In 1959, Remington improved its technology and introduced a new form of the Model 58 known as the Model 878, but it lasted barely three years. Many current shotgunners and gun show enthusiasts don't even know about the Model 878. It had the same profile as the Model 58, but without the indexing "Salt shaker" magazine cap. The Model 878 was made to handle all standard-length 12-gauge loads interchangeably *sans* adjustment. Before it had much of a chance, however, the Model 878 was elbowed aside by the great Model 1100 in 1963. Personally, I feel that the Model 58/878 design was one of the best profiled and best swinging gas guns to come along. It's unfortunate that the guns' mechanisms proved less than optimum. By placing the piston inside the magazine tube, as on both the Model 58 and 878, Remington gave the guns a less rotund forearm and somewhat less weight up front. As gas guns go, the Model 58 with a fitted stock is probably my all-time favorite.

Remington's Model 1100 has become the number one autoloader ever used in skeet and trap, and it more than holds its own in Sporting Clays and field-gunning. But the "Eleven Hundred" didn't reach the ideal of total load interchangeability, either, because the three-inch Magnum models in 12 and 20 gauge wouldn't cycle with light loads; the bleeder valves in magnum barrels were too small to transfer enough gas into the piston chamber. A hunter, however, could make the Model 1100 Magnum work with everything from light to whopping magnum rounds by simply switching to a barrel with the standard-length chamber and different valves. The standard-length-chambered Model 1100 barrels had two valves; the magnum-chambered Model 1100 barrels had one valve (which was sufficient because of the prolonged intensity of the pressure curve with progressive-burning propellants).

The Beretta Model 302 and the Browning B-80 had identical capabilities — versatility dependent upon barrel switching.

Although the Model 1100 has not reached the ideal state of complete load interchangeability, it has had a long and proud history. It was the gun which made autoloaders acceptable in trapshooting. It was the soft-shooter that won countless skeet tournaments. And it has bagged nearly every type of game. Reportedly, the Model 1100 is the one autoloader that the British will use. The gun's stock dimensions came as close to being universal fits to all hunters and shooters as any mass-produced gun. Anyone who says a Model 1100 doesn't fit him, normally doesn't know how to hold a shotgun. Anyone who can't score with a Model 1100, normally can't shoot! Well over three million Model 1100s were sold between 1963 and 1988, which says more for the gun than it does for those who criticize it.

Breakthrough

The most important breakthrough in autoloading shotgun technology was unveiled by, of all manufacturers, Smith & Wesson. The gun was a variation of the Model 1000, a semiautomatic S&W had been importing from Japan's Howa Machinery, Ltd., to expand sales volume beyond their normal handgun line. This advanced variant was named the Super 12. It was the first 12-gauge autoloader built to handle everything from one-ounce target loads to two-ounce, three-inch magnums without necessitating *any* mechanical manipulations. A hunter could chamber a trap load, then stuff a $1\frac{1}{4}$-ounce duck load with a $1\frac{7}{8}$-ounce three-incher into the magazine and trigger them in rapid succession while the gun automatically adjusted for the gas pressure variations. Never before had that kind of versatility been available.

How could one autoloader be made to handle the entire spectrum of 12-gauge loads? The Super 12 did it with a gas relief valve, something the firearms industry calls "self-metering." Located at the very tip of the magazine tube, the Super 12's self-metering device is controlled by a coil spring that holds a flanged metal seal (valve cover) tightly pressed against the leading edge of the piston chamber. The pressure of the powder gases working against the seal compresses the coil spring to permit varying amounts of exhaust according to the individual load's potency. The coil spring can hold against the lesser gas pressures of light field and target loads, thus, sealing in all gases to operate the piston. As the pressure mounts from heavier loads, the coil spring yields and compresses according to the force being applied, and excessive gases are pushed forward to jet out of the perforated magazine cap. The action's dependability, therefore, is based on the strength of the coil spring: It must hold against lower pressures but yield progressively under steadily higher pressures.

The Super 12's presence in America undoubtedly prompted a flurry of research and development activity. Stateside gunmakers and other importers wanted to remain competitive. In 1987, the battle was joined by Remington, Beretta and Browning.

SHOTGUNNING TRENDS IN TRANSITION

The Remington Model 1100 was famous for its excellent pointing qualities which made it effective on grouse in the thicket as well as high-winging geese and skeet or trap clays in the open.

MODERN AUTOLOADERS: THE CLOSEST THING TO PERFECTION

Remington's entry has since superseded the famous Model 1100. It is catalogued as the Model 11-87, but its profile is identical to its predecessor. Internally, however, the Model 11-87 differs from the Model 1100: It has a thicker extractor for added strength, redesigned firing pin retractor spring, heat-treated piston and piston seal for longer wear, stainless steel magazine tube, a more securely attached feed latch, stronger barrel support ring, a pinned forend, and a detent spring feature in the magazine cap to hold it in place.

More importantly, the Remington Model 11-87 has its own self-metering gas system which permits the random, mixed-up use of any and all commercial 12-gauge loads up to three inches without requiring any mechanical adjustments. It, too, is built around a relief valve. Interestingly, the Model 11-87's relief valve is not an integral part of the magazine tube or piston assembly. This self-metering system is located on the barrel loop which fits around the magazine tube. The gizmo is simplicity personified. There are two bleeder valves coming down from the bore, just as on the standard Model 1100; however, to allow excess gas exhaustion, there are also two additional venting holes opposite each other on either side of the barrel loop. These venting or exhaust holes are sealed by a flat spring which fits circumferentially about the forward edge of the barrel loop. The flat spring opens according to gas pressure from each load. In principle, it is identical to the Super 12's self-metering, gas-relief valve, only it utilizes a flat rather than a coil spring.

The Beretta Model 303 is made with an equally simple device, namely, a self-metering stainless steel piston. To date, the Beretta Model 303 has not topped the popularity lists as the Model 1100 and Model 11-87 have. It is not a high-profile winner at skeet or trap, but it is making some headway in Sporting Clays.

In the Model A-500, however, Browning dared to be different. This gun is *not* based on gas operation. It utilizes recoil energy in connection with a short-recoil system and a novel behind-the-breech coil spring feature. When fired, the barrel and breechblock of the A-500 remain locked together for a rearward travel of about half an inch. This is the short-recoil feature in operation. (The long-recoil mechanism, as on the Browning Auto-5 and Remington Model 11, was so named because the barrel and breechblock remained coupled until the breechblock reached the full extent of its rearward thrust.) During this half-inch rearward stab, a massive coil spring, nested in the breechblock directly behind the breech face, is heavily compressed. As the barrel and breechblock separate, the coil spring comes into play. The energy it supplies from uncoiling now initiates an inertia-block action which drives the breechblock the remainder of the way to its fully open and locked position. Another coil spring buffering device curled around the tubular magazine acts as a buffer to the barrel's forward return. Likewise, a shock absorber mounted in the receiver's stern cushions that point. The breechblock is returned to battery by a pair of coil springs housed in the receiver, not in the grip as is so common among autoloaders. The use of a coil spring in the breechblock assembly

SHOTGUNNING TRENDS IN TRANSITION

The Remington Model 11-87's self-metering gas system is predicated upon a flat spring that nearly encircles the barrel loop. Shown here in its normal position, it closes a pair of exhaust valves, but . . .

MODERN AUTOLOADERS: THE CLOSEST THING TO PERFECTION

when powder gases arrive, the spring yields (as illustrated here) to release excess gases. This simple device uses the lower pressures of light loads while releasing, variously, the higher pressures of heavier field and magnum charges.

isn't unique with Browning's A-500, of course. The Italian-made Benelli has a similar mechanism, but the Benelli doesn't self-compensate for the entire range of 12-gauge ammunition as the A-500 does.

One outstanding feature of the Browning A-500 is its use of double coil springs on both the hammer and action return. Thus, the barrel bounce of the A-500 is not uncomfortable. Perhaps the most prominent attribute of the A-500 is its upper tang line which can only be described as a "swoop" as it falls away from the hump-backed receiver. At this point, I cannot perceive the A-500 as a serious trap or skeet gun and how it will score in Sporting Clays remains to be seen. In general, it's a hunter's gun, and my experience with it on geese and pheasants indicates that it should perform extremely well afield.

The point is that, after nearly a century of tinkering, gunmakers have finally brought the soft-shooting autoloaders to the state where hunters can load any legitimate ammunition in any order and expect the guns to function without adjustments by the shooter. Compared to the technology that has been applied to other products, the new shoot-any-load self-shuckers were long overdue![1]

Pointing/Handling Qualities

Mechanics aside, autoloaders have other qualities that elevate them to a niche directly below the best doubles as effective fowling pieces. In fact, if one can tolerate something less than the delightful balance he gets in a fine double, he will find that some semiautomatic shotguns can be close to perfection.

Just as a double barrel's underlines are important to its pointing/handling qualities, so is an autoloader's exterior dimensions vital to its dynamics and pointability. If one critically examines the autoloader's receiver depths and gripping features, he may be pleasantly surprised. A vernier caliper will prove that some autoloaders are not fat and deep, and that various models have more than held their own in metallic trimness vis-a-vis over/unders of the same gauge.

In my earlier book, *The Double Shotgun,* I set down the arbitrary figure of 2½ inches as the dividing line between high and low-profiled 12-gauge over/unders. That dimension hasn't been questioned by any noteworthy source. As I place a vernier caliper on the midsection of a Model 11-87 Remington that reclines on my lap, I measure a depth of just 2.30 inches at the center of the ejection port. On the other hand, many of the vaunted and supposedly elegant low-profiled over/unders measure to 2.43 inches (or thereabouts) through the standing breech, meaning the Model 11-87 (as well as the Model 1100) actually is trimmer than the toggled low-framed over/unders. The Remington Model 1100 28-gauge skeet gun leaning against my desk measured only 2.19 inches at the same mid-port point. Thus, autoloaders aren't naturally slab-sided or gross. Compared to certain 12-gauge over/unders, they actually are trimmer.

MODERN AUTOLOADERS: THE CLOSEST THING TO PERFECTION

Browning's newest, the Model A-500, which can handle interchangeably all loads from one-ounce target to three-inch two-ouncers without necessitating any adjustments. Activated by recoil, it is one of the new breed of autoloaders which offers optimum versatility.

What makes so many autoloaders appear beefy is the beavertail forend which, of necessity, must encase the gas gun's piston, springs and action bars or rods. Although the beer-belly forend isn't truly aesthetic, it must be noted that many gas guns point excellently, thanks to their designers' concern for underlines which keep the shooter's hands in line relative to the bore axis. As will be explained more fully later, this hands-in-line relationship is an important factor in employing optimum eye-hand coordination.

Hands coordinate best when they are working on the same plane and having one higher or lower than the other simply thwarts accurate and easy shotgun pointing. Fortunately designers have recognized this need to keep the hands in line with each other, and they have balanced off gas-operated autos with pistol grip geometry to bring the trigger hand level with the leading hand's position on the forend. A gun like the Model 1100 or Model 11-87, therefore, may depress the hands somewhat below the bore axis and not provide the same hand-to-bore proximity that side-by-sides do (or over/unders do relative to the lower barrel), but I've come to conclude that one can sacrifice some hand-to-bore distance and still point very accurately and quickly *if* the hands remain in line with each other and the bore axis. Frankly, I believe I can point a Model 58 Remington and its successors, the models 1100 and 11-87, as accurately as any stackbarrel. There is very little difference between the over/under's upper barrel and the leading hand and the Model 1100/11-87's barrel and the leading hand. When it comes to hand location and hand-to-hand coordination, then, shooting the autoloader can be equated with using an over/under's upper tube.

Of course, no one will argue that gas-operated autoloaders have the responsiveness of trim, spirited doubles. Gas guns have too much stuff up front, and manufacturers have been making the barrels heavy to withstand the pressures of slow-rate powders, magnum loads and steel shot. All this leaves the basic 12-gauge autoloader variously muzzle-heavy.

There have been, and still are, some autoloading designs that come extremely close to the handling and pointing dynamics of responsive over/unders. My own feeling has always been that the Browning Double Automatic, created by Val Browning back in 1958, was the first semiautomatic to approach the handling qualities of a good upland double. The first time I picked up a Double-Auto I felt like I was swinging a spirited over/under.

Val Browning, son of the famous John M. Browning, worked this bit of design magic by eliminating the forward weight necessitated by his father's long-recoil system and combining what has become known as the short-recoil system and inertia block. Whereas the original Browning Auto-5's long-recoil mechanism had the barrel lock to the breechblock for virtually the full length of the block's rearward travel, the Double-Auto's barrel had only a 1½-inch maximum rearward jab, which was controlled by a short but massive coil spring laid in the slender semi-beavertail forearm. This short recoil thrust overcame the block's inertia and gave it rearward momentum so that, coupled to a short inertia weight working back and forth in a tube extending from the receiver's rear into the stock, it continued backward to open via its own energy.

Moreover, the Double-Auto, as its name implies, was a two-shot affair, and it held the second shotshell in the receiver directly below the breechblock. Consequently, a long tubular magazine wasn't needed, and the front recoil spring did not need a large diameter. These innovations kept the Double-Auto trim, and when the alloy-framed models (the 7-pound "Twelvette" and 6½-pound "Twentyweight") came along, hunters found them extremely responsive. A grouse-hunting friend uses the Twelvette enthusiastically and wouldn't trade it for any over/under. Regrettably, the massive coil spring that returned the barrel to battery could make the 6½-pound Twentyweight jump forward, and this made the Twelvette more popular. Unfortunately, however, not many hunters cared for a semiautomatic that held only two shells, and the Double-Auto was dropped in 1971 before the sporting world caught on to its qualities. Since this was also before the over/under was "discovered" by rank and file shotgunners, there was no basis for comparison.

The Italian-made Benelli, which is sold stateside by the West German firm of Heckler & Koch, is another autoloader that has pointing qualities akin to a thin over/under. A photo of a Benelli may not give that impression, but handling one certainly does. A considerable number of mass-produced, heavy-barreled over/unders have worse dynamics and definitely more noticeable recoil than the Benelli.

The Benelli's operating system is a unique blend of recoil and gas-operated concepts, but it is unbelievably simple and compact. The heart of a Benelli is found in the breech bolt design, which features a three-part mechanism. The bolt is a two-part design, having a head which locks up firmly against the chambered shotshell and a floating body whose purpose will be discussed shortly. The third component is a strong coil spring sandwiched between the bolt head and the floating bolt body. the plot should be thickening!

Upon firing and the inception of recoil, the bolt head remains fixed in place and recoils backward. However, the floating breech body hangs in place relative to the recoiling gun, thanks to its own inertia, and the coil spring is compressed between the bolt head and bolt body. At this point, the spring takes over. Its energy pushes the breech body backward, whereupon the moving body trips a locking bar to unseat the bolt head. All of this happens so rapidly that, once the bolt head has been unlocked, the bolt head is forced open by residual bore pressures. The whole thing is amazingly swift, so swift that the Benelli is thought to be the fastest-firing autoloading shotgun. Moreover, once the bolt head has released, the Benelli's gases work against a floating breech assembly rather than against a solid breech, thus lessening apparent recoil.

SHOTGUNNING TRENDS IN TRANSITION

The Benelli is one modern autoloader that points amazingly like an over/under, but has considerably less recoil than any stackbarrel ever built.

MODERN AUTOLOADERS: THE CLOSEST THING TO PERFECTION

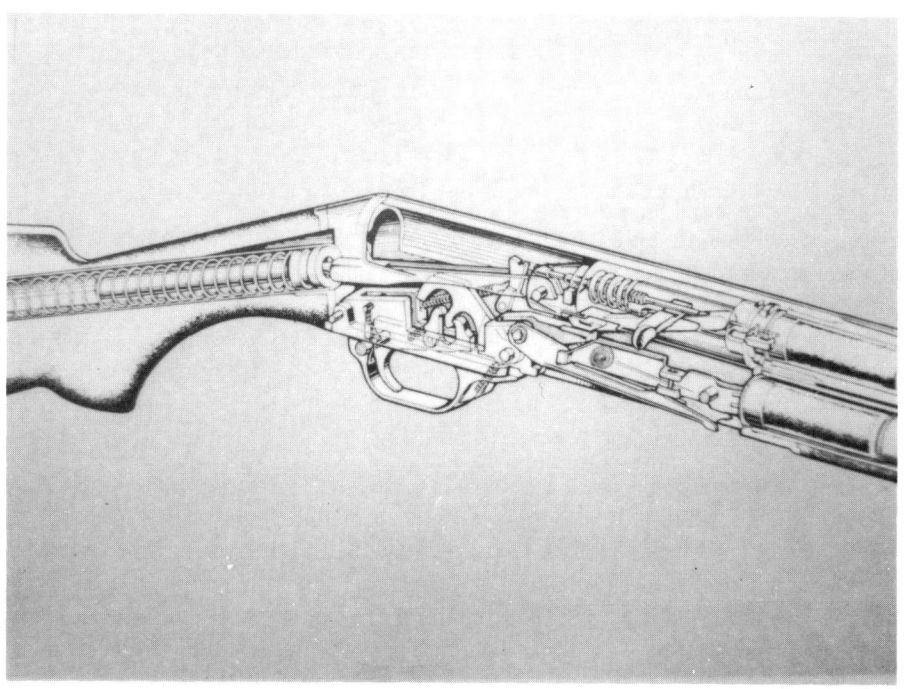

The Benelli is based on a recoil-operated system with stationary barrel and none of the "double-shuffle" effect of the Browning long-recoil types. Note the massive coil spring in the breechblock assembly as mentioned in the text.

SHOTGUNNING TRENDS IN TRANSITION

At this time, American shotgunners haven't discovered the Benelli, but with its stationary barrel eliminating the "double shuffle" of recoil-operated guns, and its utilization of powder gases against a floating breech assembly, the gun has much to offer bird hunters and, perhaps, Sporting Clays shooters.

A post-World War II American autoloader that also applied its recoil forces against a floating breech assembly was the Winchester Model 50. It had a slipping chamber that jabbed backward under recoil, overcoming the breech bolt's inertia and sending it backward. The Model 50's opening was assisted by a small inertia weight linked to the breechblock. While this tandem traveled backward, there was no recoil imparted to the gun. Unfortunately, debris tended to get trapped between the slipping chamber and its counterbore, whereupon the gun would jam. I have always felt that the Model 50 was softer shooting than any gas-operated autoloader yet devised, but the public didn't want it.

One cannot argue that the Model 50 pointed or felt like an over/under. Actually, it felt more like the famous Winchester Model 12 pumpgun.

A variant of the Model 50 was the Model 59 Winchester, an ultra-light 12-gauge autoloader with a high-strength barrel formed by wrapping fiberglass strands around a thin steel liner. An alloy receiver and trigger guard turned this into a 6½-pound field gun of surprisingly light recoil. The Model 59 was well ahead of its time, and was the first modern commercial shotgun to utilize the screw-in choke system, the Versalite. But the Model 50 died around 1961 and the Model 59 tumbled from favor in 1965. I have a hunch that the alloy-framed Model 50 and the Model 59 would have been more successful in the 1980s than in the 1960s.

In general, modern autoloaders have better pointing and handling qualities than many dedicated doubles shooters realize. Unfortunately, some of them have gotten barrel-heavy and don't come close to matching the fine weight distribution of elegant side-by-sides. But the gas guns win like crazy at clay target events, while the weight-forward hang of many autoloaders undoubtedly has translated into momentum which has helped more than a few waterfowlers or dove shooters into positive follow-throughs. Indeed, it becomes increasingly difficult to argue with success!

That doesn't mean we must accept the modern autoloader per se. Despite the facts that autoloaders have progressed mechanically, that they are soft-shooting and have very good pointability, that they have been streamlined and are being designed and made on high-tech equipment, and that some models now shoot all the 12-gauge loads (except 3½-inchers) interchangeably and without any mechanical adjustments — the autoloader still has a way to go. More thought must go into self-cleaning concepts, into weight elimination and especially into weight distribution to bring the weight more squarely between the shooter's hands. Regardless of what advertisements may claim, we have not yet developed the perfect autoloader. More creative work remains in this adventure in gun design.

Chapter Notes

1. As this book is being written, a new 3½-inch 12-gauge Magnum steel shot load has been announced. It obviously will not feed through the Super 12s, Model 11-87s, A-500s and Beretta 303s. Exactly how the 3½-incher will fit into autoloaders is something only the future will decide. My opinion is that the 3½-inch 12-gauge should remain a specialized gun because standard-length shotshells fired in such an extra-length chamber would have to make an extremely long jump into the forcing cone, and thus be exposed to potential ballistics and patterning upsets. An autoloader that pops along smoothly with both 2¾ and three-inch loads is already quite versatile and, measured by a typical hunter's skills and needs, is entirely adequate. Interchangeability between standard-length and three-inch loads still can be considered ideal, state-of-the-art production.

Chapter 6

Gun Collecting Facts and Fallacies: A Personal View

MANY OF the reasons people are prompted to collect Rembrandts, Rolls-Royces, or grandfather clocks also apply to those who collect, or would collect, shotguns. Those reasons may include: 1) investments for future resale at substantial profit; 2) as objets d'art which simply bring enjoyment; and 3) as high-classed items which exemplify the finest features and craftsmanship built into that particular art. Whatever reason(s) motivates you — relax and enjoy your collection!

From my point of view, however, I can't believe that the typical individual shotgunner has much of a chance to make the whopping profits thought to be an integral part of gun trading. Indeed, unless one has a substantial bankroll behind him to diversify his holdings and to pay his rent and groceries while the guns appreciate and/or attract buyers, he should probably collect shotguns for enjoyment, rather than as an attempt to make a killing.

This is not to say that fine guns or certain mass-produced items don't have value or that they can't generate profits. The hand-craftsmanship that goes into the finest shotguns ranks them alongside other works of art. Like jewelry, expensive antiques, custom cars and paintings, they carry value among those who treasure them. Even in the United States, where shotguns are less cherished as works of art than they are in England and Europe, it is not unusual to find great breakaction shotguns and other rare items selling for more than $50,000. The new American shotgunner is becoming more sophisticated, and those who can afford collectibles are willing to pay higher prices than the shotgunners of the first half of the twentieth century; they were shotgunners who looked upon guns as mere tools for harvesting.

But for all that growing sophistication, and despite increased prosperity, it still is difficult for a typical shotgunner to justify gun collecting solely as an investment. The market has its own dynamics and they can be complex. Moreover,

SHOTGUNNING TRENDS IN TRANSITION

even the finest guns aren't readily liquid. It takes time to find a buyer who will pay your asking price, for although the new Yankee wingshot is becoming more sophisticated, it doesn't mean that every neighborhood, city or state has buyers who will part with thousands of dollars for a gun.

Fitting a gun sale to a person who both wants it and can pay a price that nets a profit is in itself quite a hunt. Much time, effort and money can be spent finding "Mr. Right." I know one man who, during his working years, gathered a small collection of excellent Parkers. Upon his retirement he put them up for sale at prevailing gun show asking prices. The fact that they were Parkers, all still neat and tidy, would cause one to believe that they sold in a whirlwind and that the retired gent could thereafter spend his winters lounging on Miami's beaches. The fact is that it took three full years to sell those Parkers at his prices. That's hardly considered a liquid investment compared to stocks and bonds which can be sold in minutes through practically any broker and result in immediate capital gain. Obviously, there were a lot of lower bids on those Parkers; gun trading is rife with chiselers looking for a bargain. But selling at a price below your asking level simply means lost money, and that's hardly a way to conduct business. Thus, don't be misled by the high asking prices on many guns; they may sound super, but the seller frequently must sit on them for years or settle on a lower price. And that takes the gilding off the lily.

When small investors find themselves unable to sell investment-quality guns, they frequently use the services of a broker or a large dealer, either of whom works on a commission of approximately 15 percent. Even brokers and noteworthy dealers have trouble selling some guns. Moreover, from the original owner's standpoint, the 15 percent loss from commissions may skim the profit, leaving the original owner with considerably less to show for his "investment." If it is true that a fine gun appreciates by 5 to 10 percent per year (which is subject to question), the commission cost wipes out 1½ to three years of appreciation value. Would you put your money in the bank for that length of time without accruing interest?

A would-be guns investor must realize that many of the nation's foremost dealers and brokers in fine collectibles do so with little of their own capital. They work on commissions, selling consigned guns and deriving their income from a service rather than a personal investment. If you closely follow the gun trading game, you'll learn that leading dealers won't buy a gun outright unless it is sold to them at a considerable discount from the market's general pricing.

For a small investor, then, guns can be a poor business. They sell slowly, are not readily liquid and are subject to the pricing of a vague market that operates solely on what the market will bear. Nowhere are exact trading prices carved in stone for any given time or transaction. Haggling is part of the game and success is not guaranteed. The biggest mistake a shotgun investor can make is buying at prevailing prices in hopes of a profit. Prevailing prices already are high and, in all probability, won't become fully accepted for years, possibly decades. The greatest advantage seems to be that often you can sell a fine gun and not include the Internal Revenue Service as a beneficiary, especially if the sale is made person-to-person rather than through a licensed dealer or broker.

Finally, it has been argued that fine guns are hedges against inflation, that they at least hold their values and, upon resale, return to the seller his original amount of purchasing power. While this theory isn't a complete fallacy, it does have its faults. One problem is the typical person's inability to comprehend monetary values. When inflation roars, the dollar's value, alias purchasing power, shrinks. Thus, a gun trader must think in terms of purchasing power when he prices his guns for resale, not simply in terms of dollars per se. Depending upon the severity of any given inflationary period, a gun that was purchased for $7,000 before inflation struck might actually net the seller a loss when sold for $8,000! The value is not determined by the number of dollars alone, but rather by how much each post-inflation dollar can buy relative to the purchasing power of the original investment.

If a typical wingshot with less than a bulging bankroll shouldn't get involved with expensive shotguns as sheer investments, why and how should he approach the finely made, collector-grade pieces? Again, my feeling has long been that a dedicated shotgunner will derive far more pleasure from his hobby if he buys expensive, sought-after pieces mainly to improve the quality of his own life and/or to use them on game birds or clays. In other words, don't buy anything unless it rewards you with personal pride of ownership and/or thrilling dynamics and shooting performance. If a shotgun does that, and if you can afford it — buy it, appreciate it and don't worry about the investment or possible resale profit.

More than a few hunters and clay target shooters will cock an extremely skeptical eyebrow at the suggestion that they carry thousands of dollars worth of shotgun afield or onto a clay target installation. A few seasons ago, for example, I descended from a hilly section with my Merkel over/under which is worth roughly $2,000. The hills were rugged, brush-covered and given to clawing at gun stocks. As I returned to my car with a brace of ruffed grouse in tow, another hunter drove up the gravelly road in one of those big four-wheel-drive pickups equipped with huge tires and myriad antennae sticking up, making the vehicle look like a gargantuan insect. The driver, who apparently knew something about guns, took one look at my Merkel and asked, "Hey, aren't you afraid of scratching that gun?"

"No," I replied, "I'm more afraid that I won't scratch it?" The driver didn't quite catch onto that remark, but it was my little way of saying that I intend to use fine guns exactly the way they were intended to be used. As the beer commercial stated, "You only go around once," and if you're a dedicated shotgunner, why not make the best of it with fine guns?

Since that gravelly road was narrow and had tree limbs sprawling out from both sides, I turned the question around: "Aren't you afraid of scratching that truck?"

SHOTGUNNING TRENDS IN TRANSITION

Despite high prices placed on finer shotguns, there actually is a generous supply of high-quality pieces. The author suggests that such prices are artificially inflated.

"Me? Naw," came the answer. "I take this baby through hell and high water. I want performance!"

"So do I," was my counter, "but I want it from shotguns, too!" I'm not sure if he understood that point, either. So many hunters still believe that a gun is a gun, whereas the finer examples almost always have enhanced handling qualities that endear them to knowledgeable shotgunners. Although my Merkel's high frame contributes to a somewhat slab-sided profile, the gun actually scales a tad less than 6¾ pounds which, with 28⅝-inch barrels, places it within the parameters of a British game gun. Experienced shotgunners who have handled it claim the Merkel virtually flows to the target. I tend to agree because I have scored tremendously well with the gun on everything from woodcock to geese. Thus, I have pride of ownership and a performance tool that apparently suits my technique perfectly, and when I ring down the curtain I'll never have missed the two grand! Indeed, those two thousand dollars will probably have given me more fun afield than any 15 thou spent on a four-wheel-drive!

It has always amazed me when a middle-income earner spends well over $10,000 on a recreational vehicle and then grimaces at the thought of using just a $1,000 grade scattergun. Meanwhile, most RVs and four-wheel-drives are thoroughly abused, being raced through mud, pounded into snow, spun from sand or marsh, and left outside in rain, sleet, snow, blow and subzero. Each year such a vehicle depreciates by a sum greater than I needed to buy my Merkel, but the hot-dogs who batter them into submission think nothing of *those* monies. Indeed, any enthusiastic shotgunner can afford a finer gun if he will simply reduce his truck or auto expenditures.

Things are changing, I'm happy to report. Overall, there are more expensive guns being bought and enjoyed these days than ever before. Some observers may harken back to the days of the Parkers, Foxes, Smiths and Lefevers, of course, but the historical fact is that each of those old lines sold very few high-grade pieces, which is why the A-1 Specials, Deluxes and Monogram grades are so valuable; they're rare items as hardly anyone bought them. The average gun of yore was a claptrap double selling for $5 to $10 from the Sears, Roebuck catalog.

All one need do today to see fine guns is to attend trap and skeet shoots. It isn't uncommon to find low-income wage earners mounting high-quality guns in both sports. The expenditures aren't solely for snob appeal or gun art, either. Modern high-quality target guns have advanced dynamics designed for each sport. The initial breakthrough came when Ithaca Gun Company began importing Perazzis in 1969. These were always expensive guns compared to the typical shooter's take-home pay, but the guns proved they could score; and within a short time, shooters well below the millionaire class "did without" a few other luxuries to buy a Perazzi.

Another major factor is that new shotgunners coming into the sport have a definite European slant toward hunting and shooting. Unlike older hunters, this new breed isn't afraid to pay for their sport; they like the finer things and they've generated a totally new market for upgraded equipment. Many of them are well-educated people who appreciate the finer concepts. They may not hunt as much as the rural dweller who packs his freezer with wild game each fall, but when they do hunt they enjoy going first class. Rather than being completely self-taught, the newer shotgunners tend to read more and even spend some time with recognized shotgun coaches. They are, therefore, aware of advanced ideas, values, equipment and theory.

It is interesting to note that throughout most of the world's history the number of truly fine guns being sold rises in inverse proportion to the amount of land available for free public hunting. When land is free and open, the market for knockabout guns is tremendous; people who have no interest in guns per se still buy them to hunt for "cheap" meat. But as land closes to the public and game populations dwindle, as they are at present, the demand for those cheaper guns dries up, for many people will not consider buying a gun unless it means free meat on the table, and they *certainly* won't pay to hunt on commercial preserves. This leaves the sport to people who love to hunt and/or love shotguns. The amount of game they kill is not the prime consideration — they like being outdoors and they enjoy owning fine guns. This class of person willingly pays for preserve shooting.

Thus, the trend currently is toward the better grades of shotguns, as witnessed by Remington's re-introduction of a custom-made Parker at $12,000. A decade or so ago, this market probably didn't exist. Remington was content to make all the Model 870s it could to supply a still-expanding market. But time changes all things and the knockabout market is dwindling while the demand for higher grades of guns steadily increases. This trend helps support the collectors' market and makes fine guns popular.

Caveat Emptor

Before any dedicated shotgunner treats himself to an investment or collector-grade gun, however, he must understand that the entire institution is predicated on the classic economic principle of *caveat emptor* — let the buyer beware! There are crooks in this business. There are high-pressure salesmen. There are those who badly misrepresent the condition of the guns they sell. There are outlandish prices. Luckily, there are also some reputable dealers and brokers. But never, ever buy *anything* without making a thorough study of the product and, if possible, the dealer handling it. Make certain the dealer or individual seller is reputable and that he will stand behind the piece. Don't take chances when thousands of dollars are on the line. It takes a long time to earn those dollars, so don't be in a hurry to throw them away. Mull over a possible purchase; don't panic into a helter-skelter acquisition.

Moreover, never blindly accept the asking price on any gun, as they all tend to have built-in cushions to ensure the seller a profit. Any gun dealer or broker knows that this is a bid-and-ask business and because of haggling he'll most likely set high prices. The real selling prices are often lower than those asking prices published in the likes of *Shotgun News* or *The Gun List*. If a dealer or broker holds firm, back off. Let him know you're interested and give him your phone number; tell him to contact you if and when he changes his mind, then walk away. In guns, as in any other business, a quick turnover is still the best profit. When a dealer senses your interest, he may shave the price quickly to clinch a sale. On most days, a smaller profit is better than no profit.

Be extremely careful when evaluating the condition of a used gun. The only ones that are worth the top dollars being asked these days are those with virtually new colors that scream. These guns are variously classed as NIB (new in-the-box), like new or mint. To be considered new, the guns must have 100 percent of their original case color, blue and stock/forearm finish. Anything less reduces the value markedly. Pay for a new collectible only when it is *indeed* new! Don't be duped by a fraudulent seller who says, "Oh sure, it has a little wear from handling, but otherwise it's absolutely like new." That doesn't cut it. The gun is being misrepresented and that happens a lot these days. That dealer is trying to sell a gun that's in NRA excellent condition at a new gun's price. Snicker and walk away or if you have the fortitude, point out the seller's fraud. Unfortunately, there are no laws covering such misrepresentations in gun trading and dealing, which is why the buyer must beware.

Anyone shopping for a collectible or high grade of shotgun should probably stay away from local gun shows and deal only through reliable dealers and brokers. Truly desirable guns seldom appear at such local gun shows, anyway. Great guns tend to be in collections already, and when they change hands they normally do so through strategically placed and informed dealers rather than over a wobbly table in a dimly lighted dance hall setting. Experts know that few people who attend these gun shows will pay for an excellent collectible, and the smaller traders who populate local gun shows invariably try to make a fortune on each gun, asking new-gun prices for "beaters." Knowledgeable shotgun men find local gun shows boring these days. Choice items are seldom seen and the tables are heaped with pure junk. The only gun shows worth attending are the huge national displays like those at Las Vegas, Houston or Dallas where there's enough money showing up to tempt the better dealers.

Although the expression "fine old gun" has been applied very broadly (too broadly, in fact), it means nothing regarding shotgun values and desirability as investments, personal possessions and effectiveness afield. Many gun show people who speak knowingly about shotguns have no business acumen, no honest in-depth knowledge and certainly no shooting ability. Ignore such worthless chatter. To be an investment, a collectible of value, or a sought-after "shooter," a shotgun

SHOTGUNNING TRENDS IN TRANSITION

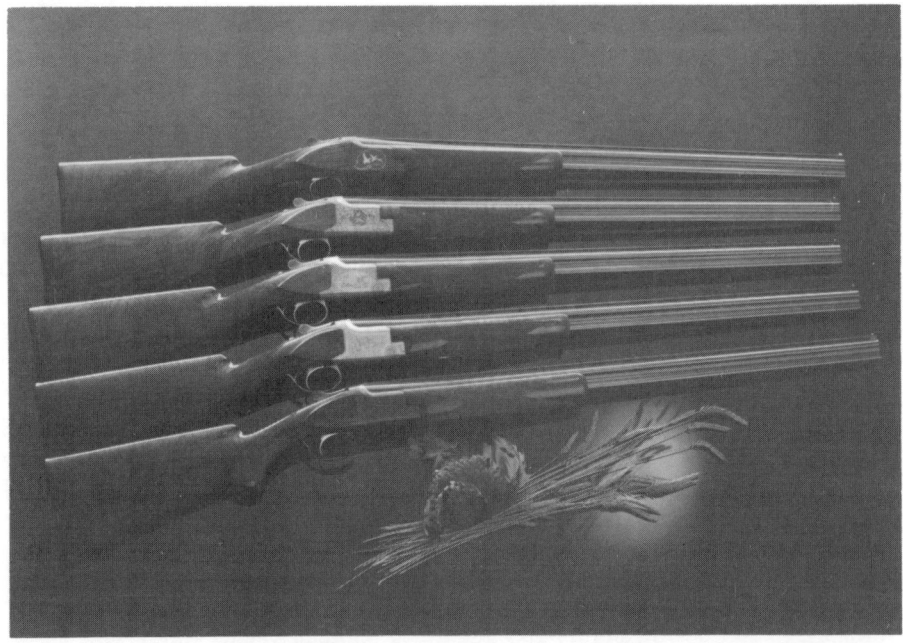

Once the leading over/under, the Browning Belgian-made Superposed guns have lost favor among most target shooters and are now virtually a glutted market. They can, however, be finely built and finished smoothbores. From the bottom: the Field Grade, Pigeon Grade, Pointer Grade, Diana Grade and the famous Midas.

must be in demand and/or have cherished qualities. Demand alone, however, doesn't rank a shotgun as a great shooter. Nor does age automatically mean quality.

Naming Some Names

Collectibles and shooters can be found at every price strata. My feeling has been that the biggest mistakes are made by buyers of lower-priced guns, say, those which range from a couple of hundred dollars to those which reach a couple of thousand. But even at the top, collector prices can be ludicrous. Many of the higher-priced doubles, for instance, are said to be exceedingly valuable because they were made entirely by hand, and prices can range from about $6,000 to well over $50,000. Even when these supposedly handmade objets d'art were originally built, the actual production costs were but a portion of their selling prices. Firms like Purdey, Holland & Holland and Boss did *not* put $10,000 worth of labor into a gun they sold for that price! Much of the handmade gun's original selling price was pure profit for the company, in which case one pays $10,000 for roughly $3,000 or $4,000 worth of skill. The high original price is normally justified, of course, because operating overhead must be covered, and everyone needs to make a little profit. Buyers are fools, though, if they pay a premium for an older fowling piece which already had its original price pumped up by profit rather than pure workmanship.

Although I love the great British and European doubles, and I find them more dynamic, sophisticated and refined than anything America has yet produced, I also question the figures put on those in the stateside fine gun market. A tremendous British game gun made for $2,000 in the 1930s or late 1940s probably didn't have $1,000 worth of craftsmanship in it — so why is it now, in the late 1980s, suddenly worth over $10,000? Scarcity can't be the answer. Check the advertising media and you'll see dealers stocked high with used Purdeys, Holland & Hollands, Bosses, Powells, Westley Richards, W. & C. Scotts, Greeners, Sauers, Heyms, Merkels, etc. Indeed, if there is a scarcity of anything in this fine gun market, it is a paucity of buyers. But dealers (mainly consignment dealers) retain ultra-high prices for the utmost profit, thus ensuring a higher commission. There are just enough people around who occasionally buy at stratospheric prices to keep dealers hopeful. Remember, although the great and truly fine guns do have *some* value, the market is badly inflated when compared to the actual artwork in them.

The same is true for many American collectibles and shooters from yesteryear. In the United States, for example, the name of Winchester fires the imagination at gun shows. The primary Winchesters of interest are those made prior to 1964, a time when Winchester quality dropped like a rock, as did the former models such as the Model 12 pumpgun, the Model 42 .410 and the Model 70 rifle. Many of these Winchesters were classic in mass production, of course, but one wonders if they were *really* as valuable as modern traders and dealers would have us believe!

SHOTGUNNING TRENDS IN TRANSITION

Take the Model 12 pumpgun, for instance. This segment of the used gun and collector's market has been hyped for over 20 years. It is not uncommon to find like-new Model 12s with price tags topping $700 in the plain field grade. Put that new Model 12 into its original box with its hanging tags, and the dealer may ask a cool thou! To hear dealers and traders talk, one would think the Model 12s had dried up and were about to disappear, but if any shopper were to pay close attention as he visits various gun shops, gun shows and major trapshoots (such as the Grand American at Vandalia, Ohio), he will literally trip over Model 12s! Moreover, the demand doesn't appear to be anywhere near the intensity level traders and dealers would have us believe. Indeed, Winchester made over two million Model 12s, and there are plenty around so that, with a minimum of shopping and negotiating, an interested party should be able to secure one without paying a steep premium.

In many instances, the Remington Model 31 was a better pumpgun than the Model 12. When both guns were extant, gunsmiths invariably complained that the Model 12 was difficult to time, whereas the Model 31 Remington had a smooth, short stroke. From what I have seen, the Model 31's design produced greater longevity; the Model 12's takedown feature always was a weakness.

Of all the once-standard Winchester pumpguns, the Model 42 .410-bore rates utmost attention these days. A few more than 160,000 were made, and finding them NIB is difficult. The skeet grades rate the highest, and those with factory-engraved receivers are gems. Between their popularity and their low number, the Model 42s seem destined to be attractive collectors' guns for years to come. It is one of the few pumpguns for which I would pay close to the prevailing prices and expect the gun to hold its own or appreciate. A quail hunter who enjoys a little snob appeal might very well find the Model 42 a joy, especially if he's a pumpgun aficionado.

A gun with surprising collector appeal is the Winchester Model 24, a knockabout side-by-side introduced in 1939 when Winchester saw that the higher-priced Model 21 was spinning its wheels. In my opinion, the Model 24 was one of the first economy doubles made in the U.S. with reasonably modern stock and forend dimensions. The forend was a semi-beavertail, while the stock had a full comb with elevated heel dimensions for a drop tandem of $1\frac{1}{2} \times 2\frac{1}{2}$, which is akin to post-war configurations drawn up to suit our lean-into-it style. This step away from the dogleg stock aided pointing, but it didn't temper recoil! The Model 24 kicked viciously at a shooter's fingers as he worked the twin-trigger arrangement. Why some collectors are willing to pay high prices for the Model 24 puzzles me, but a good one remains an attraction at most local gun shows. A look inside the gun should change one's mind!

Although Winchester's autoloaders never have been commercial successes, the Model 50 and its variant, the Model 59, still find favor among hunters. The Model 50 was well made and, based upon an inertia block system plus floating chamber,

Although repeaters seldom carry the same collectors' value as doubles, the little Winchester Model 42's price has been driven upward by a sustained demand. This is a skeet grade, one of the Model 42's most desirable and sought after versions.

was one of the lightest-kicking shotguns ever made, lighter even than some of our best gas-operated shotguns. Its fit and feel closely resembled that of the Model 12. The Model 59 had the same profile and recoil-operated mechanism as the Model 50, but it was a considerably lighter gun with a most unique barrel that consisted of a steel inner liner wound by a covering of fiberglass. The Model 59 also was the first modern gun to champion the screw-in choke tube system, the Versalite. The Model 50/59 appear somewhat more popular and valuable in the southern half of the United States, although some northern hunters of the woodcock and ruffed grouse also swear by them. As sheer collectibles, only the pigeon-grade Model 50s appear promising. The only other Winchester semiautomatic of collection value is the skeet grade Model 40 with burl wood and factory-attached Cutts Compensator (of which very few were made).

Winchester's Model 21 side-by-side has been America's best domestic double for years, and they have the potential for future appreciation. The buyer must be selective, however, as advanced collectors know that there were various levels of quality in the Model 21's history. Whereas the Model 21 became a custom gun with substantial hand-craftsmanship, the earlier ones came up lacking in quality. They were little better than high-priced, semi-production doubles with added attention given to the final fit and assembly.

In *The Shotgunner*, Bob Nichols recalled that, "The first units of the Model 21 double-gun that came to market were far from outstanding. They gave the impression that the great repeating-arms manufacturing concern was floundering a bit beyond its depth in the field of double-gun making." Thus, don't believe that any and all Model 21s are alike. Make a study of the gun, its history and production changes before buying. Those with splinter forends and double triggers tend to have less value than the rest. The smaller gauges also command attention, although the .410 and its boxy breech area is hardly fashionable. Skeet grades seem popular, especially the so-called skeet-grade trap guns. As of this writing, the collector and shooter demand for Model 21s is still less than overwhelming, and it may take years before it materializes. For the money, British guns are better shooters, original Parkers are better investments, and Remington's born-again Parker of 1988 is better handling.

Remington shotguns have not, on average, fared as well as Winchester's. However, many Remington models were excellently made and equal to anything Winchester turned out. It seems that collectors are simply obsessed with Winchesters because they tend to bring more money in the current market, and the shooting qualities of Remington guns have been overlooked. Along with the previously mentioned Model 31 pumpgun, Remington made the best over/under ever assembled stateside — the Model 32. In the last few years, collectors and shooters have shown an interest in the Model 32 and values have jumped appreciably because so few good ones are available.

Nostalgia also triggers some buying responses. The American doubles — A. H. Foxes, Parkers, Lefevers, Bakers, L. C. Smiths, Ithacas, Colts, Remingtons — currently are riding a crest of popularity, and the activity involves some of the least intelligent buying and ridiculously high pricing. With many of the higher-grade Yankee doubles gone, or with the lower-income collectors wanting to enter this market, the former economy-class American side-by-sides have suddenly taken on bewildering, if not insane, values. The guns in question include the Fox Sterlingworth, Parker Trojan, Lefever Nitro Special and the various low-grade Smiths from Hunter Arms. Unbelievable sums of money are being demanded, and received, for these doubles. The sad fact is that, even in their heydays they were nothing but simple knockabouts made cheaply by the foremost manufacturers of doubles to enhance sales volume. These are *not* handmade classics; they are not refined guns.

I believe that Peter H. Johnson overdid his eulogy of the original Parkers when, in *Parker, America's Finest Shotgun*, his coverage led readers to believe that the Trojan was a "hand-made, hand-finished gun..." akin to the finest that Parker or the British had to offer. All guns from that era had some hand-involvement, of course, just as they do today, but it's the careful attention to detail that counts, and such time and work could not have been put into the Trojans which came onto the market at $27.50! With the company, distributors and retailers all taking profits out of that $27.50 figure, the actual cost of production could not have topped ten bucks! Pardon me if I chuckle when I hear of somebody paying $1,000 for a Trojan or $500 for a Sterlingworth! (By the way, Johnson's book also says that Trojans were made only in field grade, but if you'll visit the Remington Museum in Ilion, New York, you will see a Parker Trojan skeet gun with beavertail forend.)

The only early American doubles that are worth reasonably high prices are those with like-new colors. Ditto for those with the most advanced engraving. These would be at the level of the Parker A/AA grades, the L. C. Smiths in Monogram and Premier plus Deluxe, and the Lefever AA and Optimus. Below those levels, the engraving quality on American doubles was exceedingly grade-schoolish. It lacked detail, had minimal background and depth, and the figures were often unnatural. The L. C. Smith 2E and 3E, for example, had totally amateurish art. Their current prices on the collecting market are far in excess of their quality. For example, the birds had round little bodies supported by stick legs, something one would expect from a third-grade art class.

Good Stuff and Greater Fools

Thus, shotgun collecting can be enjoyable, upon occasion it can be profitable, and it is fun to hunt with the guns of yore, but don't make blind thrusts into the market or the business. "The greater fool theory" is operative in this field. That means that someone pays more than he should for something in hopes that, later on, he'll find an even greater fool to take it off his hands at a higher price.

SHOTGUNNING TRENDS IN TRANSITION

A Parker Trojan and a mixed bag of woodcock and ruffed grouse. The Trojan is a nice shooter and blessed with some nostalgia, too. But why is a former $27.50 knockabout suddenly valued at nearly $1,000?

GUN COLLECTING FACTS AND FALLACIES: A PERSONAL VIEW

This is not to say that fine shotguns aren't desirable — you owe yourself one. I heartily recommend them, but don't be cheated. Shop patiently, carefully and intelligently only after investigating the entire market, the dealer or other seller, widespread pricing, the overall demand and supply ratio, and the individual gun's condition. Don't jump at the first asking price! Anyone who buys in the collector's market at or near the peak cannot expect a sizeable profit for decades. Also, don't let periods of economic prosperity or inflation (times when there can be some wild gun trading and buying going on) lull you into believing that fancy prices are the norm. Today, most fine guns have artificially high prices, totally unsupported by a favorable supply-demand situation. If you will follow advertisements, you'll see that many dealers today are stuck with some mighty fine guns, a condition almost solely created by the desire to try for every last penny of profit. What the gun trading business and fine gun market really needs is a crash similar to the one experienced by the stock market in October 1987. That would bring prices — and people — back to reality!

Chapter 7

Modified Choke — Myth and Confusion

FOR MUCH of my high school career, I was a country kid who made my daily trek to the big city edifice with a lunch bag under one arm. In those more casual years, the school day included a noon break that stretched for more than an hour. Rather than sit around the school's lunchroom every day, I made at least twice-weekly tours of downtown hardware stores and the sports counters of department stores to see what new guns had arrived. The one thing which stands out in my mind is that, for those three years in senior high school, I didn't see any shotguns with barrels shorter than 28 inches. Not one! I would have remembered, because even then I was a budding gun nut with a critical eye. Back home I had a stack of the most recent catalogs, and kept up to date on the offerings and different models. About all that ever populated the local gun racks were relatively long-barreled pumps and autoloaders, with just a couple of Stevens doubles occasionally thrown in. Even then, the doubles invariably poked 30-inch tubes downrange.

The retailers' stock, of course, only reflected the demand. Hunters at the time were rather obsessed with long barrels and full chokes. The sleeker the barrel and the tighter the choke, the easier it was to sell. Hunters wanted smoothbores that shot like rifles; they wanted to snap the head off a cottontail at 20 paces, reach out for a ringneck (of which there were quite a few when I was a kid), and drop mallards at estimated 60-yard distances on a local marsh that had red-hot action in those days.

About that time, gun writers were beginning to point out the errors in such gun selections. Not only were the long-barreled repeaters laggard in their handling qualities, the scribes of yesteryear argued, but full-choke patterns caused plenteous missing over the closer ranges. The question was: Why miss a lot of nearby birds and running cottontails just to make a few spectacular long-range hits each season? That made sense. Typical hunters don't have the skill to score reliably with tight patterns on fast-breaking shots, be they in the thicket or over decoys. Thus, why not pick a more open choke that gives a wider, easier-to-hit-with pattern for close and moderate-range chances?

Midcentury gun writers tried to change the typical hunter's habits by recommending modified choke as the all-around choke. In the 1940s and 1950s, I read any number of magazine articles stressing modified over full choke. Scribes of the day not only correctly pointed out that a 28-inch barrel handles better than a 30-incher, but also claimed that modified choke gives added hitting area for close-in shots while still retaining adequate density for effectiveness as far as most hunters' skills could take them. I vaguely recall one magazine column in which the writer termed modified choke as the "all-American choke" because of the way it theoretically handled every aspect of stateside wing-gunning.

Once the gun writers picked up the cause of modified choke, hunters began to believe everything they heard about modified. Few hunters, if any, ever patterned to see exactly how modified choke patterns compared to full and improved cylinder patterns, or how they actually performed according to what the hunter needed. The versatility of modified choke, along with modified's vaunted all-around capabilities, has always been based on theorizing and/or hand-me-down advice. However, among rank and file American sportsmen, the boasted versatility and all-around capabilities of modified choke have never been seriously questioned or checked. Could it be that the whole thing is a myth, something that is believed merely because it has been repeated so often?

Through the decades, my own patterning, hunting results, field observations and clay target shooting have made me skeptical of the theory regarding modified choke's ability as an all-arounder that successfully splits the difference between improved cylinder and full choke. Whereas old-timers argued that modified gave more spread for close-range shots than full choke while also providing more density than improved cylinder for the longer chances, I feel it is legitimate to turn the reasoning about: Modified choke also shoots tighter at close range than improved cylinder while throwing weaker patterns at long range than full choke. Thus, instead of finding strengths in the theoretical all-around abilities of modified choke, we can pinpoint definite weaknesses. I don't agree that this is merely an academic difference of opinion as it may be when two people look at a glass of water and one says it's half-full while the other says it's half-empty. In the case of interpreting modified choke, there is scientific substance for evaluation, namely, patterns and pellet distributions.

A Working Hypothesis

After sifting the evidence, I have come to doubt that modified choke is the effective and versatile all-around choke that many writers have blatantly claimed it to be, or that hunters have casually accepted it to be. Field and clay target experience, along with a pile of patterning sheets, prompt me to hypothesize that

MODIFIED CHOKE — MYTH AND CONFUSION

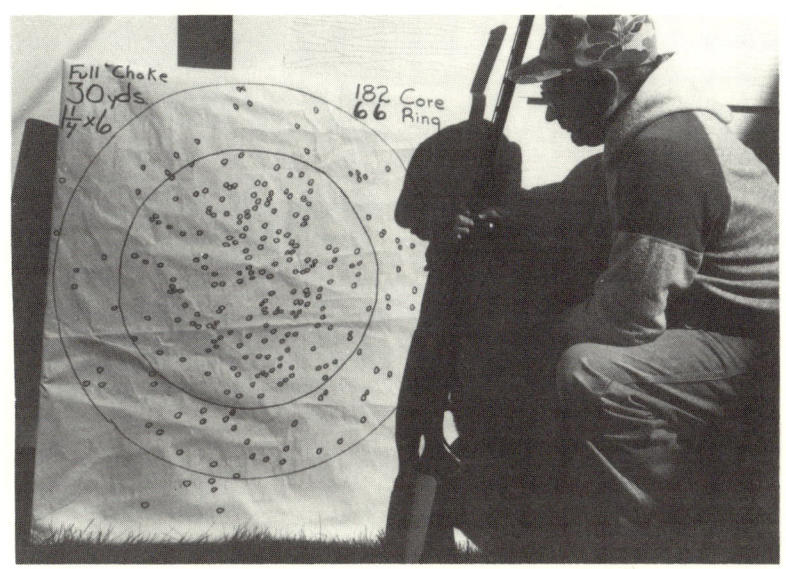

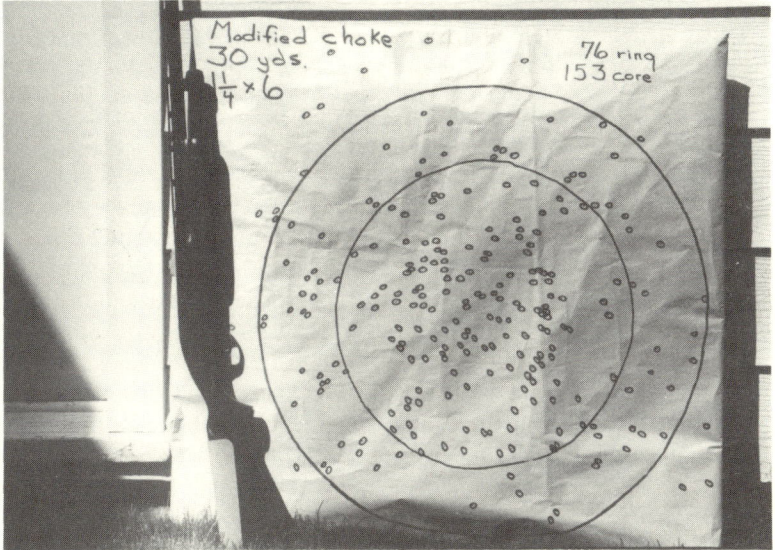

Although typical hunters dealing in rule of thumb concepts assume the modified choke to throw larger effective patterns than the full choke, this isn't always true. Above, for example, is a 30-yard pattern fired by a true full-choke gun/load combination at just 30 yards, and it shows the same basic coverage as the pattern (below) plastered by a positive modified choke. The main difference between the two patterns is found in the 20-inch-diameter core, where the full choke places more shot (182 pellets) than the modified choke (153 pellets). Overall pattern expansion on a purely effective basis is virtually the same for both chokes.

modified choke is nothing more than a true specialty choke, *not* an all-arounder, being at its best between 25 and 40 yards with a minimum of $1^1/_8$ ounces of shot. My working hypothesis is predicated upon the fact that, as illustrated by numerous patterns, modified choke offers but scant hitting advantage over the full choke inside 25 yards, and fails to provide any efficient advantage over the full choke beyond 35 yards. Succinctly put, a modified choke with no less than $1^1/_8$ ounces of shot is mainly a medium-range selection *unless* the hunter patterns carefully and alters patterns by load manipulation.

To present some data that bolsters this hypothesis, a table of nominal pattern diameters for the standard degrees of choke as established by Major Sir Gerald Burrard in *The Modern Shotgun* follows:

choke	spread in inches at						
	10 yards	15 yards	20 yards	25 yards	30 yards	35 yards	40 yards
full choke	9	12	16	21	26	32	40
modified	12	16	20	26	32	38	46
improved cylinder	15	20	26	32	38	44	51
cylinder bore	19	26	32	38	44	51	57

Although there can indeed be variations between Burrard's figures and results from other randomly selected gun/load combinations, his comparative results are reasonable. A study of those figures indicates that, at close range, modified choke offers no more than three to four inches of greater pattern expansion than does full choke. That is rather paltry; it's not much bigger than a woodcock's bill and it is much less than the length of a bobwhite's body. Anyone who speculates that those meager three to four inches of added spread will make scoring easier with a modified than with a full choke is suffering from delusions.

On the other hand, the difference between full choke and improved cylinder at 20 yards is about 10 inches, and at 25 yards it's approximately 11 inches. At 22½ yards, according to Burrard's table, the improved cylinder pattern fills a 30-inch circle, while the full choke pattern hammers only the 18 to 19-inch core. In general, the improved cylinder opens to 30-inch coverage five yards sooner than modified and 10 yards earlier than full choke. This gives modified choke a 30-inch spread at 27½ yards if we employ Burrard's figures, which is hardly short-range in shotgunning. By the time we reach 27½ to 30 yards in wingshooting, we're at medium-range. Close range for the smoothbore terminates between 20 and 25 yards. Thus, whatever benefit may be derived from modified choke over full choke inside 25 yards must be considered marginal.

Now let's turn to the opposite extreme and compare modified and full choke at 35 to 45 yards. If we check Burrard's figures, we find that modified choke offers about six additional inches of spread at this distance. At 40 yards, the full choke opens to about 40 inches while the modified flares to 46 inches.

That's where some discrepancy arises. What Burrard's figures don't spell out is how the pellets are distributed in the respective clusters as patterns open markedly beyond 30 yards. Loads don't hold enough adequately heavy pellets to fill those huge 38 to 46-inch spreads that modified chokes can toss at 35 and 40 yards, respectively. From everything I have seen on paper, expanded modified patterns are neither evenly distributed inside the 30-inch pattern at 35 to 40 yards nor capable of printing more than random and extremely irregular fringes outside the 30-inch ring at those extended distances. Modified choke, in contrast to the way some perceive it, simply doesn't open in a linear, cone-shaped manner with progressively even pellet distribution. Pellets that fly outside the main 30-inch working mass tend to flare quickly; the pattern scatters like the curve of a trumpet's bell, not like an ice cream cone's linear lines. And when those flaring pellets fly, they seem to depart posthaste; they often fail to impact on a 40-inch-square patterning sheet.

The main point is that modified-choke patterns may arrive at 40 yards in lower percentages inside the 30-inch circle, but their fringe areas don't pick up the missing shot. There is no guarantee that modified throws a wider *effective* pattern than full choke beyond 32½ to 35 yards! Modified choke only delivers a lower percentage of the original pellets at 35 to 40 yards. Thus, after having read a lot of patterns, I believe the sole difference between full choke and modified choke at 35 yards and beyond is that modified choke places less shot into the working pattern. The respective hitting areas are basically similar.

Some readers may be puzzled by my acceptance of full choke as the practical hitting-area equal of modified by 35 yards. Take another look at Burrard's figures. He shows that the full choke reaches a spread of 30 inches at about 32½ yards, which is in keeping with the old rule of thumb that full chokes open at the approximate rate of one inch per yard of flight. If modified choke pellets don't group together to thicken the area immediately outside the 30-inch circle (which they normally don't), where is the advantage in modified choke at that range? Since full choke begins to reach a full 30-inch spread by 32 to 33 yards, and definitely does so by 35 yards, there is scant, if any, advantage in modified choke between 35 to 40 yards.

While armchair theorists may scoff at that last statement, the case is well-documented by trapshooters who switch to modified choke for 16-yard singles in hopes of picking up more targets with a theoretically larger pattern — only to switch quickly back to improved modified or full choke. The trap lines are densely populated by such shooters who are now disenchanted with modified chokes because they found that modified not only did not help their scores, but the lighter, chippier hits did not give them confidence. The interesting thing about this trap-shooting application of modified chokes is that 16-yard trapshooting finds targets

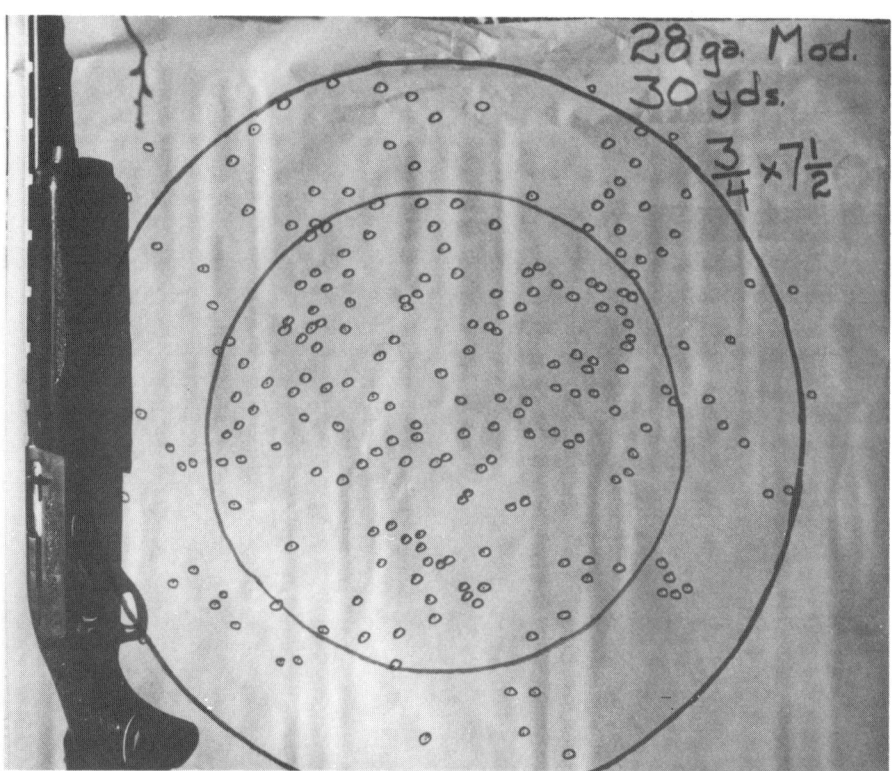

At 30 yards, this pattern shot by a modified-choked 28 gauge using ¾-ounce of No. 7½ shot shows why smallbores can be cripplers. The annular ring of the pattern is filled with "patchy" areas. The author's preference in smallbores is for a full-choke beyond skeet ranges to get the maximum number of pellets into the pattern. Let the swing take on importance rather than a theoretically wider pattern.

MODIFIED CHOKE — MYTH AND CONFUSION

being hit between 32 and 35 yards, the very point where full choke starts reaching a 30-inch pattern and modified begins to weaken. Indeed, if you're one of the doubters who believes modified exceeds my findings, take a gun that's throwing bona fide modified patterns and shoot some 16-yard trap with it, then observe the impact of the hits and record your scores. Next, switch to a gun doing honest full choke percentages and fire the same course. Note the greater impact due to more pellets and the same or higher scores, plus greater confidence in the way you hit them. That comparison on trap clays will demonstrate something about pattern density and diameter in comparative action as one nears 35 yards.

There is one final important technical point that I must make about the comparative performances of modified and full chokes as their patterns develop between 32½ and 35 to 40 yards (i.e., after they've both reached 30-inch-diameter pattern spreads): Aside from establishing their relative percentages, patterning sheets have proved to me that the main difference in their pellet distributions is in the core of the patterns, *not* in the annular ring, as so many typical hunters and trapshooters assume. Time and again, I have patterned modified chokes vis-a-vis full chokes only to find that, by 35 yards, their respective annular rings held approximately the same number of pellets. The reason why the modified choke averaged, say, 58 percent while the full choke did 72 percent was determined solely by core counts. The full chokes put more pellets in the middle of their patterns, while the modified chokes had fewer core shots. In the outer ring, however, pellet counts are frequently quite similar, whether with the five-inch annular ring of a Thompson-Oberfell pattern or the 12-field, 7½-inch annular ring of a Berlin-Wanasee patterning outline.

Some patterning I did with a Beretta 687EELL illustrates that point. Bored modified and full, the Beretta was patterned at 40 yards using Remington 1⅛-ounce loads of copper-plated 7½s. The modified barrel averaged around 58 percent; the full choke averaged 78 percent. Both patterns had quite similar outer ring characteristics. The main difference was that the near-80 percent full-choke cluster had heavy center packing, while the modified pattern had less center density. The modified patterns didn't show any more perforations immediately outside the 30-inch circle than did the full-choke patterns.

In another test, patterns were run through a Beretta BL-3 also bored M&F using this reload:

> Winchester AA hull
> Winchester 209 primer
> 23.5/473AA Ball powder
> Winchester WAA12F114 wad
> 1¼ ounces of hard No. 6s
> Pressure: 9,500 LUP
> Velocity: 1,150 fps
> (Source: *Winchester data booklet*)

Average results were 60 percent for the modified tube and 74 percent for the full choke.

It was interesting to note that the full-choke barrel actually put more pellets into the annular ring than the modified. Over the five patterns, the modified placed from 123 to 130 pellets in the various outer fields, whereas the full choke's delivery ranged from 134 to 141. Thus, in this comparison, the full choke actually outshot the modified in core *and* ring density despite being known as a "tight choke."

In the 15-inch-diameter core of the Berlin-Wanasee patterning outline, the full-choked Beretta barrel badly outshot the modified member. It placed 84 to 90 pellets in the core; the modified choke, 47 to 55 pellets. Although each barrel shot within the parameters of its respective degree of choke, then, the modified choke gave noticeably less density in both the core and ring sections. In turn, we are forced again to ask: Where's the advantage in modified choke between 32½ to 35 yards and the next five yards out to a full 40 yards?

Assessments of 40-inch-square patterning sheets don't prove that modified does give wider *effective* patterns than full choke once the 35-yard range is approached. About all modified choke delivers are lower-density patterns than full choke as the 35-yard distance is neared. That explains why trapshooters get chippy hits with modified chokes and don't see appreciable improvements in their scores, for all they're doing when they switch to random combinations of modified choke and load combination is lowering their pattern percentages without experiencing a concomitant filling of the pattern's outer rim.

Once shotgunning ranges snuggle up to 35 yards, modified choke becomes a questionable choice. Its patterning weaknesses appear quickly. My feeling is that a hunter is better off with full choke as early as 35 yards, because full choke places more shot into the overall pattern and offers as much *effective* hitting area as most basic modified clusters. The same is true for trapshooting unless a given shooter has lightning-like reactions and movements so that he can snap the target inside 30 yards where modified patterns retain more shot.

For the purpose of this book, some patterns were fired at 37½ yards to illustrate the difference between a modified and full choke with hunting loads using 1¼ ounces of copper-plated No. 6s. Accompanying photos illustrate the average pattern for each choke. Again, note how the main contrast is found in the core density, not the annular rings or the number of pellets immediately outside the main 30-inch-diameter circle. Both chokes placed 75 to 80 pellets in the annular ring, shot to shot, but the modified invariably trailed the full choke's core density by 15 to 20 pellets per pattern, the full choke averaging 115 hits per pattern while the modified averaged 97.

As stated in my hypothesis, therefore, I can find room to argue against the aged concept that modified choke is a great all-arounder. At short range (inside 30 yards) it doesn't open up much faster than full choke. At 35 yards it begins to weaken

MODIFIED CHOKE — MYTH AND CONFUSION

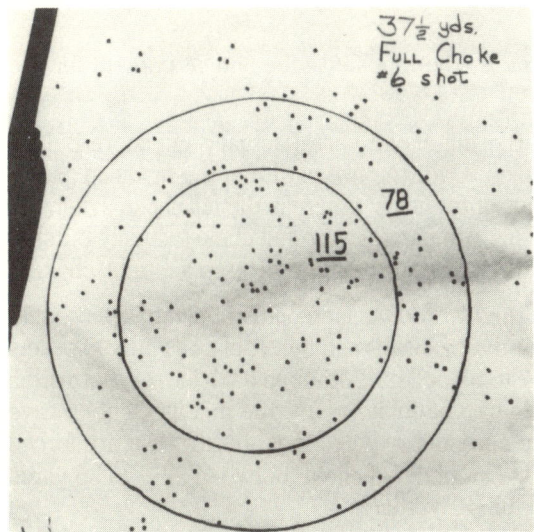

These patterns were fired at 37½ yards to illustrate the similar overall pattern width and different pellet densities of a bona fide modified choke as compared to a definite full choke. This average performance for the full choke places 115 No. 6s in the core and 78 in the annular ring with a nominal count immediately outside the main 30-inch circle.

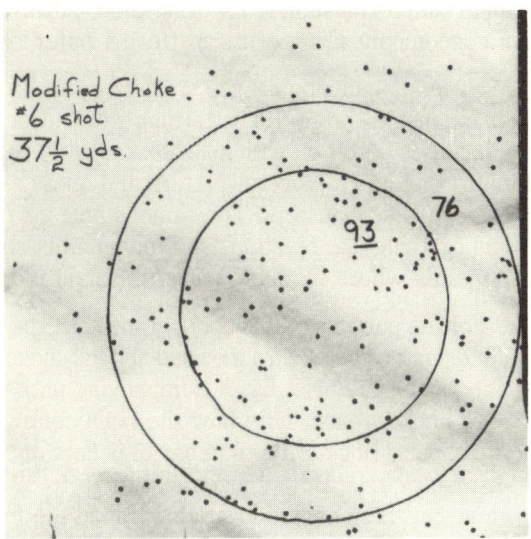

On the other hand, the modified choke differed solely from the full choke because of its lower core density. Otherwise, the annular ring densities and outside distributions were practically the same as those of the full choke. Thus, by 37½ yards, this particular full choke is giving the shooter as much effective hitting area as the modified, and is doing it with more shot.

and provides a wingshot with nothing but lower pattern percentages and precious little added effective hitting area compared to the full choke's output. Thus, instead of viewing modified choke as a jack-of-all-trades, I prefer to classify it as a specialized choke — one that is at its best between 25 and 35 to 40 yards. If a hunter gets his shooting at those distances, *especially between 25 and 35 yards*, modified will work just fine. If you really want to see how tight modified still holds at close range, shoot a round of skeet with it and watch the clays turn into smokeballs (as compared to the less violent hits of skeet or improved cylinder chokes). And if you want to see how weak it becomes by 38 to 40 yards, shoot some trap handicap from the 24 to 25-yard handicap stripes and watch the plinky, chippy hits as compared to what a good full choke will do.

State of Confusion

Added to the aforementioned hypothesis about modified choke's role in winggunning is one more problem, namely, the definition of a modified choke is in a state of confusion. There are various standards for it. For example, the British have always called modified choke "half choke," assigning it approximately half the amount of constriction used in full choke. According to tables in British writer Gough Thomas' book *Shotguns & Cartridges for Game and Clays* (A. & C. Black, Ltd., London, 1963), the standard British half-choked 12 gauge would have 20 points (thousandths) of constriction and be expected to throw a 60 percent pattern at 40 yards. The *Winchester Ammunition Handbook* of approximately the same vintage, however, suggests that American modified chokes pattern at 45 to 55 percent, leaving the tighter 55 to 65 percent performances under the style of improved modified. Moreover, an interior dial caliper slipped into many American modified-choked guns will come up with dimensions below the 20 points published by Gough Thomas and the British gun establishment. So many American modified chokes that I've measured, along with American-distributed guns made in Asia, have had modified-choke constrictions of 14 to 18 points. When put on paper, their patterns often fall short of 60 percent even with high-quality ammunition. This, I feel, is ample justification not to support the modified choke as an all-arounder; for those light constrictions don't generate ample pattern density as one approaches middle shotgun range extremes.

To obtain a modified choke pattern that's adequately effective beyond 35 yards, and even able to smoke up trap clays at 32 to 33 yards, a minimum of 20 points of choke constriction is needed. I find my best open-pattern trap choke to be about 22 points. Likewise, the 22-point modified choke chalks up cleaner kills in hunting. This dimension places modified closer to improved modified, which tends to have constrictions of about 25 to 28 points in many trap guns.

There is a conjecture that American gunmakers reduced their modified-choke constrictions when plastic shotcups were developed because they were shooting too tight at 20 or more points of constriction. I have seen no evidence of this, but there may be some truth to it. Unfortunately, if such a relaxation of choke dimensions did occur, it has given us nothing more than European improved cylinder patterns. I may be called an Anglophile, but I would prefer this modified choke dimensional dispute be decided in favor of the tighter British/European methods with at least 20 points of constriction used in modified chokes. What meager amount of hitting area would be lost at close range would be more than offset by increased efficiency at the longer ranges that a typical hunter might try. Too, a 20 to 28-point constriction jibes with steel shot, often producing the equivalent of full-choke percentages with the larger steel BBs, BBBs, Ts and Fs without causing ring bulging.

If there is anything positive to be said about modified choke in general, it is that it handles buckshot better than the other degrees of choke (at least in my experience). Speaking in terms of lead buckshot, the modified choke allows reasonably good load fluidity as opposed to the tight full-choke exit, but that modified still manages to apply excellent control to the big balls for optimum downrange density. Although some people theorize that cylinder bore and improved cylinder are suited to lead buckshot, I haven't found that to be true. Cylinder and IC chokes invariably tend to deliver open patterns with buckshot (which is fine, if that's what you want), but for the tightest hunting patterns with buckshot, modified stands out despite a wide range of actual constrictions. The American modified with 15 to 18 points of constriction seems to jibe reasonably well with lead buckshot.

In all of shotgunning, there probably is no bigger controversy than modified choke. There are different performance expectations for it, gunmakers employ different dimensions and the guns themselves operate differently when fed various loads. Although I have been critical about modified choke beyond 35 yards, I must note that some of my earlier writings stated that a favorite waterfowl gun of mine is the Model 1100 Remington 12-gauge Magnum with 28-inch, modified-choke barrel. That may sound like hypocrisy, but it isn't. I've patterned the gun assiduously, and in the process established handloads that gave excellent lead-shot patterns for long-range waterfowling. I also have developed equally snug patterns using steel BBs and BBBs. When fed random loads of either lead or steel (the way casual hunters select ammunition), however, that same modified choke which can do 85 percent or better with specially selected loads of steel BBs and BBBs, will fall to patterns averaging just 60 percent or a mite less. Thus, if one wishes to get the best from a modified barrel, he cannot take anything for granted. I have seen American modified-choked barrels that would deliver improved cylinder percentages with one load, jump to a 60 percent modified act with another loading, then reach 70 percent full choke with buffered lead-shot magnums and No. 2 copper-plated shot. In my mind, this is not versatility per se — it's a mess. Since few hunters ever pattern, and most buy their ammo according to price rather than performance, they simply don't know what pattern they're *really* getting. The potential for versatility in modified choke is therefore latent, and it will take a patterning effort to uncover it.

Changes in Choke Combos

Because of the erratic performances and weakness of modified choke, it might be well for serious hunters to consider different choke combinations in doubles. Instead of the conventional modified and full, and improved cylinder and modified combinations, there could be more effective variations, especially in the smaller bores. In 20 and 28 gauge, for example, an IC&F combination would often be more efficient on game; for by the time a second shot is thrown in, the range will have increased to the point where a full-choke pattern is as broad as a modified's effective charge. With the light shot loads of 20s and 28s, the extra density would help ensure clean kills. In 12 gauge, the IC&M tandem could be changed to IC&IM or IC&F, again for the purpose of getting more shot into game. And if a hunter is going to do some long-range shooting, why bother with modified choke at all? Go right into a pair of full-choked tubes for a full and full duo.

When it comes to single barrels, be skeptical about choosing modified choke as *the* all-arounder. Pick it only if your shooting will be primarily from 20 to 35 yards; it is this basic 15-yard range in which honest modified patterns excel and can contribute both pattern diameter and density. If your shooting will be closer, stick with skeet or improved cylinder; if it's longer, go directly to full choke and its greater density with, at 35 to 40 yards, about the same effective pattern spread as modified. Like the other degrees of choke, modified is a specialty with limited capabilities, *not* a panacea!

PART 2
THE LOADS

Chapter 8

Our Sophisticated Shotshells

DESPITE technological progress in World War II, shotshells of the 1940s and early 1950s were still on the primitive side. There were some improvements in priming and progressive-burning powders, and there seems to have been a more widespread use of chilled shot in the post-war years, but overall the loads weren't much different in concept than those rammed into muzzleloading smoothbores of the nineteenth century. They were merely powder charges compressed beneath card/filler wad stacks, and the pellets were still relatively soft. The paper hulls got scuffed, and in damp environs the tandem of fiber wads and paper tubes swelled so that they either wouldn't chamber or had to be pressed home by heavy thumb pressure. About the only change was a broader application of the folded crimp, which may very well have been an overrated advance; for in my patterning, the overshot wafer from roll-crimped loads didn't disrupt patterns as much as was commonly believed by armchair "experts." Instead, it was mainly the card/filler wad column that hindered patterning by blasting into the shot charge from the rear. The public had a difficult time understanding that, and hunters who didn't know what was inside a shotshell or how it all worked insisted on believing that shotshells had been perfected by the inclusion of a "pie" crimp. Nothing could have been further from the truth, and whatever patterning improvements came about after World War II were primarily due to the use of additional antimony as a pellet hardener.

It is true that the three-inch 12 and 20-gauge magnums that were being developed in the 1930s, combined with the new copper-plated (Lubaloy) shot sweetened long-range patterns. But despite the fact that Nash Buckingham lugged a legendary three-inch 12 named Bo-Whap! through many of his magazine articles, casual hunters didn't buy many magnums during the 1930s and 1940s. Magnum shotshells, including the 3½-inch Magnum 10 gauge, are essentially post-World War II items.

The first meaningful step toward improved shotgun effectiveness came in the late 1950s when the so-called "baby" or "short" magnums were introduced.

SHOTGUNNING TRENDS IN TRANSITION

These were standard-length shotshells in 12, 16 and 20 gauge with considerably heavier shot charges than had ever before been associated with those gauges. The 12 gauge, which had been handling 1¼ ounces of shot for decades, was increased to a monstrous 1½-ounce shot charge. The 16 and 20 were jumped by $1/8$-ounce measures to 1¼ and 1$1/8$ ounces, respectively. In one fell swoop, the patterning potential of these guns was advanced to such a degree that the 16 was now throwing as much shot as the 10 gauge had been launching just a couple of generations earlier.

The unfortunate thing about baby magnum loads is that they were badly misinterpreted by rank and file hunters. The industry's introductory advice was to use baby magnums for filling patterns with heavier pellets for clean kills *over normal ranges* via higher levels of per pellet energy. In other words, if a duck hunter had been using 1¼ ounces of No. 6 shot, he could now chamber 1½ ounces of No. 5s or 4s and have greater penetrating power without sacrificing much, if anything, in pattern density. As the industry theorists viewed it, the baby magnums were a conservation effort. They led to clean kills and positive retrieves so that natural resources weren't wasted, thanks to adequate amounts of heavier pellets.

But the public didn't quite understand that noble purpose. They insisted that the word *magnum*, which translated from Latin simply means "larger," actually meant "almighty," and within a very short time, the baby magnums were mistakenly accorded the role of long-range loads. This only proves how totally ignorant the modern shotgunner can be when applying sophisticated concepts, for the differences between the former maximum shot charges in the 12, 16 and 20 gauges and the newer baby magnum charges aren't enough to warrant the skyblasting they appear to encourage. If a hunter is using the standard 20 with a one-ounce charge of No. 2s, for example, he will gain only a dozen pellets by going to the 1$1/8$-ounce short magnum (approximately 90 versus 102), and those extra 12 or so pellets do not add 15 to 20 yards to the 20's range! Likewise, going from 1¼ ounces of No. 2s in the 12 gauge to 1½ ounces of No. 2s increases the pellet count by only 24 pellets, and that doesn't extend the range by much, either. I once calculated that, with patterns opening at the rate of 10 percent for every five yards beyond 40 yards (which isn't a disputed rate of pattern breakdown), a full-choke pattern doing 70 percent at 40 yards would gain only about five extra yards using the 1½-ounce baby magnum over the 1¼-ounce maximum load. With the 16 and 20 gauges and their lesser $1/8$-ounce increases, the added range isn't even as great!

Thus, the public's widespread acceptance of baby magnums is not based on intelligence. Rather it is predicated on a terrible misinterpretation because of a lack of shotgun knowledge. The industry outran the consumer's ability to understand and to apply the concept correctly. The industry, however, couldn't be happier as it dribbles in a few extra pellets, uses a couple extra grains of progressive-burning powder, and charges dollars more for just a few cents' worth of added components. Is it any wonder why, after initially advertising the baby magnums

OUR SOPHISTICATED SHOTSHELLS

Progressive-burning powders eventually made possible heavier shot charges, finally reaching the so-called "baby magnums" of the 1950s. Fanciful thinkers immediately equated magnums with ultra-long range shooting, which wasn't the case at all. The magnum charges added only a few more pellets to the load for increased pattern energy over normal ranges. For example, the large spread of shot on the right equals a one-ounce load of No. 4s from the 20 gauge, and the smaller batch of pellets on the left constitutes the number added to make it a 1 1/8-ounce baby magnum. Will 17 to 18 pellets extend the standard 20's range by 20 to 25 yards as so many unsophisticated hunters believe? Nope!

for greater pellet energy over normal distances, the industry gave up in despair and fed the flames of misunderstanding by booming baby magnums for long-range gunning? If that's what the people want to believe, sell it to 'em!

When baby magnums were introduced, the 12-gauge loads were given about 1,300 fps, but some of those first batches left much to be desired. These still were assembled in paper hulls with card/filler wads, and I found most of them patterned horribly. Full-choked guns dropped to 35 to 50 percent. I had one modified-choked 20 that averaged 35 percent with early $1^1/_8$-ounce short magnums. I believe these terrible patterns were caused by the then-new progressive-burning powders which were too slow; they created continuously high bore pressures, and they frequently pushed the card/wad stacks forcefully into the emerging shot string. The powders today are more refined for better pressure curves, and the petals on plastic shotcups open to act as air brakes on exit, thus slowing the wad and keeping it from ramming into the shot charge. Likewise, some manufacturers have published a lower velocity of 1,260 fps for the 12-gauge baby magnum, and charges exiting at that level seem to pattern better than the more robust rounds.

The Plastic Revolution

Historically speaking, we are barely more than 10 years into the new, sophisticated shotshell. The world detonated uranium and plutonium bombs before it began developing significant improvements in shotgun ammunition! A perusal of Nichols' *Shotgunner* uncovers nothing of consequence at midcentury. Although Major Sir Gerald Burrard was able to discuss pattern-tightening shot concentrators in *The Modern Shotgun*, such innovations were either unavailable on a widespread basis or merely so much experimental fiddle-dee-dee. Indeed, all the theories and experiments in the universe don't mean anything unless they contribute to more effective and efficient shotgun performances for rank and file sportsmen.

Hints of improvements began in 1960 when some of the first plastic shotshell hulls were presented. However, considerable time would pass before plastic was employed for all gauges and in all types of ammo. I remember buying paper-cased 10-gauge Magnum loads until nearly 1970. The plastic hulls, of course, promised scuff resistance along with a self-lubricating characteristic for smooth chambering and extraction, especially in repeaters. They were also less inclined to be influenced by moisture, and some were given the center plug treatment in the crimp's core to eliminate the possibility of moisture entering there. Finally, plastic hulls gave impetus to handloading, as they had cost-reducing longevity.

I must pause here to confess that, although the plastic case was a definite advance in shotshell technology, there are two things I always loved about the paper tubes. One was the smell of a smoky, waxy tube on a crisp, still morning when the aroma curled upward. The second is that paper hulls deteriorate in the wild and disappear, whereas plastic hulls remain eyesores. It's impossible for hunters to retrieve all their empties because ejection mechanisms fling them wildly. (It would be a sign of sportsmanship and environmental concern if all hunters made positive attempts to recover as many spent hulls and wads as possible. I do not like to preach, but I have strong feelings on the subject, for there is little difference between pitching a beer can from a car window and dropping empty plastic hulls into the marsh. Neither the beer can nor the plastic component is biodegradable.)

Although the first plastic hulls excited many hunters, there was much about them that was superficial when considered alone. It remained for the plastic shotshells' interiors to be advanced for significant ballistics and patterning improvements. Time has telescoped these advances, but they developed slowly at first and were only partly understood by the public.

The first major step was the flanged plastic overpowder cup. Laboratory data quickly proved that powder charges could be cut 10 to 15 percent with a plastic overpowder obturator without hindering velocity levels. This "efficiency" meant more velocity was generated per grain of powder than had been the case when card/filler wad columns allowed gas seepage. The earliest plastic overpowder wad was sold by the old Alcan works, which called it the Plastic Gas Seal (PGS).

For a number of seasons, plastic overpowder wads were used in commercial loads with fiber or felt wads. Remington-Peters employed an H-shaped wad with a moulded fiber cushion that did yeoman service.

By the mid-1960s, however, one-piece plastic wads were becoming common. Hunters again jumped to unwarranted and unproved assumptions about them when they incorrectly assumed that they made open-choked guns throw tighter patterns, and contributed to lower recoil levels because they were lightweight. Closer examination proved that neither assumption was automatically true. The law of individual differences prevailed.

When the industry introduced plastic shotcups, its claim was for more pellets in the *original* pattern spread, not tighter patterns. An improved cylinder, for example, would still scatter shot liberally when fed plastic shotcups, but there would be added density. This was accomplished by two factors: First, there was less pellet deformation because the shotcup mitigated against abusive bore scrubbing, and the one-piece wad's cushioning straps variously reduced the ramming effect of firing setback.

Secondly, the shotcup's petals performed like an air brake on exit, slowing the wad so that it couldn't slam into the shot charge and jumble or otherwise influence the charge's integrity. From the patterning I did with shotcup wads, the industry's claims were honest and accurate; open-choked barrels still threw basically open patterns, although they increased somewhat in center density because more pellets remained in-the-round. Moreover, many of my patterns showed that open-choked barrels gave better and more uniform annular ring densities with shotcupped wads than they did with the old card/filler stacks. Patterns don't open in linear fashion, and pellets deformed by bore scrubbing often flip away quickly to leave the pattern's annular ring patchy. The point is that improved cylinder and modified chokes did *not* immediately start throwing full-choke patterns when plastic shotcups came along.

From armchair or bar stool, however, fanciful shooters told the sporting world that plastic shotcups had turned every modified choke into a full choke, and that skeet guns and improved cylinders were now patterning like modified chokes once did. Some of this nonsense continues to plague casual shotgunning. Some people still claim that the shotcup's thickness increases the *de facto* choke constriction of any gun so that they all shoot tighter by at least one degree of choke. As I said before, there is a fanciful, unscientific daydreaming going on among new shotgunners who should know better. Nothing can be taken for granted in shotgun patterning, certainly not ultra-tight patterns solely because of shotcups. Variables occur in shotgun performances for reasons aside from wad design. Poor quality shot, for instance, can deform in the best shotcup and throw nothing better than 55 percent from a full-choke barrel. My own patterning, which involves guns made before and after the advent of plastic wads, proves that cylinder bores, skeet guns, improved cylinders and modified chokes still average generally within their parameters for most loads using plastic shotcups or wrappers. It takes a tremendously thick wad to increase the mechanical choke of a shotgun.

To a major extent, then, the effectiveness of plastic shotcups has been exaggerated by typical shotgunners. While the shotcup does protect against bore scrubbing, it doesn't eliminate setback; and setback is the main deformer of lead pellets. Recover some fired shotcups, and you'll see massive dimpling where setback pressures forced pellets into the plastic. A further inspection will disclose that setback acts more brutally on the lower half or one-third of the shot charge than it does on the upper half, mainly because the lower half is sandwiched between the surging gases and the resistance of the crimp and the inertia of the upper layers of shot. Thus, the lower pellets still are subjected to deformation. Such deformed pellets, of course, flare from the shot string and/or slow down markedly after muzzle exit to produce weak patterns and long shot strings.

The Pellet Hardness Factor

Overall shotshell performance has come a long way since midcentury, and those improvements are due mainly to increased pellet hardness. Except for Winchester's pre-World War II development of copper-plated shot, little was done to enhance the quality of lead pellets on a grand scale. Much of the lead shot used in the first half of the twentieth century was relatively soft and easily deformed. The cheaper pellets were known as "soft shot" and were formed from a combination of pure lead with a bit of arsenic added to provide the surface tension that produces a spherical shape while the molten droplet is falling down the shot tower. Perhaps some soft shot had a pinch of antimony in it to act as a hardener, but that normally wouldn't have exceeded .05 percent.

Also called "drop shot," this soft pellet often wouldn't pattern better than 50 percent even from a bona fide full-choke barrel; for under modern chamber pressures of 7,000 to 11,500 psi, soft shot is readily deformed. Today, soft shot has faded from the market, but the so-called "promotion loads" that unsuspecting hunters buy at bargain prices have come close to it, and I have never had those cheap loads pattern better than 57 percent from any full-choke gun. These bargain basement "mallard and goose" loads are low priced because they consist of inferior lead with a very low antimony content. Antimony, a hardener of lead, is expensive, thus excluding it lowers costs, but it also lowers performance more than any casual hunter suspects.

Southern quail hunters also have been buffaloed by the extensive deformation of soft shot by firing setback. Generations of such quail hunters have believed that soft shot "mushrooms" on impact, thus making soft shot a positive stopper. This idea was undoubtedly started when Southern hunters found badly deformed pellets in their quail while cleaning them. The fact is that the deformation took place inside the gun when setback forces worked on the pellets, not when the pellets hit the target. I doubt that any Southern quail hunters ever knew about the setback phenomenon in shotshells, which demonstrates how such a lack of knowledge translates into mistaken beliefs among myth-prone shotgunners!

Pellets were made in varying degrees of hardness prior to World War II, but their use wasn't all that widespread. To be competitive, manufacturers didn't want to increase prices by employing a lot of antimony unless the customer complained. And few customers complained, because most typical hunters thought — as many still do — that a pellet is a pellet. Put a high-brass head on the load, and most hunters will jump to the conclusion that it's automatically "powerful." But pattern a high-brass load of low-antimony shot or drop shot, and you'll come up with improved cylinder patterns in a full choke. Since hunters don't pattern, who knew?

Things began changing after World War II, however. Bob Nichols reported as much in the late 1940s when he wrote in *The Shotgunner* that, "the loading industry in this country today is almost definitely committed to the exclusive manufacturers of hard shot." Exactly what is "hard shot?" It varies with time and place. What Nichols termed as hard shot around midcentury was generally different — still softer, if you will — than is available today. In fact, there really are two levels of hard shot in American history: The level Nichols described that was called chilled shot, and the current level known today as high-antimony Magnum grade shot.

The basic difference between chilled shot and Magnum grade hard shot is the amount of antimony employed. I do not know the precise antimony percentage used in all chilled shot, but Taracorp Industries, which makes Lawrence Brand chilled shot, advises the amounts used today are as follows:

SHOTGUNNING TRENDS IN TRANSITION

Although many hunters lament the demise of lead shot for waterfowling, they often fail to realize that lead shot was far from perfect. It may have been overrated, in fact. Lead shot almost invariably deformed on firing setback, and misshapen pellets, such as these lead 2s, had poor aerodynamics, low energies and may have flipped from the main shot string when battered by air resistance.

shot size	antimony content (percent)
Nos. BB, 2, 4, 5, 6	1
Nos. 7½, 8, 9	2

Although used sparingly, such antimony amounts helped improve patterns by approximately 10 percent over clusters fired with soft shot. Thus, the tighter patterns hunters began to experience around midcentury were not mainly attributable to the new folded crimp or plastic overpowder wads as most sportsmen speculated, but to the harder pellets.[1]

Before exploring the subject of Magnum hard shot, I must dispense with a lingering myth about chilled shot. Naive hunters believe that it is hardened by some mysterious process involving cold air at the time of formation. This is nonsense. Air and temperature have nothing to do with it. Chilled shot is badly misnamed; its only claim to fame is antimony content.

Magnum hard shot has a higher antimony content than chilled shot. This explains why many books and magazine articles refer to it as high-antimony Magnum shot. One of the foremost makers of Magnum-grade shot is Taracorp, droppers of Lawrence Brand Magnum shot. Latest information available lists the following antimony content for the respective sizes:

shot size	antimony content (percent)
BB, No. 2	2
Nos. 4, 5	3
Nos. 6, 9	4
Nos. 7½, 8	6

As a rule of thumb, the larger the pellet the less it is thought to require optimum hardness for patterning; therefore, the larger numbers require less antimony. On the other hand, Nos. 7½ and 8 are the primary trapshooting sizes and they are made with very high antimonial contents for maximum pattern density.

How much better is Magnum hard shot than chilled shot? Using a full-choked Perazzi trap gun, I used scaled powder and shot charges in a control reload with 18.0 grains of Red Dot and the Winchester 209 primer in Double-A cases to test over 40 yards. Five reloads were given 1⅛ ounces of Lawrence chilled No. 8s, while five of the same reloads were supplied 1⅛ ounces of Lawrence high-antimony Magnum No. 8s. A check with the micrometer proved they were No. 8s with nominal diameters of .090-inch. The results: Patterns with high-antimony Magnum 8s averaged 74 percent; those with chilled 8s, only 60 percent. Because of greater

SHOTGUNNING TRENDS IN TRANSITION

The hardness factor in lead shot is important to patterning. Ordinarily chilled shot will deform en masse under setback pressures, whereas the higher antimony content of hard shot, alias "Magnum grade," will mitigate against pellet deformation.

deformation, the chilled shot loads did no better than modified choke. Thus, if one wishes to get the optimum performance from a full-choked gun, he needs high-antimony hard shot. Chilled shot is a distant second best today, and handloaders who buy chilled shot because it's cheaper are being penny-wise and pound-foolish.

Buffered Shot Charges

Another step toward pattern improvement was taken in the late 1960s when Remington introduced a line of buffered buckshot loads — the so-called "Power-Pakt®" items. These advertised significantly improved buckshot patterns, and they lived up to their promise. At the time, typical hunters acknowledged that such buffered rounds "cushioned" the pellets to help preserve their best aerodynamic shape, but there was more to it.

The buffering media, which is normally granulated polyethylene or expandable polystyrene, acts differently than is typically believed. It doesn't cushion a pellet the way a feather pillow cups your head. Instead, the buffer, when it is under the pressure of firing setback, forms a mouldlike encasement around the pellet and deprives it of any space into which it can deform. Thus, it isn't a true cushion at all, but an entrapment or encasement which holds the pellets in shape.

Although preserved pellet form is essential to good patterning, the buffer serves another important purpose, namely, improving the fluidity of the shot charge's flow from chamber through choke constriction. The fluidity of buffered loads is especially vital when coarse pellets like buckshot, BBs, No. 2s and No. 4s are used, for these bulky units often wedge and mash against each other in an unbuffered load, perhaps even tumbling and spinning as they rumble through the bore and up the choke's incline, which obviously hinders patterning. The ideal situation would have coarse pellets flowing smoothly the way smaller 7½s and 8s do, as such lesser numbers can shift about within their masses for heightened fluidity. By putting buckshot, BBs, 2s and 4s in a buffer, this fluidity is advanced; the coarse pellets can shift about within their charge's mass as they flow through the cone, bore and choke to exit more smoothly.

In general, modern loading technology has enabled the industry to buffer shotshells of all sorts. At one time, it was believed that pellets smaller than 4s and 5s didn't need a buffer because they flowed with adequate fluidity, but currently the industry is ignoring that early concept and buffering turkey loads with copper-plated No. 6s for either tighter patterns or sales appeal.

My own shooting indicates that best patterns result from loads with full helpings of buffer. This ensures the total encasement of each pellet and provides an opportunity for pellet shifting on acceleration and bore travel. The mere addition of a smattering of buffering agent, therefore, doesn't automatically produce significantly tighter patterns than would occur in the same commercial loads without buffer but with hard shot. In some loads, the less-than-filling charge of buffer does

SHOTGUNNING TRENDS IN TRANSITION

Buffer improves patterning by encasing pellets and preventing them from deforming under firing (setback) pressures.

very little. As with magnum loads, the addition of a few inexpensive grains of buffer allows manufacturers to establish much higher over-the-counter pricing without being a definite advantage. Instead of being blindly gullible, the new shotgunner should pattern scientifically to determine if the cost of buffered loads is justified over loads with high-antimony shot. The final point is that buffer can do a terrific job of pattern improvement when everything is right, but buffer used incorrectly isn't much better than no buffer at all. If a load has only a partial measure of buffer, and if that buffer is up front, the lower pellets will still be subjected to brutal setback forces — they'll deform, and will not flow fluidly.

Some handloading techniques also have applied buffer to steel shot. The leadership in this goes to Don Vizecky, who developed the Supersonic® line of steel shot reloading components. Why use buffer if steel shot doesn't deform? For the other stipulated purpose — improving the load's fluidity through the bore. All of Vizecky's published reloading data includes full-to-the-brim buffering. That traps the individual steel pellets, holding them apart and reducing the binding and wedging. Used with Supersonic buffer, the larger steel pellets have patterned beautifully for me through improved modified and full choke, normally ranging from 85 to 95 percent at 40 yards. Some patterns have printed 100 percent. Components and data covering the Supersonic line are distributed by U-Load, Inc. (14952 Martin Drive, Eden Prairie, Mn 55344). Don Vizecky also helped pioneer the use of pellets heavier than BBs for improved steel shot effectiveness on geese. To date, the commercial shotshell manufacturers have not been using buffer in their steel shot loads.

Hull and Wad Developments

During the 1960s, sport shooters and the loading industry assumed there eventually would be an all-plastic shotshell hull, but for nearly 20 years that goal wasn't attained. True, there were some serious attempts at the concept, including the ill-fated Wanda and Eclipse lines. Herter's, the large mail order house located in Minnesota, also sold a loading that was the spitting image of the Wanda. But for various reasons, the all-plastic hull didn't materialize as rapidly as theorists predicted. Perhaps the plastics weren't right, or maybe the shooters shied away from anything that didn't have the brass head symbolizing strength.

Nevertheless, out of this melange of designs, concepts and configurations came some very efficient hulls: The Winchester compression-formed, alias the Double-A; the Federal Gold Medal and plastic-based field hulls; the Remington Premier and its predecessor, the Peters blue target cases. With selected one-piece plastic wads, they all generate a considerable amount of velocity with light powder charges. When I first started handloading in the 1950s, for example, a typical 12-gauge trap load rolled into a paper hull consumed anywhere from 21 to 23 grains of Red Dot for velocities around 1,145 fps and 1,200 to 1,220 fps with $1^{1}/_{8}$ ounces of lead shot and card/filler wads. That was a lot of powder and blast and as tough on one's wallet as on his ears.

SHOTGUNNING TRENDS IN TRANSITION

Today, however, plastic components have greatly reduced fuel requirements, thanks to the gas-sealing proclivities of one-piece plastic hulls. Compare, for instance, the charges of 21 to 23 grains of Red Dot called for back in the 1950s with the following recipe from Hercules' 1988 *Reloaders' Guide for Hercules Smokeless Powders*:

> Winchester 12-gauge AA hull
> Federal 209 primer
> 1.75 grains Red Dot
> Winchester WAA12 wad
> $1^{1}/_{8}$ ounces lead shot
> Published pressure: 10,600 psi
> Published velocity: 1,200 fps

The difference between 23 grains of Red Dot and just 17.5 grains is substantial, both on recoil and the reloader's wallet.

As excellent as the AA, Gold Medal and Premier plastic hulls have performed, however, they all require the added step of drawing metal case heads and rims. Ditto for Federal field-style plastics and Remington "unibody" hunting hulls. A foreign concept became the first commercially successful all-plastic case — ACTIV. Today ACTIV ammo is manufactured in Kearneysville, West Virginia, but it originated in Puerto Rico.

What makes ACTIV hulls so interesting is that they are the first shotshells that function reliably through autoloading and pump-action shotguns without an exterior metal head/rim for strength. The Wanda and Eclipse designs could not do this flawlessly, but I have fired cases of ACTIV rounds through the Remington Model 1100/11-87 autoloaders without so much as one failure. Moreover, the ACTIV is an excellent reloading candidate and the company has introduced a new wad (TG-30) which performs excellently.

The ACTIV hull is made by a two-step process. The cylindrical tube segment is first made by a simple extrusion method. Then the tube is placed in a die and the head/rim segment is moulded to the tube via the injection moulding process. It is in this moulding procedure that the ACTIV case's rim is strengthened by the insertion of a thin metal disc prior to the actual moulding of the head/rim feature. Upon ejection from the die, the ACTIV case has a strong, thick case head and metal-bolstered rim (albeit internally bolstered). It is the competition and creativity of firms like ACTIV that keep the industry hopping and progressing.

Aside from somewhat different designs through the cushioning straps, plastic shotshell wads have experienced only one major change. Initially, they were all made with linear high-density plastics, but more recently the plastics industry has applied linear low-density plastic to shotshell wads. A low-density wad gives better performance in cold weather, whereas high-density plastics become stiff and brittle in the cold and fail to seal gases efficiently. Certain low-density wads, such as the Remington TGT-12 and FIG-8, also seem to contribute to very uniform ballistics, thanks no doubt to their equally uniform compressibility as compared to the harder resistance of high-density wads' cushioning straps. Some of the best patterns I've gotten with low-antimony chilled shot have come from Remington TGT-12 wads in the Remington Premier hull.

For steel shot, the wads must be extra hard and tough to prevent "piercing" under setback pressures. If a steel pellet pierces the shotcup, it can score the bore wall. Steel shot wads do not have cushioning sections; all possible room is utilized for powder and shot, especially shot. This is no great sacrifice with steel loads, because steel shot doesn't deform, anyway, but it does eliminate the chance for powder gases to find early expansion room, and therefore has a bearing on interior ballistics.

Because steel shot wads are so tough, some manufacturers have been giving them more than the conventional four shotcup slits so that each petal, being smaller, can be laid back quicker by air resistance. If the petals don't open and provide an air brake effect, there is a chance that the heavy steel shot wad can bump into the rear pellets and disrupt patterns.

Pellet Size Combinations

Ever since their inception, commercially loaded shotshells have been given only one size of shot. That size is clearly stamped somewhere on the hull or, as in the case of the old rolled crimp, the overshot wad. Unfortunately, the manufacture of lead shot is not perfect, and anyone who takes a micrometer to a handful of pellets from any shotshell will find variations. The best loads have shot charges in which the pellets vary by no more than ±.002 to .003-inch. However, it is not unusual to find some loads with pellets that vary by as much as one full size (.010-inch). For example, measuring the diameters of pellets coming from a load of No. 7½s could uncover a few pellets with diameters like those of No. 8s or 8½s. I have found shot that measured out to No. 5 dimensions in field loads of No. 6s, and vice versa. The fact is that shot loads are made from a "blend" of pellets which come close to duplicating the established count per ounce. Thus, the mixing of shot sizes has been going on forever, although not purposely and for no scientific reason. The industry simply has not perfected lead shot technology.

In 1986, however, Remington began marketing specialty loads with two different shot sizes in them. These are called the "Multirange®" "Duplex®" Special Purpose (SP) loads, and they combine such numbers as lead No. 4s and BBs (BBx4) and lead No. 6s with lead No. 4s (4x6). The Remington Duplex ammunition has been widely accepted, and is now being made in steel shot loads, too. But why combine shot sizes?

The buying public unknowingly believes the reason is to provide heavier pellets in any load for greater ranges than a hunter would normally try. For instance, if

SHOTGUNNING TRENDS IN TRANSITION

REMINGTON "DUPLEX" SHOTGUN SHELL

- TOP LAYER OF LARGER SHOT
- OLIVE DRAB HULL
- "COPPER-LOKT" EXTRA-HARD COPPER-PLATED PELLETS
- SHOCK ABSORBING BUFFERING FILLER
- BOTTOM LAYER OF SMALLER SHOT
- "POWER PISTON" ONE-PIECE SHOT PROTECTING WAD
- NON-REFLECTIVE BLACK BASE CAP

The newest concept in shotshells is Remington's "MultiRange®" "Duplex®" load, which combines two shot sizes to provide both deep penetration for optimum damage and multiple hits for shock.

a hunter normally used No. 4s for his pheasants, the inclusion of some No. 2s would give him added range if a rooster flushed well out. So, too, would the heavier pellets supposedly act as insurance if a hunter innocently misjudged range. In other words, here we go with range again: Every time John Q. Hunter sees something new in shotshells, he automatically thinks in terms of yardage and of stretching shots. But here again there's another motive...

Back in 1976, I wrote an article entitled "Thoughts on the Shot Size Controversy" which was published in *Handloader* magazine No. 62. In that article, I discussed the opposite schools of thought regarding pellet size selection and pellet on-target function. At one extreme was the older school of thought, the so-called "heavy shot" position, which argued that deep penetration was the most important factor in clean kills or at least anchoring hits. For that reason, the heavy shot adherents advocated the largest practical shot sizes for any type of game to ensure optimum penetration.

At the other extreme was the "small shot" school. This group maintained that multiple hits were more important than deep penetration, insisting that multiple hits dropped birds by shock. As if to lend mathematical proof to their contentions, they constantly claimed that the impact of shot upon a game bird was the square of the actual number of hits. Therefore, if a bird received four pellet hits, the impact on its nervous system was supposed to be the equivalent of 16 hits! No one has ever proven this mathematical contention by placing electrodes on a bird just before it's shot, but the calculation has remained a part of shotgunning theory. Obviously, the small shot school recommends using the smallest practical shot sizes for any type of game so that multiple hits are more likely.

It is not my purpose to debate the two extreme theories of shot size selection here as I did in the previously mentioned *Handloader* article. I merely set them down here in their succinct forms so that readers may realize that such schools of thought exist among sophisticated shotgunners. Moreover, this is where the duplex load concept re-enters. Ed Herring, a Remington ballistics technician, informed me that he read the *Handloader* piece one day when he was thumbing through back issues and after finishing it he asked himself, "Why not give hunters both in one load?" In one pattern, there would be heavy pellets for penetration *and* a lot of lighter ones for multiple hits and shocking power. Remington gave Ed Herring the go-ahead to develop the project, and the result is history — the Multirange Duplex SP shotshells. As I've just related, though, the purpose behind them was not to give hunters shotshells that stretched ranges by including extra-heavy pellets, as is the popular theory among weekend hunters, the actual purpose was to combine the extremes of the heavy and small shot schools and put both penetration and shocking power into one shot string.

Anyone who cuts open a Remington Duplex load will see that the heavy pellets are layered atop the smaller ones. Why? Heavy pellets retain their velocity better than the lighter ones, and this stacking keeps the heavy pellets up front in the mass. If the heavy pellets were placed on the bottom of the charge, they might (and probably would) overtake the lighter pellets and bump them into poor, erratic patterning.

I have had excellent results with Duplex loads on upland game. Loads like the BBx4 and 4x6 combinations have done well on long-range pheasants. Frankly, I believe the Duplex concept still has a distance to go, and that it could be used with the lighter shot sizes for close-range upland work and/or trapshooting. Remington already has begun making steel-shot Duplex rounds. When it comes to steel shot, however, I must confess to having enrolled in the heavy shot school and tend to prefer Remington loads with just one size of pellet, namely, the heaviest practical for any given waterfowl.

Since Remington's introduction of Duplex loads, Federal has attempted a oneupsmanship marketing venture by introducing a magnum with *three* different shot sizes, calling it the "Tri-Power®." Their advertising maintains that a hunter can now use one shotshell for all ranges, because there's a combination of lighter shot, intermediate sizes and heavy pellets to handle all ranges. While I enjoy creativity, I'm not positive about the use of more than one pair of closely related pellet sizes. The presence of light shot reduces the amount of the heaviest pellets, and it is the heaviest size that does the job at long range where one wants optimum density and energy. Thus, although it's very early in the Tri-Power's career, I remain skeptical of the concept. The product appears a bit gimmicky to me and this is the first time a product from Federal has struck me that way.

Turkey Loads

The widespread restoration of wild turkeys has generated considerable hunting interest. Areas that had lost their native turkeys 150 years ago are suddenly conducting limited seasons on the birds, and this has enlivened the shotshell industry. Most turkey hunting doesn't involve true wingshooting; the birds are taken by aimed shots at the head/neck region as they are called into relatively close range. The best loads historically have been magnum doses of No. 6s from a tight-patterning full choke for optimum target saturation. To meet this new market, domestic shotshell makers quickly began offering all sorts of magnum-length loads with copper-plated No. 6s, including the three-inch 12. Subsequently, this was followed by the introduction of whopping two-ounce No. 6 loads in the three-inch 12 for even greater potential density. Moreover, whereas it was once believed that buffer wasn't needed with the smaller or intermediate shot sizes, the companies began to employ some buffer with No. 6s.

Not all hunters were content with No. 6s. They wanted more pellet energy for definite performance against this bony vital area. Hence, the manufacturers answered with other turkey-type magnums using two ounces of No. 4s or 5s in the three-inch 12. Remington went one further step with its Duplex concept,

OUR SOPHISTICATED SHOTSHELLS

The Remington Model 11-87 and Duplex loads of No. 2s over 6s turned in this impressive bag.

offering buffered magnums with No. 4s on top trailed by No. 6s (all of them copper-plated), which combines both requirements of penetration and multiple hits. Winchester has brought out a three-inch 12-gauge load with two ounces of No. 5s for turkey hunting, which I found patterned splendidly from a full choke. Federal has put 2¼ ounces of lead shot into the 3½-inch extra-length 12-gauge Magnum for a truly robust turkey pattern. In many respects, the industry's packaging of turkey loads may be its quickest response to a specialty market. It may also be its most lucrative, as the turkey rounds are being packaged mainly in boxes of 10 at considerably high prices.

The Powder Picture

One would think that, by this time, shotshell powders would be established and in a virtual state of perfection. Although we do have some exceptional powders stateside, there is still some experimentation going on. Moreover, there are some overseas manufacturers who profess to turn out better sporting propellants. Experiments and competition undoubtedly will cause some future changes in shotshell powders.

In mid-1988, for example, a brand new stateside powder company announced that it would not only make available Scotland-made propellants, but that it intended to offer 12-gauge ammunition, in both lead and steel, to American hunters and clay target shooters. Behind this venture — known as the Scot Powder Company — is the primary argument that powders made from nitrocotton are invariably more uniform than those made of nitrocellulose. This should stir some interest in the United States, because stateside sporting powders are normally made from nitrocellulose, not nitrocotton. There are some American military powders being made of guncotton, but that nicety has not yet been extended to sporting propellants by many, if any, stateside suppliers. Thus, the Scot Powder Company will have some leverage on Yankee manufacturers *if* it can supply its refined powders at popular prices.

The main difference between nitrocellulose and nitrocotton is that nitrocellulose is a product derived from wood, and wood cellulose can vary. Cotton, on the other hand, is a more consistent material. Therefore, the Scot Powder Company has presented three selling points for its product (which is made in Scotland by ICI's Nobel Explosives Company):

1) Powders made from nitrocotton are said to be cooler-burning and to have a lower recoil level;
2) they are clean-burning because they aren't heavily coated with deterrents as are progressive-burning powders made of nitrocellulose;
3) they are said to flow very fluidly through reloaders, metering accurately.

One further point must be made about nitrocotton's clean-burning characteristics. The burning rates of these powders are adjusted by porousness and the concomitant amount of air in each particle, not by chemical inclusions or coatings. Fast-rate

OUR SOPHISTICATED SHOTSHELLS

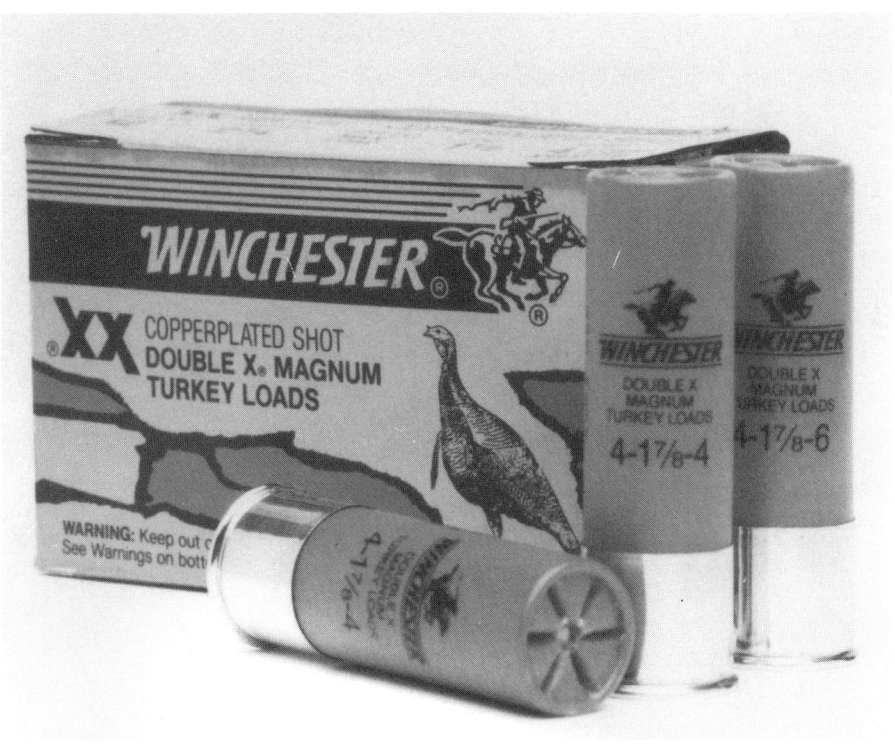

One of the more recent shotshell specialties has been the buffered turkey load, which is engineered for ultra-tight patterns for head/neck shots.

powders made from nitrocotton simply will have more pores and air in them than will the slow-rate particles. The results are greater uniformity, plus less debris.

Although the advent of nitrocotton-based powder for American sporting ammunition is new at this writing, it is as old as the Scottish moors. American gun powders apparently have centered on nitrocellulose because it is readily available and less expensive. Moreover, nitrocellulose works. One glance at the skeet and trap records hung up by American-made shotshells using nitrocellulose, and one trip down memory lane with a bird gun stroking grouse and geese, will cause many American shotgunners to question the need for nitrocotton-based powder. Should nitrocotton actually impress stateside trapshooters with a lower recoil level, however, and should nitrocotton do a better job with steel shot loads, there may be a conversion from our traditional reliance on nitrocellulose to a new demand for nitrocotton. On a purely theoretical basis, there is no doubt that nitrocotton is a more refined material for ammunition. But on the practical side, there is always the question of whether typical American hunters will pay for such refinements the way British wingshots do! In a nation where most hunters don't know the difference between soft, chilled and hard shot, it will be extremely difficult to sell them on a need for refined gun powders when their rusty pumpguns still go *"Bang!"* with the old stuff.

Nevertheless, the American shotshell has become more sophisticated. I attribute much of this progress to advanced handloaders who prove that concepts work and have commercial value as specialties. Other contributions to progress are due to improved manufacturing technology that permits the profitable loading of specialty "cartridges." We can only hope that, one day, the typical hunter and shooter becomes as sophisticated as the ammunition he uses.

Chapter Notes

1. My information is that the 3¼-1¼ live pigeon loads, along with some trap loads which still hosted 1¼ ounces of shot, were loaded with significantly higher antimony percentages even before World War II. That may be why so many upland hunters swore by the live pigeon loads for the field, especially on big birds like pheasants and sharptails. The No. 7 pellet, then properly loaded, was a great upland size. Although some hunters mistakenly believe there was something magical about the 3¼-1¼ recipe which made it pattern so beautifully, in reality the presence of high-antimony shot is a better explanation.

Chapter 9

Exploding Some Ballistics Myths

THE PUBLIC is constantly exposed to a lot of nonsense about shotgun ballistics and patterning. Much of this is perpetuated by word of mouth, while some of it, unfortunately, appears in print when writers address shotgun performance ideas using hand-me-down theories without questioning the lingering logic and without putting anything to a scientific test. Is it any wonder why modern would-be experts still parrot ancient advice which either doesn't hold up or needs qualification and clarification?

There are currently several popular *assumed* truths making their way among hunters and trapshooters, and it will be the purpose of this chapter to poke holes in them.

Powders for Short Barrels

One of the generalizations offhandedly accepted is that the best powders for the radically short-barreled upland guns have fast burning rates. On the flip side of that, of course, is the belief that propellants with slow burning rates are basically unsuited for the bobbed barrels of 21 to 23 inches. It is easy to understand how hunters and handloaders can theorize in that manner, for it sounds perfectly logical that powders with a fast burning rate will convert more of their chemical energy to kinetic energy during the short run through a stumpy barrel, than will powders with slower rates.

But logic and science aren't always perfectly compatible, and this is one of those times when complexities enter the picture. Such factors as chamber pressure and available energy (powder charge weight) begin to have an impact. There is also the question of whether one is discussing sheer velocity (optimum speed) or efficiency (velocity per grain of powder). To provide a guide for my readers, let me note that I intend to demonstrate that slow-rate powders are far from useless in radically short shotgun barrels, and that chamber pressures play a vital role in wringing out top performance from such stubby tubes.

SHOTGUNNING TRENDS IN TRANSITION

The data accompanying this chapter was taken from a pair of Remington barrels — one a 22-inch slug barrel and the other a 26-inch "Rem" choked barrel. Chronographing was done with the Oehler Model 33 plus the Skyscreen III hook-up at a five-foot instrumental range. Handloads were scaled charges of both shot and powder, and No. 5 shot was used.

The first example illustrates that fast-rate powders alone do not ensure optimum ballistics from short barrels, but rather that they also need adequate charge weights and heightened chamber pressures to reach their best levels. There can be no doubt that Hi-Skor 700-X is a fast-rate powder, and it was used in the following reloads:

Reload A-1

Remington "Premier®" hull
Remington 209P primer
17.0 grains Hi-Skor 700-X
Remington TGT-12 wad
$1^1/_8$ ounces lead shot
Published velocity: 1,140 fps
Published pressure: 9,600 LUP

Reload A-2

Remington Premier hull
Remington 209P primer
18.5 grains Hi-Skor 700-X
Remington TGT-12 wad
$1^1/_8$ ounces lead shot
Published velocity: 1,200 fps
Published pressure: 10,800 LUP
(Sources: Remington/DuPont)

After five loads of each had flown over the Skyscreens, the averages read:

barrel (inches)	velocity (fps)
Reload A-1	
22	1,126
26	1,159
Reload A-2	
22	1,199
26	1,222

The difference between the two reloads is significant because in the lighter Reload A-1 the shorter 22-inch barrel was still below the reload's published average velocity, while heavier Reload A-2 generated a full 1,199 fps from just the 22-inch barrel. The lighter powder charge and its lower chamber pressure simply didn't provide the heat and the continuing pressure needed for a full thrust from a short barrel. Thus, as just stated, optimum velocity comes from radically shortened shotgun barrels mainly when the load has *both* adequate charge weight for gas intensity into the bore *and* maximum or near maximum chamber pressure to ensure substantial early combustion.

It is easy to prove that a relatively high chamber pressure with only a very light powder charge will not generate enough gases for stiff performances in short barrels. For if any legitimate shotshell powder has a fast burning rate, it is Bullseye, and one would think that Bullseye, loaded to near maximum chamber pressure in the 12 gauge, would produce a high percentage of its energy within the confines of a 22-inch barrel. However, that didn't happen with the following load:

Reload B-1

Federal Gold Medal hull
CCI 209 primer
18.0 grains Bullseye
Federal 12S3 wad + one .200 inch 20-gauge card
one ounce lead shot
Published velocity: 1,200 fps
Published pressure: 10,200 psi
(Source: Hercules)

When fired in the 22-inch barrel, it produced only 1,141 fps. From the 26-inch barrel, it clocked 1,155 fps. A full 30-inch barrel was needed to reach 1,191 fps, on average with B-1. Since the chamber pressure with fast-rate Bullseye was certainly nearing maximum, the only explanation for the low speed in the 22-inch barrel was the lack of gas intensity: Bullseye burned rapidly and began experiencing decay quite soon. Therefore, chamber pressures alone won't suffice for high speeds in short barrels.

Another reload with Bullseye proves that charge weight and gas mass do a better job even though the chamber pressure is lower. In the following reload, the chamber pressure is influenced downward by the Winchester WAA12F1 wad. However, the powder charge is increased to 19.5 grains of Bullseye for more available chemical energy:

Reload B-2

Federal Gold Medal hull
CCI 209 primer
19.5 grains Bullseye
Winchester WAA12F1 wad + one .200-inch 20-gauge card

(continued)

Reload B-2 (continued)

> one ounce lead shot
> Published velocity: 1,200 fps
> Published pressure: 6,900 psi
> (Source: Hercules)
>
> 22-inch barrel: 1,157 fps
> 26-inch barrel: 1,200 fps

Thus, despite the significantly lower chamber pressure, the 19.5-grain charge of B-2 delivered more velocity from both the 22 and 26-inch barrels. In fact, B-2 reached the published velocity of 1,200 fps from the 26-incher, while B-1's 18.0-grain charge didn't come close to reaching its published velocity from the 22 or 26-inch barrel. Chamber pressure aside, then, it appears that powder mass is vitally important to performance even with the very fastest burning propellants in short barrels. The more gas, the more velocity. And it takes powder to produce gas.

Before moving from this point about bore-gas intensity, I must discuss an experience a friend had with the 21-inch-barreled Remington Model 1100 Special Field in 20 gauge. His skeet loads with $7/8$-ounce of lead shot over light charges of Green Dot or Unique didn't operate the gun. A 14.5-grain charge of Green Dot merely jiggled the action. What was wrong? Obviously, too little gas at the bleeder valves. He then changed to Winchester's recommended load of 17.5 grains of 473AA for the $7/8$-ounce skeet load in Winchester AA surroundings and found that the gun worked perfectly even though the chamber pressures for the Green Dot and 473AA reloads were quite similar. The heavier charge of 473AA simply supplied more gas despite being a slower burning rate than Green Dot.

What I've been leading up to, of course, is the performance of heavy charges of slow-rate propellants in short barrels. Popular doctrine tells us that such fuels are terribly inefficient in short barrels and woefully unable to generate effective velocities, but my own chronographing doesn't agree with armchair experts! As case in point, consider the results from this pair of 12-gauge short magnums run over the Skyscreens:

Reload C-1

> Winchester AA case
> Winchester 209 primer
> 36.5 grains 571 Ball powder
> Winchester WAA12R wad
> 1½ ounces lead shot
> Published velocity: 1,260 fps
> Published pressure: 10,300 LUP
> (Source: Winchester)
>
> 22-inch barrel: 1,211 fps
> 26-inch barrel: 1,235 fps

Reload C-2

Winchester AA case
Winchester 209 primer
34.0 grains Blue Dot
Winchester WAA12F114 wad
1 3/8 ounces lead shot
Published velocity: 1,245 fps
Published pressure: 10,500 psi
(Source: Hercules)

22-inch barrel: 1,233 fps
26-inch barrel: 1,267 fps

As the final averages show, even the 22-inch barrel acquitted itself with adequate energy for field applications with the heftier pellets used in short-magnum loads. Its average velocity of 1,211 fps isn't at all bad when one remembers that the three-inch 20-gauge's 1¼-ounce load is regulated for only 1,185 fps, and nobody hesitates to use that at 40 yards in the uplands where stubby 12-gauge barrels are also wielded. In fact, Reload C-2 is a very efficient number from the 22-inch barrel.

If we can apply any rule of thumb to load selection for the highest velocities from short-barreled shotguns, then, it is that the best results tend to occur 1) when a load's chamber pressure is maximum or near maximum for any respective gauge and 2) when the powder charge is heavy to provide an intense, prolonged gas mass for a lengthened pressure curve. Instead of slow-rate powders being hopeless, taboo and inefficient in radically short upland barrels, they definitely can contribute to optimum velocities from stumpy guns. Contrary to what the public tends to believe, fast-rate powders aren't automatically superb in short barrels unless they, too, are thrown in generous amounts at maximum or near maximum chamber pressures.

Powders and Patterns

Back in the 1930s when powders with slower burning rates were being improved, Winchester cleverly used this so-called "progressive-burning" fuel to popularize the short shot string concept with its widely known Super-X waterfowl loads. To many hunters, such advertising was extremely attractive, although they didn't have the faintest idea how it all tied together. What ballistic magic had Winchester worked to develop high-velocity (1,330 fps) duck loads that patterned like a rifle and didn't tail out?

The answer, of course, was that Winchester based much of its skyhooting on the theory that progressive-burning powders deformed fewer pellets on firing setback than did the faster-rate powders; consequently, there were more still-round pellets with optimum aerodynamic shape to remain in the main shot mass. Unless

SHOTGUNNING TRENDS IN TRANSITION

Popular theory has it that powders with a fast burning rate are needed to obtain the best velocities from a short-barreled shotgun, but chronograph sessions with various reloads and powders indicate that slow-rate powders can also deliver very effective velocities when taken to maximum or near-maximum chamber pressures. The stubby slug barrel on the right, for example, can generate some relatively high velocities with 1½-ounce short magnums using the slowest progressive-burning powders when maximum chamber pressures are employed.

Winchester gave the pellets a higher antimony content than normal in those days, that was all there was to the Super-X's vaunted short shot string brag — a theory based on slow-rate powder and its more gradual acceleration.

Today that same theory exists, namely, that handloaders can tighten patterns and trim shot string lengths by using powders with the slower burning rates to reduce chamber pressures for any given velocity level. This thinking has become part of many trapshooters' approach to reloading for handicap; ditto for handloading hunters who strive for turkey or goose loads that hammer the target with exceedingly high center densities.

There are, however, complexities. As my patterning indicates, slow-rate powders will *not* automatically enhance pattern density, for patterns aren't solely the product of chamber-end pressures. Reducing the sharp impact of firing setback may eliminate *some* pellet deformation, which in turn can improve patterns variously, but that amount of setback deformation may not be as great as theorized, and there's another factor that may be more important to patterning — the relationship of muzzle-region powder gases to the exit of wad/shot tandems. For pattern disruption can, and does, occur when wads shoot into the shot charge at emission. When shotshells were loaded with the old card/filler wad stack, it wasn't uncommon for the wad column to be blown into and through the pellets to cause a so-called "donut" or "blown" pattern.

Field E. White, who developed the Poly-Choke, was said to have proved the influence of wad columns by running an experiment with one cylinder-bored 12-gauge barrel using various degrees of bore smoothness. When the bore was left rough, the barrel printed full-choke patterns, and when it was given a high degree of polish it threw open clusters. The reason for these changing patterns, it was believed (and correctly so, in my opinion), was that the rough bore condition gripped with wads to slow them and let the shot charge escape without rear-end ramming at exit. Conversely, the smoothly polished bore condition let the wads slip slickly along and be driven into the tail of the shot charge. Thus, whenever we think of pattern development, we must consider the wad's role at that split instant when the ejecta clears the muzzle and is in its first inches of free flight; for wads have weight and momentum, and they can affect shot charge integrity and pattern development if they are driven into the pellets.

On a purely theoretical basis, the less gas pressure there is in the final barrel segment, the less chance there is for wad disruption of the pattern. Stated another way, the powders and loads with faster powder gas decay offer better patterning potential because they have less muzzle-end pressure acting on the wad/shot tandem, either to blow the wad into the pellets or to scatter them by emerging gas. The point is that although slow-rate powders may deform fewer pellets than fast-rate fuels, the slow-rate powders generate more bore gas (i.e., have longer pressure curves) than do fast-rate propellants. Hence, the slow-rate powders have more potential for ramming wads into emerging shot masses, and trapmen who use slow-rate powders for their handicap ammo without bothering with comparative patterning may find such practices to be counterproductive.

My current interest in trap load performance stems from my column work with *Trap & Field*, the official trapshooting magazine. But my curiosity was piqued well before I began at *Trap & Field* by some experimental shooting I did for an article entitled "What's a Good Trap Load?" which ran in *Handloader* No. 33. In that article, I included a table detailing the performances of three full-choked trap guns — a Browning BT-99, a Remington 870 and a High Standard pump — with reloads assembled from powders of different burning rates (including Red Dot, Green Dot, Hi-Skor 700-X, DuPont PB [now IMR PB] and SR-7625). Contrary to what theorists would have us believe, the slower-rate powders did *not* give the best patterns. That honor went to fast-rate Red Dot.

Of course, if we invoke the rule of gun/load individuality, we must assume that one series of patterns shot back in 1971 doesn't alter the course of history or theoretical science. Through the years, however, I have patterned a lot of reloads for my *Trap & Field* columns, and I invariably found that unaltered full chokes (meaning guns not regulated for a specific load) didn't throw naturally tighter patterns with the slower-rate powders like Unique, Green Dot, PB, SR-7625 and 473AA, or Johnny-come-lately Hi-Skor 800-X. In fact, good ol' Red Dot, Hi-Skor 700-X, and the Ball-type twins — Hodgdon's Trap-100 and Winchester's 452AA — frequently printed the best patterns.

The question in my mind was: Why didn't the slower-rate powders deliver as assumed by the theorists? Accordingly, I set up another series of tests using a Winchester Model 12 trap gun and data from the 1987 Hercules *Reloader's Guide for Hercules Smokeless Powders*. These were all to be nominal three drams equivalent target or light field reloads with velocities of about 1,200 fps from a 30-inch barrel. Because Remington's new Premier® components were then relatively new, I selected the following trio of "recipes" to keep all reloads the same except for the powder charges and pressures:

Remington Premier hull
Remington 209P primer
19.0 grains Red Dot
Remington TGT-12 wad
1 1/8 ounces lead shot
Pressure: 10,100 psi

Remington Premier hull
Remington 209P primer
21.0 grains Green Dot
Remington TGT-12 wad
1 1/8 ounces lead shot
Pressure: 8,800 psi

Remington Premier hull
Remington 209P primer
22.5 grains Unique
Remington TGT-12 wad
1 1/8 ounces lead shot
Pressure: 8,200 psi

These reloads were all given scaled powder and shot charges, the shot being Lawrence Brand high-antimony Magnum No. 7½. All firing was done over a 40-yard range on a calm day.

Now, if one follows the rule of thumb established by those theorists who expound loudly around gun clubs, the reloads with Green Dot and Unique would have printed the tightest patterns because they had the lowest chamber pressures and, therefore, would have deformed fewer pellets than the higher-pressure Red Dot rounds. But it didn't happen that way! Again, as so often happened in the past, Red Dot walked off with the prize. Red Dot averaged 76.5 percent with some individual patterns reaching 78 to 79 percent whereas Green Dot did only 70.5 percent and Unique ran 72 percent.

The interesting, if not truly amazing, aspect of this test came when I switched from hard, high-antimony shot to ordinary chilled shot and found that Red Dot still patterned best among the three loadings. It averaged 74 percent with chilled 7½s, while the 21.0-grain Green Dot load and 22.5-grain Unique load both gave 66 percent. Thus, Red Dot was still shooting like a full choke despite its higher chamber pressure, although Green Dot and Unique had dropped off to a strong modified choke performance.

Thus, after years of observing powder with fast burn rates and higher chamber pressures outpattern slower-rate powders operating at lower chamber pressures, I finally was forced to conclude that there was more at work here than chamber pressure influences. But what was it?

The one element I kept returning to was gas pressure in the bore and at the moment of ejecta exit. My thinking emphasized the fact that powders with slower burning rates have greater retained energy well down the bore, and it is possible that those higher bore pressures do shove the wad into the shot. Being without any means to check bore pressures, I contacted John C. Delaney, chief ballistician for Hercules. His reply was: "Your thoughts on muzzle region barrel pressure are in line with this theory: Red Dot reaches peak pressures faster than Green Dot or Unique, and the pressure also decays faster. Lower pressure at the muzzle could allow the barrel/wad friction to slow the wad enough to separate [it from] the shot."

Apparently, then, the patterning advantages theorized for low chamber pressures can be offset by muzzle-end disturbances when husky charges of slow-rate powders are employed to match the velocity level of fast-rate powder. What is saved in

SHOTGUNNING TRENDS IN TRANSITION

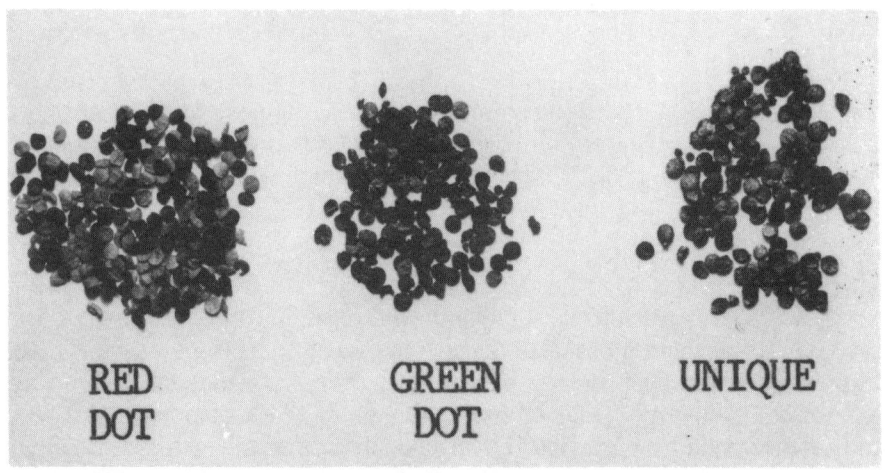

Although popular reloading notions hold that slower-rate powders, such as Green Dot and Unique, will invariably deliver tighter patterns than fast-rate Red Dot, the author's test results indicate that such is not the case *unless* the charge of slow-rate powder approximated the weight of the fast-rate powder. Increased charges of slow-rate powder merely increase muzzle region gases which can ram the wad into the emerging shot charge to scatter it widely.

the way of fewer deformed pellets via lower chamber pressures is lost at the exit end when higher lingering pressures deny smooth shot/wad separation.

The question that immediately came to mind was: Can shooters, especially trapshooters, use the slow-rate powders and obtain any advantages? Further patterning has indicated to me that slow-rate powders do offer advantages for pattern tightening, but that it generally doesn't happen when the slow-rate powders are loaded to equal the muzzle velocity of loads using fast-rate propellants. For example, my testing required 21.0 grains of Green Dot and 22.5 grains of Unique to match the velocity of just 19.0 grains of Red Dot, and those heavier charges of slower-rate powders produced bore pressures that didn't decay as rapidly as those of Red Dot. Consequently, there was less exit pressure on the wads driven by 19.0 grains of Red Dot.

Since the heavier charges of slower-rate powders generated the undesirable muzzle-end pressures, my only course of action was reducing the charges of Green Dot and Unique. Because Hercules makes no 2¾ dram equivalent recommendation for Unique, I concentrated on Green Dot and tested a load rolled thus:

> Remington Premier hull
> Remington 209P primer
> 19.0 grains Green Dot
> Remington TGT-12 wad
> 1⅛ ounces lead shot
> Pressure: 7,300 psi
> Velocity: nominal 1,145 fps

This reduced the powder charge, which obviously reduced the potential gas mass, but still generated totally adequate target-load velocity. When I patterned it through the same Model 12 full choke, the results were astounding! Chilled No. 7½s bunched into an 80 percent average, the highest average I'd ever attained with ordinary chilled shot in 1⅛-ounce loads. When I switched to hard, high-antimony shot, patterns increased to 85 to 87 percent. Of course, these averages outshot those of Red Dot by several percentage points. Over my chronograph, the reloads did indeed reach their velocity levels, some going to 1,165 fps.

Eventually, I used the same 19.0-grain reload of Green Dot in the Browning BT-99 with its extra-full-choke tube, and it again patterned at an 87 percent clip. Used in other randomly selected trap guns, the charge of 19.0 grains of Green Dot has patterned famously for me and is highly recommended for trapshooters who want optimum handicap density with hard No. 7½s or excellent practice reloads with inexpensive chilled shot. I also have found this same 19.0-grain load of Green Dot exceptional in modified-choked trap guns throwing hard No. 8s.

My work with this 19.0-grain charge of Green Dot, then, may well have been the key to sorting out the subtleties of shotgun/shotshell performance vis-à-vis comparative powder burning rates: The old rule of thumb about slow-rate powders

SHOTGUNNING TRENDS IN TRANSITION

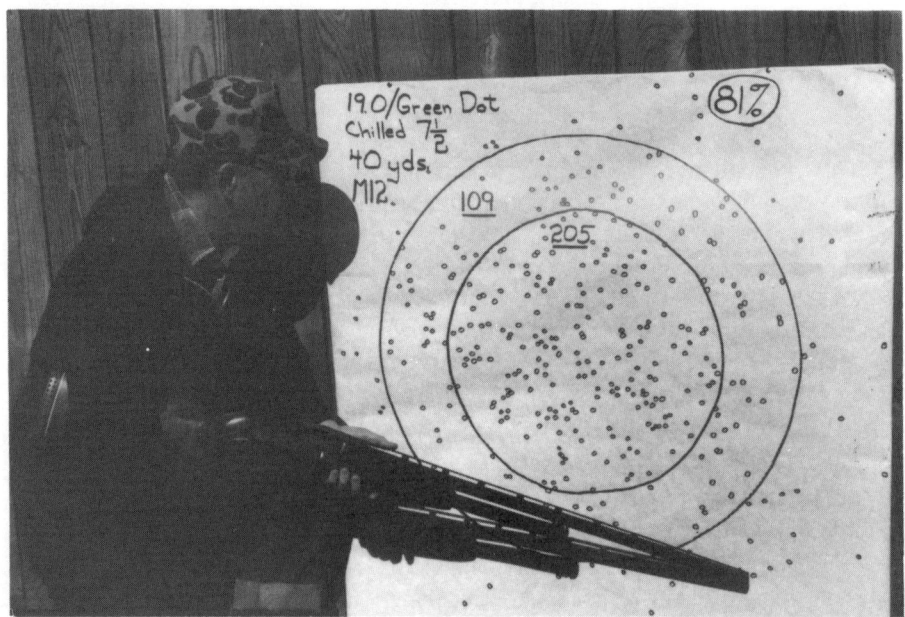

One of the best-performing reloads the author has ever found with ordinary chilled shot appeared when he used Green Dot in nearly the same amount as Red Dot. This 19-grain charge turned in an excellent trap handicap pattern. Adding more Green Dot for greater velocity tended to open the pattern due to extra muzzle region gas.

patterning better than fast-rate powders works best when the charge weights are similar, if not identical. Chamber pressures aside, a heavier charge of slow-rate powder that brings a reload up to the velocity of a fast-rate powder can, and does, generate more muzzle-segment gases which, in turn, have the potential to impact patterns adversely.

To make the aged rule of thumb function efficiently, therefore, we have to consider the charge weight rather than just thinking in terms of chamber pressure comparisons. In my patterning experiences, there is the potential for detrimental pattern influences due to muzzle-region gases whenever a slow-rate powder is thrown in charges heavy enough to match the velocity level of a faster-rate powder. Of tremendous importance, it seems, is the powder charge's decay rate. When we can have lower chamber pressures *and* reduced muzzle-region gas pressures, we have something exciting! My 19.0-grain reload of Green Dot strikes me as just such a concoction!

One final example to bolster my argument about the importance of decay rate on patterning: Some of the tightest patterns I've ever seen with chilled shot came from my Merkel over/under when it was tested with one-ounce target loads. This Merkel had an ultra-tight choke and bore, and it easily reached 75 to 80 percent with normal factory one-ounce trap loads. But when Hercules released data for one-ounce target reloads using fast-rate Bullseye powder, I immediately began getting 40-yard averages of 90 percent or better with chilled No. 8s and 7½s.

What was the difference between Bullseye and the other target-grade powders? Bullseye has a faster decay rate! It peters out down the bore, leaving the shot to escape fluidly without being rammed by the trailing wads.

Thus, when thinking about manipulating ammunition for pattern, we must consider the gas pressures at both ends of the barrel. Low pressure in the chamber with slow-rate fuels can spell too-high pressures at the muzzle.

Little by little, then the old rules of thumb and hand-me down advice — ballistics myths, if you will — are being chopped up by scientific subtleties and new components, by experimenters and those who question clubhouse theories bandied about by shooters who have never patterned or chronographed so much as one measly shotshell! When it comes to shotgun performance, have an open and inquiring mind!

Chapter 10

A Flame Still Flickering: The 16 Gauge

WHENEVER we see a flickering candle, we know that one of two things will happen: Either the flame will catch and glow brightly again, or it will fade, dim and extinguish. Under normal circumstances, such flickering doesn't last very long.

Those who hold a candle for the 16-gauge shotshell and bird guns so-chambered have set a new long-run record for flickering. The 16 gauge's flame has sputtered and flickered ever since the 1950s, never dying entirely but not bursting back to brilliance either. Indeed, as candle-watching goes, the 16 gauge's plight during the past 30 to 35 years has been a marathon vigil!

Hunters who are versed in the shotgun literature of midcentury still find the 16's disappearance a mystery. Some of the most popular writers praised the 16 gauge, and two of the most famous ruffed grouse hunters of all time — William Harnden Foster and Burton L. Spiller — focused in their books on the 16 in some memorable, if not classic, chapters. Perhaps the most famous shotgun in all upland writing is the 16 gauge Parker hammer gun. That gun forms the pivot for the very first chapter, "The Little Gun," of Foster's *New England Grouse Shooting*. And when Burton L. Spiller, considered to be the poet laureate of grouse hunting, narrated the ordering and purchase of his first custom bird gun in *More Grouse Feathers* (1938), it turned out to be a 16-gauge Belgian piece.

Other important writers also admired the 16 gauge. In *Shotguns by Keith*, the late Elmer Keith, who loved big holes in the ends of his sporting gun barrels, opined that the 16 was "perhaps the nicest of all upland guns and a very useful gun for average range duck shooting as well with the heavy $1^1/_8$ ounce loads with progressive powders." Jack O'Connor of *Outdoor Life* magazine didn't mind saying pleasant things about the 16 in his columns, and in *The Shotgun Book* went on record as finding it to be "a fine choice as an all-around gun, as it patterns about as well as the 12, kicks less, handles enough shot for most purposes, and makes

SHOTGUNNING TRENDS IN TRANSITION

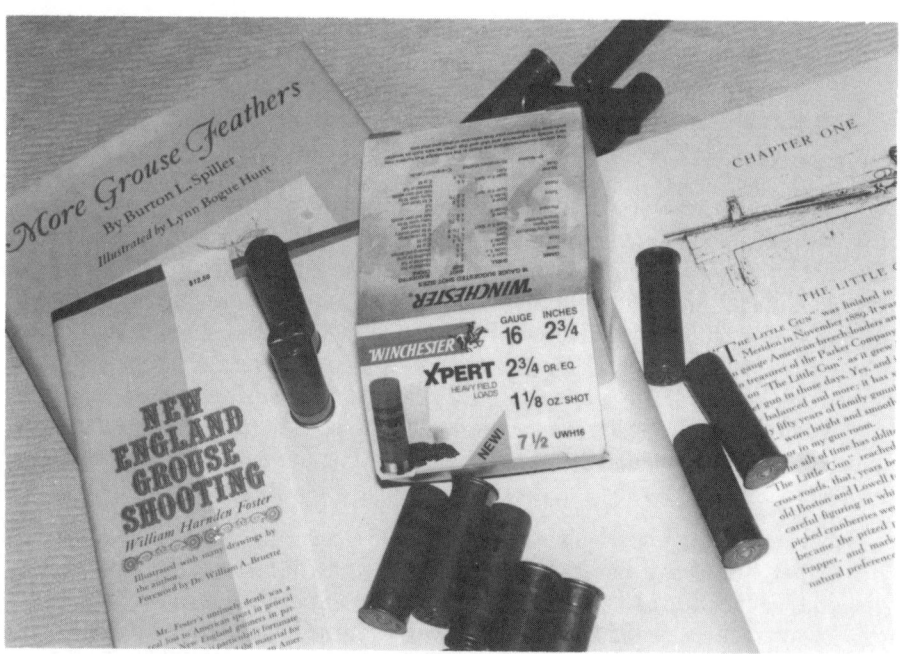

The 16 gauge is steeped in American literature, being a focal point in both Burton Spiller's *More Grouse Feathers* and W. H. Foster's famous first chapter, "The Little Gun," in *New England Grouse Shooting*.

up into a trimmer gun." And the influential Charles Askins Sr., blessed the 16 by claiming that, "it is without a doubt superior for upland work ... [and] is a corking good little gun in the duck blind ... where the birds are decoying well..." as he discussed gauges in *The American Shotgun.*

Why, then, did the 16 gauge's flame begin to flicker and fade even though the ranking experts and most popular writers endorsed it heavily? My feeling is that it did *not* do so because of any lack of public support. In the 1940s, the *American Rifleman* published a survey which showed that roughly 50 percent of the shotguns bought stateside were 12 gauges, approximately 25 percent were then still 16 gauges, and that the 20 gauge attracted only about 17 percent of the business. At that time, the .410 bore sold just 4 percent with the 10 gauge and 28 gauge claiming but 2 percent of the total. Time changes all things, of course, but just before midcentury the 16 gauge was holding its own. Twenty-five percent of all shotgun sales isn't bad.

Moreover, hunter interest in the 16 gauge still isn't lacking. In my capacity as a handloading and gun editor for various magazines, I continually receive letters from hunters who are enthusiastic about the 16. Some of them will have no other gauge; they're dedicated to carrying a 16. And I'm sure there are many others who would try the 16 if they were available, but during the 1950s, 1960s, 1970s and the first half of the 1980s, it was extremely difficult to find a well-made, well-designed 16 gauge and the ammo to go with it. Thus, I'm positive there was a market for 16-gauge guns and loads during those decades. The demand may have been less than 25 percent of the total market, but if gunmakers were willing to crank out .410s and 28s at a time when they contributed no more than a total of 4 percent of the trade — why not continue the 16 when it surely would have generated more sales than the 28 and .410?

The answer, it seems, is twofold: 1) the manufacturers didn't give much time to the design and development of 16-gauge guns, and 2) the industry attempted to kill off the 16 so that it would have fewer items to catalog, produce, inventory and distribute. Therefore, it wasn't the sportsmen whose lack of demand stopped the 16 in full stride — it was an industry decision. Those hunters who might have bought the 16 as a light piece or as an all-arounder bought a lightweight 12 instead, and, if they weren't true gun nuts, they didn't complain. Unfortunately, the demise of the neat 16-gauge guns and loads frustrated those who truly loved the intermediate bore.

One look at some of the best-selling guns after midcentury will illustrate how badly the 16 was treated. The Remington Model 1100, for example, was destined to become a great autoloader; I personally love it in 12 gauge. But when Remington made 16-gauge Model 1100s, the guns weren't scaled to 16-gauge proportions; they were merely 16-gauge barrels stuck on 12-gauge frames. Who wants to carry a 12-gauge Model 1100 to shoot a 16-gauge load? The advantage was gone, for the glory of the 16-gauge bird gun is that it can pattern like the 12 with loads up to 1¼ ounces while handling and carrying easier, thanks to the potential for trimness. A critical look at other 16 gauges, including some from before World War II, will show that they, too, were not bona fide 16s but were mainly improvised 16s assembled on 12-gauge receivers.

The 16 gauge's flame is beginning to glow just a bit brighter as we speed to the year 2000 A.D. With the gunmakers now searching out niche markets that are capable of generating profits because advanced manufacturing technology allows for profitability on short production runs, some 16s are appearing. Browning tested the market by introducing a 16-gauge version of the popular Japanese-made Citori O/U. The gun was made to look and handle like the old Belgian Lightning Superposed. Given the Invector choke system, the Citori came as close to being an all-around 16-gauge over/under as we've ever had. The only other 16-gauge over/under obtainable is the German-made Merkel, and they are both more costly and difficult to pin down.

Browning also has re-introduced the "Sweet Sixteen" version of the Auto-5; a joy among autoloaders because it is scaled to the gauge. The only 16-gauge autoloader I enjoyed more was the Remington Model 11-48, which, though mechanically inferior to the Sweet Sixteen, had streamline profiling and excellent pointing and carrying qualities. The Model 11-48 was sized just right for a 16-gauge repeater.

Manufacturers must be sensible, and recognize the 16 as a niche product, one that appeals mainly to hunters who split fine hairs or are for various reasons totally taken by it. The advent of steel shot will certainly work against the 16 — unless an adventurous company comes up with a three-inch version of it! For although I once thought the 16 gauge would be a better steel shot vehicle than the three-inch 20, thanks to the 16's wider bore and better pressure/velocity ratios, things haven't turned out that way. The early commercial 16-gauge steel shot loads either hold no more shot than the three-inch 20 or a mite less. Thus, given no steel shot advantage, the 16 won't lure hunters away from the three-inch 20 until a three-inch 16-gauge Magnum arrives. Then the 16 could go on to become the stellar all-around smallbore that early writers always said it was, perhaps becoming *the* outstanding smaller piece of the steel shot era.

The final fate of the 16 gauge as a production-run bird gun may very well hinge upon the success of Browning's offerings. Other manufacturers will be watching. If the 16-gauge Citori and Asian-made Sweet Sixteens sell, other gunmakers would be inclined to follow with their own limited runs. I believe the Parker Reproduction would make up into a splendid American-style upland piece, and Remington's new computerized designing and machining equipment could easily scale the Model 11-87 and Model 870 to fit the 16-gauge hull. If hunters are reluctant, however, the 16 gauge's flame may very well begin flickering again only to fade and die.

A FLAME STILL FLICKERING: THE 16 GAUGE

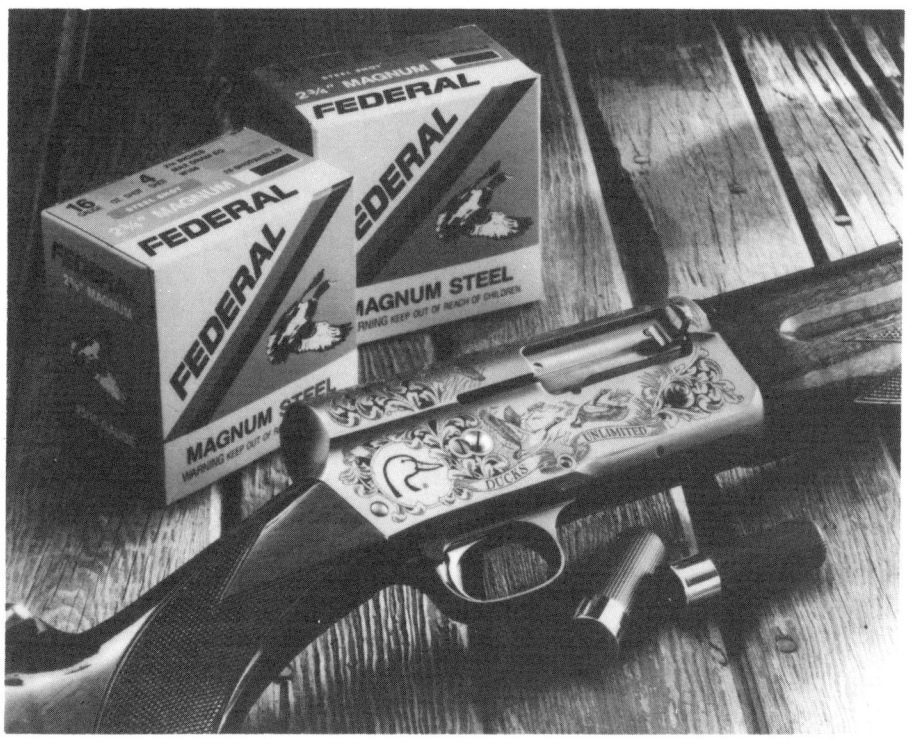

Browning not only brought back the Sweet Sixteen, but offered it in a 1988 special Ducks Unlimited version. Much of the 16 gauge's future will depend upon how well the Browning 16s are received.

Chapter 11

Barrels of Fun

WHEN A beginner or unsophisticated hunter/shooter peers down a shotgun's barrel, he sees nothing but a bright, shiny hole. Despite the shadowy effect, the main reason for examining a barrel is to check for cleanliness, but there's considerably more to a shotgun barrel's interior. Let a thoroughly knowledgeable shotgunner or machinist peer through the same tube, and he'll see all sorts of important features that influence interior and exterior performances. By changing the interior configurations of a shotgun barrel, one alters recoil, velocity, patterning and even chamber pressure. This chapter will detail some of those conditions and alterations along with their proven or potential results.

Before exploring the nuances of shotgun barrel influences on shotshell function, however, let's briefly establish the four main segments of a shotgun's barrel. Beginning at the open breech end and running to the muzzle are, in sequence, the chamber, the forcing cone, the bore or main bore, and the choke constriction.

The Chamber

The chamber seems to be a simple enough segment. It receives and holds the shotshell for and during firing. Chambers are designed with a minor back-to-front taper, not a perfectly cylindrical configuration. For the best ballistics and patterns, the chamber's length should be the same as the unfolded hull's length. If the chamber is shorter than the unfolded hull, the case's mouth will uncrimp into the conical forcing cone and impede ejecta movement due to the too-narrow passage. Rather than opening to its full diameter, the case mouth/crimp section will be restricted according to the degree of taper in the cone. The result will be heightened chamber pressure as the wad is pinched abruptly at the puckered case mouth forcing it to swage down to fight its way clear. This can create a sharp recoil jolt. Some duck seasons ago, I had a Browning Belgian-made Auto-5 in the three-inch 12-gauge Magnum model. It kicked severely with three-inch loads. When a gunsmith dropped a chamber length gage into it, he found the chamber was nearly $1/8$ inch

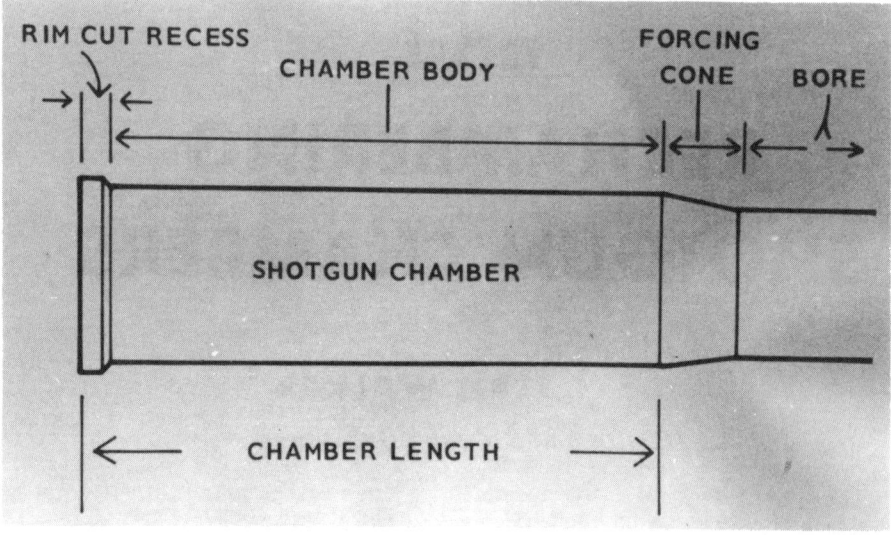

The lower segments of a shotgun barrel.

too short; the crimp was opening into the cone, and the wad had to bump its way out while chamber pressures soared. After the chamber was cut to a full three inches, the objectionable recoil vanished.

Conversely, chambers that are too long can permit some gas seepage with the concomitant lowering of temperature and pressure for lower ballistics. This situation does not appear as serious today as it was prior to the 1960s' plastic revolution, as the plastic shotcups tend to do a better job of filling the cone than did the old card/filler wads which provided no circumferential protection from spurting gases. Indeed, the former card/filler wad stacks were suspected of letting gases fuse pellets so that patterning sheets picked up tightly welded clusters. Called "balling," this condition simply doesn't appear in patterns shot with plastic obturating and shotcup units even when short hulls are employed in magnum-length chambers. In my experience, the pre-plastic 2½-inch .410 loads left much to be desired when used in the three-inch .410 chamber.

Shotgunners who like to use the older guns should pay strict attention to chamber lengths, as shotshells have gotten progressively longer. Commercial 10-gauge hulls have run from 2⅝ to 2⅞ inches, and then they jumped to 3½ inches. The 12 gauge has had chambers cut from two inches to the new 3½-inch ultra-length magnum for steel shot, while the 16 gauge has gone from 2⁹⁄₁₆ inches to 2¾ inches. The 20 gauge at one time was a 2½-inch hull, and firing 2¾-inchers in a rickety old 20 may exert too much pressure in its chamber/cone portion. At one time, the 28 gauge was just 2½ inches long, but it now opens to 2¾ inches. And the original .410 load was just two inches long, but subsequently stepped up to 2½ and then three inches. I once had a beautiful old A. H. Fox 12-gauge double that I loved to swing on mallards, but it had a 2½-inch chamber and I didn't want to recut it because that would spoil its authenticity. Thus, I went through the process of reloading 2½-inch duck loads until I sold the piece.

The chambers of foreign shotguns often will be stamped in metrics. For instance, a 70mm equals the U.S. 2¾-inch chamber, and the 75 to 76mm chamber designation is a full three-incher.

Although we take chamber dimensions for granted, that dimension can have an impact on ballistics. I have not run any of my own experiments on this, but British writer Gough Thomas reported in *Shotguns & Cartridges for Game and Clays* that, in a 12-bore game gun, increasing the mean diameter of the chamber by .005-inch lowered the chamber pressure by about a quarter of a ton and the velocity by about 30 fps. Thus, since shotgun chambers are hardly identical, they may account for various ballistic irregularities on a gun to gun basis. Unless the chamber is excessively oversize, there seems to be little to worry about as legitimate hunting loads can spare 30 to 50 fps without losing their downrange potency. When two hunters obtain different chronograph results from a given load, though, the chamber/bore diameters may be one reason.

Forcing Cones

The forcing cone, alias simply the "cone," is a conical segment of the barrel immediately ahead of the chamber. Its job is to funnel the ejecta into the main bore, which all seems simple enough. But the cone actually can be a complicated subject. The complication hinges upon the cone's length. The shorter the cone, the more abrupt will be its angle; and the more abrupt the cone's angle, the more difficult it is for the ejecta to swage down rapidly for the chamber-to-bore transition. What this adds up to is recoil as the powder gases pile up behind the ejecta which is briefly jammed at the case mouth as the shot charge and wads squeeze down. In effect, a short and steep cone acts as a minor obstruction, as do the leading pellets that pile up there to halt the lower pellets and the wad.

A longer forcing cone, on the other hand, automatically means a shallower angle, which translates into less obstruction for the ejecta. The result is a smoother chamber-to-bore transition for the wad/shot mass with concomitant reduction of recoil.

Belgian Browning Superposed guns often had very short forcing cones, and my first 12-gauge Superposed kicked like the proverbial mule. After I had those cones lengthened somewhat, the gun acted almost civilized.

Along with recoil reduction, forcing cones influence patterning. Long cones that allow ejecta to flow fluidly from chamber to bore deform fewer pellets, whereas a short, steep cone that impedes ejecta flow causes deformation by raw pellet-against-pellet mashing when the leading layers of shot bump into the cone's wall-like obstruction.

An important question is: How long should a forcing cone be? Experimenters and barrelsmiths have various results and different opinions. My own work indicates that the lighter target loads with fine shot need less cone length than do magnum charges of coarse shot. I still haven't made up my mind about cone length and steel shot because of some test results. For lead shot, however, cones of $5/8$-inch to two inches seem appropriate for the various specialties, with the shorter lengths for the lighter loads and smaller pellets. That, of course, is somewhat vague, but there seems to be a lot of individualism in shotgun performance to justify hedges and the advice to pattern each gun rather than living with a rule of thumb or hand-me-down generalization.

Some years ago, for example, I had a pair of autoloaders cut with two-inch forcing cones. Before those barrels were altered, though, I patterned with them to obtain some data from their factory-length cones. Then I patterned with the same control loads after the cones had been modified to compare performances. The data follows:

One gun was a Remington standard-chambered Model 1100 with 28-inch full-choke barrel. When patterned at 40 yards, it averaged thus for five-shot strings:

load	original cone (percent)	lengthened 2-inch cone (percent)
Factory load: 1½x5 (Federal High-Power)	73	81
Factory load: 1½x2 (Remington Express)	70	74
Handload: 1¼x5 hard shot (35.0 grains 540 Ball)	67	76.5
Handload: 1½x5 hard shot (35.0 grains HS-7)	77	90
Handload: 1³⁄₈x4 chilled (31.5 grains SR-7625)	57	63
Factory load: 1¹⁄₈x8 (Peters target)	74	67

The second gun was a Browning Belgian-made Auto-5 in 12-gauge Magnum with 32-inch full-choke barrel. Its before and after results were:

load	original cone (percent)	lengthened two-inch cone (percent)
Factory load: 1⁷⁄₈xBB (Federal Premium)	72	84
Factory load: 1¹⁄₈x2 steel (Remington steel)	86	70
Factory load: 1³⁄₈x1 steel (Federal steel)	84	92
Handload: 1⁵⁄₈x4 chilled (40.0 grains Blue Dot)	57	71
Handload: 1⁷⁄₈x2 hard shot (39.0 grains Blue Dot)	71	80
Factory load: 1¹⁄₈x8 hard shot (Peters target load)	71	65

The interesting conclusion gathered from this material is that the shorter shot charges failed to improve as the cones were lengthened to two inches. Note especially the 1¹⁄₈-ounce target loads which lost density through the longer cones. Ditto for the 1¹⁄₈-ounce steel shot load through the Browning Auto-5. Meanwhile, the heavier loads of coarse lead shot and magnum-length charges of steel shot increased their efficiencies. As a further note, I must add that the loads which improved their averages after the cones had been lengthened also tended toward higher center densities. Thus, although factory barrels normally will produce their stipulated choke percentages with quality loads and hard shot, longer cones frequently will improve performances for less recoil, less pellet deformation and tighter patterns. I seriously doubt that the lighter loads need cones beyond an inch, and it is possible that a smoothly cut ¾-inch cone is adequate for target loads. However, some combination of long cone and bore/choke configuration that I'm not aware of might generate excellent target-load clusters. In any case, the forcing cone is a very vital segment of any shotgun barrel despite its relative brevity.

The Main Bore

Once the shot charge and wad negotiate the forcing cone's incline, they reach the main bore. Here they travel in a restricted tubelike condition until they reach the inception of the choke constriction. Here, too, a typical hunter or collector might deem the segment as simply another hole, but the bore plays a role in ballistics, too. The diameter of a shotgun's bore determines 1) how much powder gas can get to the base of the wad and 2) how much friction will be exerted upon the ejecta's circumference. Let's start at the beginning:

A shotgun's bore size is related to its "gauge," and for many people that reference is a mystery. In "shotgunology," the term goes back a long way and it refers to the exact number of round lead balls per pound that fit a shotgun's main bore. Thus, it would require 16 lead balls the size of a 16 gauge's bore to make one pound. If we cast similar lead balls to fit the 12 gauge's nominal bore, there would be one dozen per pound. For the 20 and 28 gauges, there would be 20 and 28 lead balls, respectively, per pound. The only exception to this bore system is the .410, which actually is a bore, not a gauge. If the .410 were a gauge, it would be roughly 67.

During the past decades, manufacturers established relatively standard bore diameters for the gauges. These are not followed precisely by manufacturers, but they serve as nominal dimensions from which variations can be judged. The current standards are:

gauge	inch
10	.775
12	.729
14	.693
16	.662
20	.615
24	.580
28	.550
32	.501
.410 bore	.410

Variations on those diameters can be due to manufacturer preference and/or manufacturing tolerances. In the last year, I have measured any number of 12-gauge shotgun bores, and they have ranged from .725 to .732-inch. At present the 12-gauge seldom is given a true .729-inch bore diameter. The tightest 12-gauge bore I have owned is my Merkel over/under's which ran .722-inch. That gun kicked robustly with loads heavier than $1^1/_8$ ounces as all that shot and wads from high-velocity duck loads or short magnums forced their way through the narrow bore. To improve that Merkel's efficiency with heavier loads, I asked the people at Briley Manufacturing to bore out both tubes to the normal .729 to .730-inch diameter, which also shaved the barrel weight slightly and made the gun handle a bit more like the fine side-by-side game guns.

The current trend is toward increased bore diameters, sometimes radically increased diameters, for *lead* shot. Such barrels are said to be overbored because their diameters are larger than minor manufacturing tolerances would leave them. Another new term added to the modern wingshot's vocabulary which means the very same thing is backboring. Backboring is a term coined by Seattle barrelsmith Stan Baker. He thought the original description of *overboring* misled people into mistakenly believing that there was something disastrously excessive about bores machined larger than standard specs would require. The fact is, however, that with modern lead shot loads an increased bore diameter has much to offer.

At first glance, it appears that any expansion of a shotgun's bore would create a reduction in pressure which, in turn, would cause a velocity drop. As mentioned in Chapter 10, the frequency of gas molecule collisions decreases as the amount of expansion room increases, but that's mainly theory. What happens when overbored barrels are tested on chronograph rigs is something else, but it took us until the early 1980s to learn that lesson.

The practice of overboring shotgun barrels is not something totally new, of course. It met with some popularity between the two world wars when continued advances in progressive-burning smokeless powders brought about increasingly heavier shot charges for each respective gauge. When the bore diameter standards were established via the gauge system, for example, the 10 gauge was still topping out with $1^1/_4$ ounces of shot, and the 12 gauge was normally at maximum with $1^1/_8$ ounces. The 16 gauge handled one ounce at the very most, and the 20 gauge was stuck with just $^7/_8$-ounce. These charge weights tended to shoot comfortably and pattern quite well from their standard bores.

But then stouter loads came along, as did magnum-length shotshells. Suddenly the original bore diameters were less than ideal. Recoil built as the powerful loads rammed into the forcing cones; patterning efficiency varied and faltered with pellet deformation. The newer, heavier rounds were simply a lot of stuff to move through bores formerly devised for significantly lighter loads.

But the 1920s and 1930s didn't lack for innovators. Some of the earliest widespread publicity given overboring came from Nash Buckingham, a noted outdoorsman who was widely published and had a reputation for being a superb long-range duck shot. Buckingham wanted all the pattern he could get, and his primary waterfowling guns were a pair of Burt Becker three-inch 12-gauge magnums which, like other Becker custom pieces, were fashioned from A. H. Fox barreled actions. These Becker guns differed from the norm by their overbored barrels which were approximately .010-inch oversized. To these barrels Buckingham fitted three-inch loads with $1^3/_8$ ounces of copper-plated shot. When the three-inch 12-gauge picked up followers, the A. H. Fox Gun Company turned out a special waterfowl model known as the Grade H which sported overbored tubes. These are collectors' items now, and I've seen some offered at $2,000. Likewise, Remington provided overbored barrels for the models 11 and 31 during the 1930s, although they were not chambered for three-inch hulls, of course. These barrels may still be found at gun shows, but you'll need an inside caliper to identify them.

As history records, though, few hunters and shooters picked up on the overbored barrel during the first half of the twentieth century. Unless I missed something, Bob Nichols skipped the subject entirely in *The Shotgunner*, as did Askins in *The American Shotgun* (1928). The average shotgunner of their eras (as well as today's typical hunters), apparently didn't appreciate the subtleties of overbores. Today, it is mainly the trapshooter who opts for overbores; most hunters aren't "up" on the topic.

The current popularity of overboring traces back to the 1970s when trapshooters looked for other ways to combat recoil pain and fatigue. Stan Baker was one of the first to advocate overboring for recoil reduction, and he struck up a brisk business. Besides creating the term "backboring," Baker also continued experimenting with constantly larger 12-gauge bore diameters. Although the prevailing theory told him that overbores reduced pressure and velocity, he began seeing things differently. According to his chronograph, the widest bores generated the highest, *not* the lowest, velocities. Out of curiosity, Baker kept opening experimental barrels until he reached an .800-inch bore diameter (which is *wider* than the 10 gauge's nominal .775-inch diameter) and obtained significantly higher speeds. This was the ballistics world turned upside down! About then Baker began supplying writers and experimenters with his "Big Bore" barrels, and I was one of the first individuals to wring them out.

My sample of the .800-inch diameter Big Bore was for the Remington Model 1100. It had a massive maw through which a 12-gauge wad would generally fall. How could such a spacious, low-pressure bore generate higher velocities than a standard-diameter (.729-inch) 12-gauge bore that seals gases better? My own critical chronographing proved that it could do so with apparent ease.

For the sake of comparison, the Baker Big Bore, which was 30 inches long, was pitted against a Perazzi MX-8 that had the standard-diameter in its $29^1/_2$-inch tubes. The results based on a $4^1/_2$-foot instrumental reading were:

load	MX-8 (fps)	big bore (fps)
Peters trap load (3 - 1 1/8)	1,241	1,283
ACTIV trap load (3 - 1 1/8)	1,224	1,266
Peters trap load (2 3/4 - 1 1/8)	1,172	1,211
Federal trap load (2 3/4 - 1 1/8)	1,156	1,196

Obviously, the .800-inch-diameter Baker Big Bore outraced the MX-8 barrel by about 40 fps, on average, with the listed loads. What this means for trapshooters is that they can use light-recoiling 2¾ drams equivalent ammunition and actually realize the velocity of three drams equivalent rounds. And patterns? It was difficult to keep the Big Bore from throwing devastating full and extra-full-choke strings; there was a tremendous leeway in the amount of constriction one could employ and still get 70 percent patterns or better. The only point I noted was that hunting loads rolled with slow-rate propellants didn't gain velocity as readily, perhaps because the greater bore space didn't generate the high temperatures necessary for optimum burning.

The problem with Baker's .800-inch bore was that it left original 12-gauge barrel walls too thin for safety. The Big Bores, which are still being made, are fashioned by the "sleeving" process in which the original barrel is cut off just ahead of the chamber and a new tube matching the 10 gauge is fitted to the drilled out chamber in male/female fashion. This produces a weight-forward gun, of course, and some trapshooters find it a bit slower starting.

To mitigate against the expense of sleeving and the weight of a wider barrel, Stan Baker relaxed the extreme bore dimensions and designed the "Semi-Big Bore," which has a nominal bore diameter of .775-inch, i.e., the exact industry standard for 10-gauge barrels. This provides another .005-inch thickness, and the performance is practically identical with that of the .800-inch bore. I have used the .775-inch barrel extensively for both trap and waterfowling, and it made the Model 1100 Remington livelier because it lightened the 30-inch barrel. Again, I noted that slow-rate powders did not improve their velocities substantially in the Semi-Big Bore; that phenomenon was experienced mainly with powders having fast and medium-burning rates.

Why would such cavernous 12-gauge bores deliver advanced velocities with various loads and powders? This seems impossible to people who have always equated high speeds with slender, rifle-like barrels and small bores. The answer was hinted at previously: Reduced friction allows more powder gas energy to convert to kinetic energy. In a tight bore, much of the powder charge's energy is wasted by fighting friction and turning into heat. Secondly, the powder gases can reach the optimum base width and, by pushing on a broader area, make a more efficient conversion from chemical to kinetic energy.

SHOTGUNNING TRENDS IN TRANSITION

The author and what might have been the first goose taken with the Stan Baker "Semi-Big Bore," a 12-gauge barrel bored out to .775-inch, which is a nominal 10-gauge bore diameter. The wider bore reduces pellet deformation, reduces recoil and enhances patterns. With many loads, it also will increase velocity as there is less friction to overcome and the powder's energy can channel into the ejecta rather than fighting friction.

How far must a gun's bore be opened to achieve some velocity gains? In the 12 gauge, I believe velocity increases begin around .755 to .760-inch. Lesser amounts of overbore relieve recoil and help reduce some pellet deformation, but I have not seen important velocity increases until we near .755 to .760-inch. I once chronographed with a 26-inch skeet barrel that had a bore diameter of roughly .755-inch. When I tested it against a standard Remington 26-inch skeet barrel with .725-inch bore, the data looked like this:

load	standard bore (.725-inch) (fps)	overbore (.755-inch) (fps)
Winchester AA (3 - 1 1/8)	1,178	1,196
Federal Gold Medal (3 - 1 1/8)	1,185	1,204
Peters Skeet (3 - 1 1/8)	1,179	1,190
Peters Skeet 2 3/4 - 1 1/8)	1,122	1,136
Reload (19.0 grains Red Dot - 1 1/8)	1,154	1,166

With this bore diameter and barrel length, the overbore feature netted velocity gains of only 10 to 20 fps, on average, which is about one-half the gain registered by the tunnel-like .800 and .775-inch bore diameters. Exactly what might have happened in 30-inch barrels with the .755-inch overbore, I cannot say. What it indicates, however, is that velocity gains are progressive as the bore increases to .800-inch. I have not tested beyond that point. Perhaps it would be an exercise in futility, as there is a breaking point where the wad's flanged overpowder cup no longer provides any semblance of sealing.

Do the massive overbores have any shortcomings? Yes, at least two. It was learned very early that cold weather and extensive overbores, such as the .800-incher, do not jibe. Cold weather, meaning down around 0°F, will cause plastic wads to become hard and brittle, and they lose their obturating potential. The overpowder cups simply don't flare out to seal the bore. Under such conditions, the powder gases seep around the wad and produce squib effects. Overboring also remains an unknown entity insofar as steel shot loads are concerned. While one would tend to believe that greater bore expansion room would enhance steel shot fluidity, there is also the chance that a wider bore would permit the shotcup slots to open and expose steel pellets to the bore, creating damage. Likewise, steel shot loads are relatively light compared to lead shot magnums, and steel shot powders tend to start very gradually; therefore, the extra bore space could hold down ballistics and, in some cases, fail to operate a gas-operated autoloader. The .775-inch bore I used on a Remington 1100 Magnum for goose hunting wouldn't eject any steel loads, although it functioned perfectly with any and all steel ammo using the normal .725-inch bore. I believe that anything beyond a .740-inch 12-gauge bore diameter will be of questionable worth with steel shot unless unanticipated radical changes develop.

In warm weather and with lead shot, however, overboring is becoming quite fashionable and effective. Removing some steel lightens a barrel for better handling and, as already mentioned, lowers the recoil level significantly.

Commercial gunmakers are also beginning to work overboring into their production guns once again. Winchester employed it on some commemorative trap guns made on the Model 101 frame. Remington is foremost among American makers in the current application of overboring. The Remington Model 870 single-shot "Competition" pumpgun had an overbored barrel to help reduce recoil, and beginning in 1988 the Model 11-87 trap guns and Model 870-TCs were equipped with barrels overbored to roughly .740 to .743-inch.

In many respects, the hunting grade 20 gauge that uses more than one ounce of lead shot could well be overbored. The 20-gauge's bore is simply too snug for $1^{1}/_{8}$ and $1^{1}/_{4}$ ounces of shot. I'll wager that opening the .410's bore slightly will enhance performances with three-inch cartridges, too.

As chronographing indicates, then, overboring sensibly doesn't cause a loss of velocity. In many instances, the overbore makes shotguns more efficient in both velocity and pattern. If you'd like to discuss it with the leading pro in the business, write to Stan Baker at 10000 Lake City Way, Seattle, WA 98125.

Choke Constrictions

One of the funniest things in the gun world is watching someone check a shotgun's muzzle using a dime. According to popular belief a 12-gauge barrel that won't accept a Yankee dime is *indeed* a full-choke. Ask any gun show expert or old-time hunter.

But the fact is that shotgun patterning involves more than just a gun's muzzle diameter. An important factor is the choke's constriction relative to the bore's diameter. Moreover, chokes have different configurations, and shot pellet hardness has a definite bearing on the resulting patterns. That old dime trick means very little in any scientific study of shotgun chokes.

Essentially, the word "choke" is a mechanical term. It refers to the way a shotgun barrel's interior is dimensioned in the muzzle segment for pattern control. Up to a certain point, the more a shotgun's muzzle is constricted, the tighter the pattern will be. When a constriction of about .045-inch is passed in a 12-gauge barrel, however, a condition called overchoke, occurs and patterns can begin to loosen and become erratic. Thus, there is a limit to effective and efficient muzzle constriction, and working a dime around in such muzzles proves nothing. An interior dial-equipped measuring tool and/or actual patterning are the only ways to begin measuring a given barrel's worth.

Conversely, when a shotgun's muzzle diameter is larger than its bore diameter, it is said to have a reverse choke. This is produced by putting a flare into the bore walls, which results in a funnel-like exit for rapid pattern expansion.

In general, neither the overchoke nor the reverse choke is very popular nowadays. The following list presents the typical choke designations, beginning with those of the least constriction. The percentage (efficiency) figures indicate the amount of shot they are expected to put into a 30-inch-diameter circle at 40 yards from each shot charge:

choke	efficiency (percent)
cylinder bore	30 to 35
skeet	35 to 45
improved cylinder	45 to 55
modified	55 to 65
improved modified	65 to 70
full choke	70 to 80
extra-full choke	80 and above

In the past, there was also a Skeet No. 2 constriction which gave patterns around the 50 percent level and was noted for its uniformity. Unfortunately, Skeet No. 2 has become the forgotten choke, but some independent makers of screw-in choke tubes include it in their lines. Perhaps the best Skeet No. 2 performances came from Winchester guns so-bored, especially the Model 21 with Skeet No. 1 (also known as Skeet-In) and Skeet No. 2 (then known as Skeet-Out) lying side-by-each.

Choke configurations differ markedly in theory and practice. Some barrelsmiths argue that they can produce any kind of pattern with just short, abrupt choke tapers. On the other hand, some tinkerers opine that long, smooth, gradual choke tapers deliver the best patterns. In either case, chokes that flow upward to the muzzle and have their tightest point at the very exit are known as conical chokes because of their conelike configuration.

Some of the first work with ultra-long choke tapers was done by Merkel of Suhl, Germany. Most Merkel over/unders I've seen had long forcing cones, narrow bores and lengthy chokes. This worked famously with shot charges of $1^1/_8$ ounces or less in my particular full-choked Merkel, and with one-ounce loads that Merkel would print patterns of 85 to 90 percent at 40 yards. But as the shot charges got heavier, the patterns dropped off due to the overchoke phenomenon, and I eventually had the gun bored out to a nominal 12-gauge diameter of .729-inch. However, when the shot charge matches a long, sweeping, conical choke it can come very close to perfection in tight patterning. I have never had a short, abrupt conical choke perform as well as that Merkel with one or $1^1/_8$-ounce loads. Before having the Merkel's barrels opened, I worked up a buffered $1^3/_{16}$-ounce goose reload which, with copper-plated 2s, averaged 88 percent at 40 yards.

When it comes to short and medium-range shotgunning, where improved cylinder and modified chokes are involved, it is difficult to select between short and long conical chokes. In my experience, they both deliver adequate results. It is mainly in the tighter degrees of choke, from improved modified through extra-full, that the longer conical designs excel.

A variation of the American conical choke is the conical-parallel. This has a two-part development. It begins with the normal conical taper which builds toward the muzzle, but reaches its point of maximum constriction well before the muzzle. From that point of maximum constriction to the exit, the remainder of the choke segment runs straight to the muzzle with no additional taper. The barrel walls are parallel to each other; the final inch or so of a conical-parallel choke again being cylindrical. The conical-parallel design is becoming more popular among barrel-makers, custom barrelmen, and those who pattern experimentally. The "Rem®" choke system uses the conical-parallel system, and my patterning data indicates that the "Rem" Choke's full-choke tubes deliver some of the tightest long-range patterns I've yet found in the screw-in choke tubes and many fixed-choke guns. Likewise, I have seen some beautiful improved cylinder clusters from the "Rem" Choke IC tubes for closer ranges. When I had my Merkel reworked, the gunsmith regulated the upper barrel for modified choke patterns and left a conical-parallel configuration with nearly one inch of parallel after the conical climb. It is one of the most vicious modified patterns I've ever seen.

What is the strength of a conical-parallel choke? My own guess is that the final parallel section lends to shot charge stability. Even though that parallel is sometimes less than an inch, it seems to produce uniformity. A brief conical choke *sans* the parallel, conversely, launches the pellet mass immediately after swaging it to its narrowest form, and pellets may take an outward line from being released so quickly after being maximally compressed. A parallel portion, however, holds the pellets in their narrowed mass for a short distance, thereby eliminating the sudden action-reaction condition that causes outer pellets to rebound outwardly after leaving a simple conical choke.

When the choke wall between the point of maximum constriction and the muzzle are angled outwardly, the choke is said to have "flared flats." Skeet barrels have this characteristic to cause a rapid pattern expansion with uniform distribution. It is unusual to find flared flats in tightly choked guns, but I found them on a Brazilian-made IGA double in 20 gauge, and the patterns were some of the best I've seen from a full-choked 20. Moreover, the modified-choke tube of Mossberg's ACCU-STEEL® screw-in system has flared flats to engineer more open steel shot clusters for closer-range gunning, and my patterning indicates that they do open very rapidly.

The so-called Tula choke is a novel configuration swaged into guns used primarily for International skeet. Named after the Russian gunmaking center, the Tula choke consists of 1) an elongated expansion chamber with a wider diameter than the main bore, 2) an abrupt taper that forces the ejecta together again as it leaves the expansion chamber, and 3) a flared flat which runs from the abrupt taper (constriction) to the muzzle. Some writers already have observed that the Tula choke's configuration looks like a Cutts Compensator built into the barrel. The barrel, of course, is slightly bulbous at the muzzle to accommodate this interior bit of engineering. (Warning: Do not mistake all flared or belled skeet gun muzzles to be honest Tula chokes. Many such guns are merely belled like old-time muskets to inspire a reverse choke kind of performance. Indeed, in many instances such chokes are merely a reverse system. To truly be a Tula choke, there must be the listed three-point swaging with a positive "pinch-down" feature between the expansion chamber and flared flats.) The most commonly seen Tula choke is on the Rottweil Model 72 skeet gun.

What does a Tula choke do? There is some debate on this subject, but it seems apparent that true Tula chokes give extremely uniform pellet distribution and cause a slightly longer shot string. Both qualities are helpful in skeet where the ranges are close and the birds are swift. But I must point out that, in considerable test patterning, I have found the Tula at its very best with loads that do not have shotcups or plastic shot wrappers.

Having previously described the Cutts Compensator, which was one of the very first commercially successful variable choke devices, I must note that Kolar Arms of Racine, Wisconsin, has brought back the concept in refined form, and it has been attracting skeet shooters and hunters. The Kolar Compensator's important features are twofold: First, whereas the original Cutts could be bent because of a short barrel adapter, the Kolar version can't be bent because of a lengthened barrel adapter. Secondly, the Kolar Compensator's gas vents are positioned differently than were the original Cutts' vents. On Colonel Cutts' device, the slots were diametrically opposed at the top and bottom, gases jutting equally up and down. On the Kolar device, however, the vents are angled sideways and upward, while the bottom of the Kolar Compensator's "cage" is left solid. The purpose of this design is to more effectively use escaping powder gases for reducing muzzle jump. Powder gases spurting out of any opening set up the action-reaction situation, and the gases jabbing upward apply their reaction energies against the solid bottom to help minimize recoil bounce. The result is a muzzle that hangs steadily on target for quick, accurate follow-up shots.

The screw-in choke tube systems have opened the way to various novelties, including the eccentric or off-center tubes. Trapshooters who want a high-shooting gun, but don't want their gun's barrel bent or their comb line raised, have begun employing screw-in choke systems that send the patterns variously high. Foremost in this field is Briley Manufacturing of 1085 Gessner "A," Houston, TX 77055.

One trick that has been played to improve patterns is the use of a rough spot or sharp step-taper protrusion to retard the wad. I agree with many theorists and experimenters who believe that the wad is a most destructive force in patterning when it slips too easily through the choke segment of a barrel and bumps or slams

SHOTGUNNING TRENDS IN TRANSITION

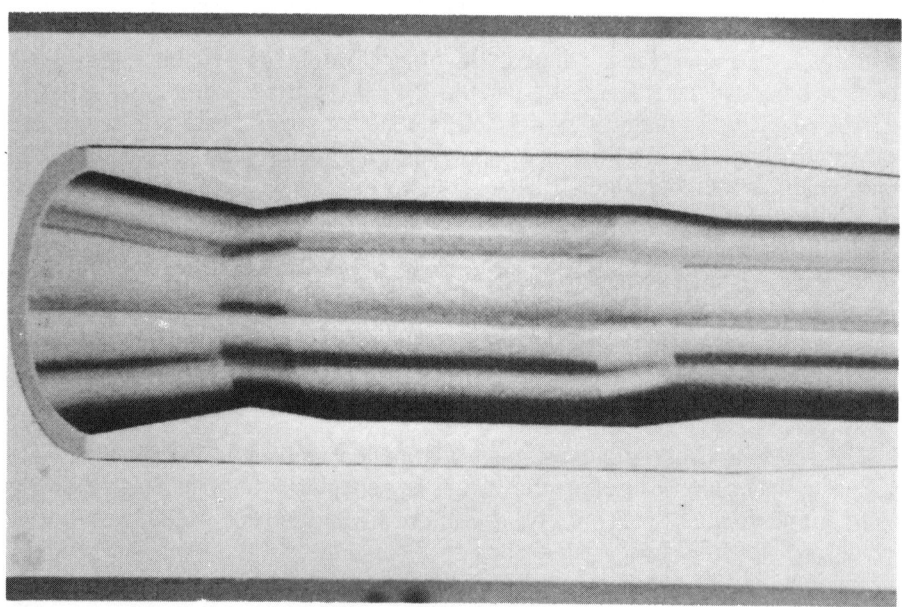

The inside of a Tula choke as devised by the Russians for greater efficiency in Olympic skeet. (Tula is a Russian gunmaking city.) The Tula throws a very evenly distributed shot pattern and, to a degree, helps stretch out the shot string for more pattern depth on this close-range game.

into the emerging shot charge. In earlier days, the card/filler wad stacks blasted right through exiting shot strings and created the "donut" or blown patterns (which typical hunters mistakenly blamed on the overshot disc). Indeed, one reason the old Cutts Compensator (and now the Kolar Compensator) patterns so nicely is that the ventilated cage bleeds off tremendous amounts of gas pressure, thereby slowing the wad so the shot charge can escape ahead of the wad. At one time, an experimenter could get everything from cylinder bore spreads to full-choke tightness from one 12-gauge cylinder tube simply by altering the bore's finish. When the cylinder-bored tube was highly polished and slippery, the wads whistled through and blasted into the shot charge to scatter it wildly, but when the bore was roughened, the wads were slowed by friction and the shot charge got out ahead of the wad to form a dense, full-choke pattern. Indeed, some of today's theorists believe that choke constriction does nothing more than affect patterning by retarding the wad to various degrees, i.e., the tighter the choke constriction, the more the wad is delayed and the tighter the pattern develops. I don't believe wad delay is the sole explanation of choke/pattern performance, but it is a definite factor. Quite possibly, the conical-parallel type of choke obtains some of its efficiency from wad retardation at the point where the taper ceases and the parallel flats continue.

Vibrational Dynamics

After going from chamber to muzzle, we reach the complete shotgun barrel itself. That, in turn, brings us to another factor that influences pattern development — vibrational dynamics. The human eye may not detect it, but shotgun barrels do vibrate on firing.

What causes such vibrations? The impact of powder gases, which is to say the relentless hammering of countless powder gas molecules against the chamber and bore walls. As explained in a previous chapter, chamber pressure is nothing more than the intensity of gas molecules colliding with each other and their surroundings, and when they beat on the inner barrel wall it's comparable to striking a tuning fork. Now, don't look at a shotgun barrel and argue against vibrational dynamics just because the tube is made of apparently stiff steel! Barrels vibrate just as the bull barrels found on target and varmint rifles vibrate, or as the heaviest Naval guns on the largest battleships vibrate. To understand firearms, one must understand that vibrations follow a pattern of nodes and overtones similar to what one would see if he were to grab a length of rope by one end and snap it.

The problem caused by vibrations is that every sporting arm — handgun, rifle or shotgun — has its own individual vibrational pattern due to its individual molecular structure as a steel entity. Stated scientifically, each barrel has its own peculiar frequency (cycles per second) and amplitude (range of movement). This may be a new concept to many casual hunters and shooters, but even though seemingly identical objects are made from the same fluid steel formula and poured simultaneously, their molecular structures can, and do, vary enough so that they have dissimilar vibrational patterns. Indeed, there is nothing absolutely perfect except scientific theory, and it is not wrong to say that each gun barrel is a physical law unto itself.

The way to obtain optimum performance from a gun barrel, be it accuracy from a rifle or a certain pattern from a smoothbore, is to find the load which is compatible with that given barrel's vibrational characteristics. When such a load is found, its gas molecules repeatedly emit the basic frequency of that barrel for uniformity. Riflemen evaluate their gun/load performances by the size of "groups"; when a load is right for a given barrel, the groups shrink and become symmetrical. Most serious riflemen test different loads for that reason.

But the subject of vibrational dynamics is generally new to shotgunners. How do shotgun barrel vibrations upset patterns? That answer was provided by Jack C. Seehase, a retired aeronautical engineer who also happened to be a trapshooter and shotgun fancier. Seehase initiated the study because he found that so many full-choked trap guns patterned poorly, packing their main masses into just the 15 to 20-inch diameter core of a 30-inch circle and leaving the annular ring weak and spotty. Seehase decided that the inferior performances emanated from the influence that erratic barrel vibrations had on deformed pellets, and theorized that if he cleared up that influence he could make deformed shot stay in the main cluster longer, rather than flipping off.

According to Seehase's approach, the flat spots and other deformations on each pellet represent airfoils which function like the seams on a baseball to make them curve away from the center of the shot string. In baseball, the pitcher snaps his wrist to put "English" on the ball, and the spin creates a boundary vortex (high air pressure spot) that moves the ball over into the opposite area of lower air pressure. How is the spin imparted to a shotgun pellet? Seehase figured it was generated by the barrel's vibrations, which he found to be about 7,000 cycles per second on randomly selected shotguns. His figures indicated that such vibrations could produce a half-pellet spin in a 30-inch barrel at the trap load's velocity of 1,200 fps. That computes to one full turn in about five feet at 1,200 fps or 14,000 rotations per minute. Seehase deemed that adequate to make a pellet curve, for he noted that a big-league pitcher's wrist snap rotates a baseball only three times from the mound to home plate when throwing at the velocity of 100 miles per hour for a rotation of just 440 rpm. A slower pitch would spin a bit more, of course, but in any case the big leaguers can certainly break off curves.

There are two methods of going about this process of matching load and barrel vibrations: One way is to test different loads until one is found that jibes with the individual barrel's vibrational characteristics; this is what riflemen do when they test round after round from benchrest. The second method is altering the stresses within the barrel to match the load. Seehase opted for the latter. He hooked various shotgun barrels to a pair of accelerometers and oscilloscopes which checked the vertical and horizontal amplitudes vs. the frequency. He then spent two years experimenting with methods for changing the stresses within the barrel metals, thus altering the vibrations or eliminating them for the best patterning performances with any given load. He calls his work "Dynamically Balanced Barrels," and although he has kept his method secret it is based on using electromagnetic force to shift molecules about in the steel.

How well does the Seehase system function? When I first met Jack, I had a Perazzi MX-8 bored IM&F. With Federal 2¾ drams equivalent Gold Medal trap loads of No. 8 shot, it averaged 73 to 75 percent over 40 yards from the full-choke barrel. If I counted every pellet that hit a 40-inch square sheet, that efficiency rose to only about 78 to 80 percent. Thus, more than a few deformed pellets curved off inside 40 yards.

After Seehase reworked that MX-8, the full-choke tube jumped to an average of 96 to 98 percent performance on the overall 40-inch-square sheet, most of them within a 36-inch-diameter circle! Obviously, Seehase had made some adjustments that brought the former fliers back into closer proximity to the working cluster. Moreover, the 15-inch core experienced a significant increase after Seehase's overhaul, raising the average number of hits from 180 to 205. Likewise, there was an approximate 100 percent increase in the number of pellets striking between the 30 and 34-inch diameter rings for enhanced potential on a loosely placed pattern.

Compared to the results with the original Perazzi barrel, the Seehase revamping definitely proved that fliers can be brought into play by damping their spins when the barrel's vibes are correct for a given load. His work is undoubtedly one of the greatest achievements ever devised by barrelsmiths, and smokeballing targets with one of his high-performance alterations is a barrel of fun!

Chapter 12

The Steel Shot Solution: The "Rule of Two"

SOME OF the world's greatest theoretical scientists lived during those exciting decades when man strove to split the atom and unleash its energy. After their experiments and mathematical bases reached the point where they actually produced chain reactions and could predict success, they theorized that the element plutonium would be a better energy source than uranium 238 for atomic bombs. There was only one hitch: The Earth doesn't contain plutonium per se. They had to make their own, through neutron bombardment of uranium ores. In the process, the great minds that guided the "Manhattan Project" to the nuclear weapons which ended World War II theorized that at one time plutonium was on Earth but it decayed and formed lead! Thus, like the other heavy metals, the lead shot we use in scatterguns may once have been a radioactive, metallic chemical element.

Although lead may have lost its radioactivity, it still is considered to be a long-lasting toxic material with no beneficial biological purpose. It has been legislated out of gasoline, paint, many plumbing uses — and now American waterfowl hunting! The reason for outlawing lead shot in duck and goose hunting, of course, is to reduce and eliminate the potential for waterfowl losses due to lead poisoning. Lead shot picked up by feeding waterfowl does not automatically move through a bird's digestive and excretory systems; therefore, it was estimated that millions of ducks and geese died unnecessarily each year.

According to current laws, lead shot will be outlawed in all waterfowling in the contiguous 48 states by 1991. Steel shot will replace it.

The transition from lead to steel shot has not been smooth. Tempers have flared. Arrests have been made and will continue to be made as hunters sneak in lead-shot ammo. Some hunters have quit the sport because they fear damaging their guns. Others have complained that steel shot slows down so quickly that it doesn't have the energy to kill ducks cleanly; hence, more birds are being lost by crippling hits than by lead poisoning. And so the dilemma continues, ad infinitum, ad nauseam ... aw, nuts!

The idea that we should return to lead shot for waterfowl hunting because ducks and geese are being crippled goes nowhere. It won't fly. The reason is twofold: First, the question is not which metal, steel or lead, will cripple fewer birds, but "Can we save waterfowl hunting from the anti-hunters, bird and animal protectionists and knee-jerk environmentalists?" These groups will refuse to backtrack and accept the return of lead shot because of the crippling issue. Instead, they will advocate an end to all waterfowling. (Wouldn't that be dandy?)

The second reason is one that hunters won't like, but it has become apparent that properly selected steel shot isn't the crippler many armchair experts claim it is. If money were to be bet, I'd place mine on a good wingshot with steel rather than a mediocre shot with the magnumest loads of lead ever devised. Honest hunters will admit that crippling existed in the days of lead shot, too, only they didn't complain because they didn't have a scapegoat. Now that we have steel shot, they blame every miss on the load instead of their poor techniques. These same people never shoot skeet or trap because they can't hit enough targets to buoy their egos. It is wrong to take the opinions of bum shots when assessing steel shot.

Steel Shot Characteristics

The new shotgunner must realize that steel shot has different characteristics than lead shot in the way it moves through the bore, the way it flies through the air and the way it impacts on game. Steel and lead pellets of a specific size do not equate in their flow characteristics, their exterior ballistics, or their penetrations. It is an entirely new world, but one that isn't difficult to comprehend once a hunter takes an open-minded, intelligent approach to it.

While a casual shotgunner may think that steel shot is a recent innovation, there are some references to it scattered about in literature from the first half of this century. Bob Nichols mentioned it in *The Shotgunner* when discussing an ultra-hard pellet which wouldn't deform. However, the 1940s were devoid of plastic wads, thus steel shot fired with just card/filler wad stacks were exposed to the bore walls and were bound to damage those bores and pattern poorly. The potential for damage with metal-against-metal at 1,200 fps speaks for itself. Patterns were undoubtedly poor because the pellets rolled and took on a spin as they progressed through the bore and up the choke taper, their "English" carrying them away from the bore's axis. Thus, Nichols' remarks about steel shot (which were based on tests conducted by Wallace H. Coxe of DuPont) were negative.

Time changes all things, however, and modern technology has, in turn, negated virtually everything Nichols said about steel in *The Shotgunner*. The development of tough, high-density plastic shotcups has made it safe to fire steel pellets through

THE STEEL SHOT SOLUTION: THE "RULE OF TWO"

shotguns without fearing automatic ruination of the bore, and the same wads have mitigated against pellet spin to produce extreme patterning efficiency.

Steel pellets have different characteristics than lead shot both in and out of the gun. Whereas even the hard, high-antimony lead shot and copper-plated pellets will compress to flow through the narrow places of a shotgun barrel (the forcing cone and the choke), steel shot will not (cannot) swage down under normal shotshell pressures. The result is that lead shot will flow more fluidly under gas pressures, while steel shot will bind and wedge and turn into a veritable steel slug under stiff setback forces. This is why steel shot *cannot* be reloaded like lead shot with thin shotcups and fast-rate powders. Steel shot requires extremely tough shotcups and ultra-slow-rate powders which get the payload moving very slowly to avoid binding in the chamber/cone bore segments. Even as this is written, the loading industry isn't satisfied with its steel shot powders and is trying to find something better. Thus, powder and wad selection, along with shot charge weight, are more critical with steel shot than with lead pellets.

Once out of the barrel, steel shot exhibits different downrange ballistics than lead shot. What most detractors harp upon is that steel shot, being lighter than lead shot of any given diameter, loses its velocity quicker in the face of air resistance (drag). This cannot be debated; it's scientific fact. On a nominal basis, a steel No. 4 pellet will weigh about 2.14 grains as opposed to roughly 3.42 grains for a No. 4 lead chilled shot. On a theoretical plane, the heavier pellet will overcome air resistance better to retain its velocity/energy values longer. (Of course, that theory can be upset easily by lead shot deformation, which reduces the aerodynamic quality of the lead pellet and actually can cause it to *trail* the steel sphere in downrange effectiveness. That's a fact of shotgunning science that shouldn't be ignored. In many respects, lead shot is overrated; by deforming, it falls well below anticipated performance levels. For the sake of this discussion, however, we will *assume* the lead pellets used for comparison retain their best aerodynamic form, if for no other reason than that the empirical nature of pellet deformation makes energy/velocity calculations impossible.)

But simply being lighter doesn't damn steel shot, for unlike deformation-prone lead shot, steel retains its best aerodynamic form; hence, it also retains optimum exterior ballistics for its weight. Although the steel pellets' lighter weight does eventually come into play, the questions hunters should ask before jumping to any unwarranted conclusions are: How much velocity is lost, and at what point downrange does that loss become important? Unfortunately, not many new shotgunners have asked those questions. I've heard more than a few hunters complain that steel shot practically faltered and fell like a wad of tissue paper just a few yards from the muzzle, which is a helluva mistaken assumption.

There are two points that must be made regarding the application and selection of steel shot sizes. First, they do not dribble out the muzzle; therefore they all have effective operating distances which hunters need to learn. Those distances will differ from lead pellets of the same size. Secondly, the downrange effectiveness of steel shot loads can be enhanced tremendously by careful pellet selection based on the "Rule of Two," which will be discussed shortly. As a basis for that discussion, take a hard look at this comparative data:

pellet	3-foot velocity (fps)	retained energy (foot-pounds)		
		20 yards	40 yards	60 yards
Steel No. 4	1,365	4.9	2.5	1.4
Lead No. 6	1,330	4.04	2.5	1.7
Lead No. 4	1,330	7.34	4.77	3.35

The velocities listed above are nominal for the fastest commercial 12-gauge loads with their respective types of pellet metals. Note that steel 4s aren't even close to the energy of lead 4s at any distance. The hunter who ignorantly declares that, "I always used lead 4s for ducks, and I'm not going to change sizes with steel!" is in fact being technically foolish. The lighter steel 4s simply don't generate the same momentum as heftier lead 4s.

A careful comparison of the above data indicates that steel 4s function more like lead 6s in the face of air resistance. Thus, we come to the Rule of Two, which essentially argues that a hunter must select steel shot *at least* two sizes larger than his normal lead shot to obtain approximately the same downrange ballistics. In other words, if someone normally hunted over decoys with lead 6s, he would be well-advised to pick steel 4s for the same chore. And if he normally chambered lead 4s for ducks, he would be wise to buy steel 1s or 2s. Here is how both those sizes of steel compare with lead 4s:

pellet	3-foot velocity (fps)	retained energy (foot-pounds)		
		20 yards	40 yards	60 yards
Lead No. 4	1,330	7.34	4.77	3.35
Steel No. 2	1,365	8.1	4.4	2.6
Steel No. 1	1,365	10.2	5.7	3.4

Note how steel No. 1s actually surpass the energy level of lead 4s at 40 yards and have practically as much energy left at 60 yards. Jumping by two to three shot sizes when going from lead to steel provides as much, or more, energy. The biggest mistake new shotgunners can make is measuring steel shot by lead shot experiences. Never do the two meet on a tit-for-tat basis. Heavier steel shot is needed to overcome air resistance.

Many states that limited waterfowling pellet sizes to BBs or smaller in lead-shot days have recently relaxed their laws to permit the use of steel BBBs, Ts

THE STEEL SHOT SOLUTION: THE "RULE OF TWO"

and Fs. The normal BB has a diameter of .18-inch, while BBBs are .19-inch, Ts are .20-inch and Fs run .22-inch. Although not officially termed buckshots, these larger steel pellets do indeed carry the mail! Steel T-shot leaving the muzzle at 1,350 fps hit with an energy just short of that of a screaming lead BB at 60 yards. Moreover, my own field observations indicate that BBBs and Ts cut cleaner than lead shot such as No. 2s and BBs, and, consequently, the steel numbers penetrate deeper, often considerably deeper. I've had steel BBBs and Ts give total penetration on geese at 45 to 50 yards, whereas nothing remotely close has ever happened with lead 2s or BBs. Why the difference in penetration? Steel pellets cut sharply; they don't wad up with fuzzy down as they impact. Anyone who has ever cleaned birds will remember lead pellets (even the tiny 7½s and 8s) carried long strings of feather and fuzz into the wound channel, something which steel shot seldom does. Not being mushy, steel shot cuts through cleanly in most instances.

In the past several seasons, I have begun to notice more lethal body hits with steel BBs, BBBs and Ts on geese than I saw when lead No. 2s and BBs were in vogue. My own impression always has been that lead pellets were deflection-prone on rounded waterfowl bodies when the down and feathers were laid back like a tough shield by a slipstream, and the mushy quality of lead shot shed energy more readily on impact. If I could now switch back to lead shot for geese, I might not do so because steel BBs and BBBs have handled things so well for me out to a full 55 to 60 yards (as checked by range finders).

Steel Shot Size Selection

Few hunters want to be bothered by physics. They like to keep things simple. For them I'll point out the strengths and weaknesses of various gun/load combinations with steel shot.

When steel shot first appeared on the market, there were only sizes 1, 2 and 4. Numbers 2 and 4 were considered duck loads, while No. 1s were often designated as goose loads. Thankfully, additional sizes have come along. When lead shot were the only pellets in use we had practically forgotten about such pellets as Fs, Ts, BBBs, No. 1s and No. 3s, but they're all available in steel. Winchester also returned the No. 5 birdshot to active duty in its line of 1988 steel shot offerings.

Hunters may scratch their brows and wonder why No. 3 steel shot has been loaded, but there is a method behind the madness. From the very beginning, many hunters, including this author, were critical about the effectiveness of steel 4s on waterfowl. As the above data indicated, steel 4s had but the punch of lead 6s, and few modern waterfowl hunters would pick lead 6s for their mallard and pintail gunning. Steel No. 3s were developed to provide somewhat greater per pellet energy while still delivering adequate pattern density for ducks over decoys. The added energy of steel No. 3s, which closely resembles the potency of lead No. 5s, seems to be quite noticeable as compared to steel No. 4s between 25 to 40 yards. Steel No. 3s are probably at their best for hunting over decoys with a modified or improved cylinder choke, in which case a 1¼-ounce shot charge is recommended for pattern sweetening. Just don't stretch either the pellet or the pattern beyond sensible decoy ranges.

Steel 5s, 6s and 7s are not recommended waterfowl sizes regardless of what advertisements say. They will take some ducks at close range, of course, but so will skeet loads of No. 9 lead shot, and nobody in his right mind advocates 9s as a bona fide duck load. By following the Rule of Two, we find that steel 5s perform about like lead 7s or 7½s and that steel 6s operate like lead 8s. These are mainly shot sizes for upland game where steel shot is mandated for all hunting, not just waterfowl.

Steel No. 6s will probably be a good dove and sora rail loading, while steel 5s will be adequate for the second shot on ringnecks and ruffed grouse. If upland ranges lengthen for sharptails and ringnecks, however, I'd opt for steel 4s or 3s. I have taken some pheasants with steel 4s and 2s, and it is interesting to note here how surgically clean the pellets cut on these lightly feathered birds, too, not pulling wads of feathers into the wound channels.

Although steel 4s and lead 6s are virtually exterior ballistics twins out to 40 yards, my experiences have shown deeper penetration by steel 4s than 6s. For ruffed grouse, steel 6s will hit like lead 7½s for the first 20 yards of flight, tapering off thereafter to reach the ballistics of lead 8s. As mentioned, steel 5s will be the choice for follow-up shots at fantails.

If the clay target games are forced into steel shot usage, No. 7s will probably be our skeet pellet. Trapshooting will pivot on steel 6s. I've used steel 6s both on skeet and trap and scored every target I deserved. The only current problem is that steel 6s still are being loaded to hunting velocities beyond 1,300 fps, and they generate too much recoil for prolonged clay target shooting. A 1⅛-ounce charge of steel 6s counts to 349 to 350 pellets as compared to 388 No. 7½ lead shot, but since steel patterns so efficiently they often duplicate the densities of lead 7½s at 40 yards.

Steel 2s are about the smallest steel pellet that one can recommend for pass-shooting waterfowl. They are best inside 45 yards. Personal experience has me leaning toward steel No. 1s as the optimum all-around duck pellet regardless of whether the duck is a teal, woodie or late-season greenhead. Steel 1s simply get the job done cleaner on ducks than any other steel pellet I've used. At this point, steel 1s are not being loaded into 20-gauge three-inch hulls, apparently because they take up too much space. Ditto for the 16 gauge steel loads. One can only hope that this is changed shortly, as steel No. 2s, which are the heaviest pellets loading into the 16 and 20 gauges, are only marginal on geese. Indeed, while 10 and 12 gauges have advanced nicely with steel shot innovations, the 16 and 20 have barely crept along.

THE STEEL SHOT SOLUTION: THE "RULE OF TWO"

For jump shooting, which often involves outgoing birds, the author prefers heavy loads of No. 1 or BB steel shot for optimum penetration.

In jump shooting, ducks almost always give the hunter an outgoing shot, and tremendous penetrating power is needed to anchor such birds for positive retrieves. Steel 1s are the smallest pellet one can rely on for driving to the vitals through rump fuzz, viscera, bone and muscle. For optimum penetration on straightaways and other lesser climbing angles, I have come to appreciate the energy of steel BBs. That may seem like a coarse concept on paper, but a solid full-choke pattern of steel BBs certainly helps hold birds where they fall. If in doubt about shot size for jump shooting, always remember the need for deep penetration and go with steel 1s or BBs. My experience with them is that there is no such thing as overkill; there are only clean kills or cripples. And 1s and BBs fold them and hold them better than steel 2s, 3s and 4s.

Geese are the big game of wingshooting, and it takes tremendous energy to drop them cleanly. Steel 1s can do the job reasonably well out to 45 yards, sometimes 50 yards, but they can also cripple when used indiscriminately at longer distances (which isn't unusual for those hunters who have no concept of range).

As seasons passed, independent experimenters learned that larger steel pellets carried energy much better than bar stool theorists ever dreamed. Steel BBs, BBBs, Ts and Fs became popular. When I first began reloading with steel BBBs delivering roughly 1,350 fps, I had 10 straight one-shot kills between 40 to 60 yards, all verified by a range finder. However, experience with steel BBs starting at 1,350 fps, or slightly above, indicates that they can be positive goose loads out to 55 yards, too.

American hunters are afflicted by the "more is better" syndrome, and they impetuously grab for the largest shot sizes legal, meaning steel Ts and Fs. Although both Ts and Fs carry energy to long waterfowling ranges, they also tend toward weak patterns. There are so few Fs per load that observers find steel Fs cause considerable crippling due to insufficient pattern density; one-pellet hits are not conducive to clean kills, and patterns of Fs beyond 40 to 45 yards seem to be dicey. Add the weakening effects of shot stringing and shooter error in exact pattern placement, and the result is a questionable load. Although my home state outlaws steel Fs, I have also noted a tendency of steel Ts to cripple when patterns aren't optimally tight. If Ts and Fs are selected for geese, then the hunter owes it to himself, the game and sportsmanship in general to make certain he's getting patterns of at least 85 to 90 percent at 40 yards, tighter if possible. Rely on definitely tight clusters rather than the "golden BB."

For goose hunting, then, more pellet weight beyond BBBs is not automatically better unless it is accompanied by maximum pattern density. There are only about 76 triple-Bs, 66 T-shot or 48 F-shot in a 1¼-ounce steel load, and if pattern percentages are low with such minimal pellet counts, there will be lots of room between pellets downrange for vital-area slippage. As a personal choice, I've come to select steel BBs and triple-Bs for geese. There are approximately 87 steel BBs per 1¼ ounces as compared to just 63 lead BBs in the same charge weight, and said steel

BBs provide the potential for greater pattern density with still-adequate energy out to at least 55 yards. Fired at 1,300 fps a steel BB travels 60 yards with 5.2 to 5.3 foot-pounds of energy, and authorities have long deemed a 3.0 foot-pound blow adequate for penetration on geese with lead shot. Certain adjustments must be made in the theoretical energy requirement when switching to steel, of course, but don't be surprised if, after more data has been scientifically collected, we find that steel shot actually is penetrating deeper per foot-pound of ballistics energy and foot-second of velocity than lead shot! The reason will no doubt be the above-mentioned matter of steel's cutting ability. If future powders someday advance steel shot loads to velocities beyond 1,400 fps, we will probably learn that lead shot must be driven 200 fps faster to achieve the same penetration as steel shot of the same basic pellet weight. Thus, the new shotgunner with an open, observant mind will begin to see a definite advantage in steel shot goose loads over lead ones.

The kills I have made with Remington and Federal 1¼-ounce loads of steel BBs out to 50 to 55 yards have not lacked for impact, penetration, or bone-breaking ability. Steel BBBs have extended that by five to 10 yards. Few typical hunters have the skill to hit beyond 45 to 50 yards with any regularity, and therefore they don't need anything heavier than BBBs if they apply common sense and improved range judgment. *Woofing* three quick rounds of Ts or Fs hopefully skyward is total nonsense, just as it was with No. 4 lead buckshot.

Choke Selection for Steel Shot Sizes

When steel shot first became available to the public, "armchair experts," who had never fired so much as one pattern, suddenly began making all sorts of dogmatic claims about the patterning characteristics of the new loads. A popular generalization was that steel shot patterned like the proverbial rifle through open-choked guns, such as improved cylinder and modified, and that full choke was taboo. Hunters in my area opened their Poly-Chokes to improved cylinder when they used steel shot, and more than a few reported light hits and lost cripples on the goose line. They blamed that on the supposed weak-hitting quality of steel pellets, of course, never once questioning the choke-selection concept that was rampant.

The fact is that steel shot isn't hopeless in a full-choked gun; in many instances, steel shot will pattern murderously tight from FCs. It also is true that, contrary to the public's pronouncements, improved cylinder and modified aren't automatically the most efficient degrees of choke for steel shot. Much depends upon the actual shot sizes. Ditto for individual gun/load combinations. The old rule that each gun is a physical law unto itself remains in effect with steel shot. You really never know what you're getting until you've patterned!

As I've just mentioned, the size of steel shot has much to do with its patterning from the various chokes. As a rule of thumb, the smaller steel shot sizes — from Nos. 1 through 6 — will pattern very nicely through full-choked barrels. There are some gun/load pairings in which No. 1s *may* balk, but normally No. 1s and full choke are still compatible. I have had steel 1s, 2s and 4s deliver 85 to 93 percent, *on average*, from various full-choked guns, which is far better than any over-the-counter lead-shot loads have ever done for me (except for a few buffered lead buckshot rounds which came close to 100 percent averages). Why do these smaller steel shot sizes still pattern so well from tightly choked guns? Because they have "flow" characteristics which permit them to respond with adequate fluidity to maximum constrictions. Thus, a hunter need not jump to the conclusion that his pet full choke won't work with steel shot. Chances are it will perform quite well with the smaller pellets.

What about the more open chokes with steel 1s, 2s, 3s, 4s, 5s and 6s? My own patterning and field work indicate that skeet chokes, improved cylinders and modified chokes don't print them according to the public's belief. In other words, such open chokes *definitely do not* tighten up when fed steel shot! I have never yet had a skeet gun or improved cylinder choke, whether a screw-in tube or fixed choke, throw a bona fide full-choke pattern with steel loads of fine shot. In my experience, skeet and improved cylinder normally continue to throw their designated percentages, or very close to them, with steel pellets from 1s through 7s. One of the worst mornings I've had with steel shot came when I tried an improved cylinder choke with steel 2s and 4s on woodies in the timber; I lost two cripples, both obviously lightly struck by the open patterns. With the finer steel shot sizes, then, don't conclude that full chokes are out and open bores are in. Actual patterning doesn't prove the public's beliefs.

The growing reliance on modified choke for steel shot isn't all wrong, but it isn't necessary, either, where the smaller shot sizes are concerned. There is virtually nothing that modified choke can do that full choke can't with the lesser steel pellets. In fact, many modified chokes that I've tested with steel shot continue to average exactly what modified should average, namely, between 55 and 65 percent. With certain loads, especially with steel 1s and 2s, modified chokes *can* upon occasion tighten up to a full-choke performance, but that's *not* automatic as some folks believe. Thus, if the public wants a more scientific rule of thumb for selecting chokes for steel shot, it is that patterns can be pretty much the same as with lead shot from the respective open chokes when steel shot smaller than BBs are fired. This is not to say that somewhere out there there isn't a modified that will throw 85 percent with steel 4s (I'll bet there is), but such performance isn't typical. When you shoot steel 1s, 2s, 3s, or smaller through an improved cylinder gun, you are probably going to get improved cylinder patterns.

Changes occur, however, when the bulkier steel pellets — BBs, BBBs, Ts and Fs — come alive. These coarse pellets do not have the same flow characteristics of the lesser spheres; they do not shift about within their masses to squeeze down when ramming through a tight full-choke constriction. Hence, this wedging and jamming with bulky steel pellets from BBs upward produce two problems: It can upset patterning, and it can cause ring bulging in tightly choked guns as it hammers into the choke constriction like a steel slug.

THE STEEL SHOT SOLUTION: THE "RULE OF TWO"

It is with these huskier steel pellets that the theory of using less choke constriction enters in, not with the smaller numbers that can flow more fluidly through a full choke. The boys were basically wrong when they recommended open chokes with the first steel 1s, 2s and 4s, but they aren't wrong when it comes to steel BBs and bigger balls. By reducing choke constriction, a hunter makes it easier for the larger steel pellets to exit without damaging the choke. Because steel pellets don't deform, these larger sizes which retain their spherical shapes fly true to the bore axis for tight clusters. Patterns I have run with commercial steel shot loads of BBs, BBBs, Ts and Fs have given some full-choke percentages from improved cylinder and modified chokes. These seldom top 75 percent, but they are honest full-choke averages, of course.

This is *not* to say that improved cylinder and modified choke naturally, invariably, or automatically give full-choke performances with the bulkier steel pellets beginning with BBs. Improved cylinder can be erratic. Remington's screw-in "Rem" Choke improved cylinder unit has been the most reliable in my shooting against paper with the larger steel shots, normally always doing a strong modified or a weak full choke, but some of the Winchester and Browning IC tubes have been mediocre, not reaching full-choke percentages. When testing Mossberg's new ACCU-STEEL extended-length choke tubes marked modified, I got more patterns in the improved cylinder or weak modified range than I did in the tight modified or full-choke category. Thus, although *some* improved cylinder and modified chokes will deliver full-choke patterns with the coarse steel BBs, BBBs, Ts and Fs, nothing is carved in stone. Don't jump to any conclusions. The possibility exists that certain steel shot loads of BBs, BBBs, Ts and Fs will deliver dense patterns from IC or M chokes, but *only* a possibility. The point is that potential for such tight patterns from the more open chokes is greater with coarse steel pellets than with finer ones.

Why does the industry boom open chokes for steel shot if there's nothing certain about such chokes throwing tight patterns? The industry is trying to avoid gun damage! It is not claiming that IC and M invariably give the best patterns, for heavy loads of coarse steel shot can hammer the choke constriction of a full-choked gun and cause ring bulging or other sorts of metal displacement much sooner than they normally distort the more open degrees of choke. That's just good business, keeping disgruntled customers off their backs by minimizing barrel/choke damage. Just don't take the association of loose chokes and coarse steel to mean that they produce the best patterns overall. Coarse steel pellets will pattern well through many full chokes. The highest pattern percentages I've yet had with Winchester's three-inch 12-gauge loads of copper-plated T-shot have come from the full-choke "Rem" Choke tube of a Model 11-87. That was followed closely by equally dense full-choke clusters from a Remington Model 1100 three-inch Magnum full-choke factory barrel. On the other hand, I have just finished patterning the IC&M choke combo in the new steel shot compatible Parker Reproduction DHE, and its lightly choked barrels mustered nothing better than mediocre modified percentages with any kind of steel shot, No. 4s through Ts. I rest my case: The looser chokes are recommended for the larger steel pellets, BBs through Fs, mainly to ward off bore/choke damage, not because they pattern magically with said bulky balls.

Is there an all-around choke constriction for steel shot and waterfowling? If one follows the old dictum that all barrels are individuals, there probably isn't a perfect all-arounder. But hunters interested in regulating a barrel for steel shot are advised to investigate a little-known degree of choke called improved modified. This fits between modified and full, and with lead shot it is supposed to average from 60 to 65 percent at 40 yards. To date IM has been mainly a trapshooting choke, and many target-grade O/Us have IM in the lower tube. Manufacturers vary their dimensions for improved modified, but for most practical purposes it falls between a .025 and .030-inch constriction in a 12-gauge gun.

There is no guarantee that improved modified will send rifle-tight shot strings while eliminating the potential for bore/choke damage, of course, but IM does split the difference between modified and full on a dimensional basis. Hunters who want to experiment with chokes will find improved modified a good first play.

A Reprieve for the 10 Gauge

How does one achieve long-range patterns filled with bulky steel BBs, BBBs, Ts and Fs? This is difficult, of course, since normal shotshells have space limitations. The industry has carried steel loads into the 10-gauge Magnum, however, and this appears to be the best bet for energy-laden patterns. To date, the heaviest 10-gauge steel-shot loads go 1¾ ounces, which isn't close to approaching the old 2¼-ouncers once available with lead shot, but still is well ahead of the normal 1⅛ and 1¼-ounce 12-gauge rounds.

The new 10-gauge Magnum steel-shot loads of 1⅝ to 1¾ ounces have introduced two interesting aspects into the steel shot arena: First, the long 3½-inch hull means an equally long shot charge, and that could translate into added shot string depth. Secondly, since the lighter steel-shot loads aren't as heavy as the former lead-shot rounds, there will be less recoil in the 10-gauge Magnum. Less recoil, in turn, may result in development of lighter 10-gauge guns for easier handling and faster swinging. The Browning BPS 10-gauge Magnum pumpgun isn't exactly a lightweight at its published 9½-pound weight, but that certainly is less than the 11-pound "iron monsters" I used to carry around in the form of European-made side-by-side 10s!

In recent years, a 3½-inch 12-gauge extra-length Magnum has been jointly developed by Federal Cartridge Corporation, Browning Arms and Mossberg. Its purpose is to increase the shot-charge weight of the 12 so that hunters have an easier-handling gun than the big 10s. However, the 3¼-inch 12-gauge load will of necessity have lower velocities than the more efficient 10 bore. Thus, a 10-gauge Magnum will still outperform the extra-length 12-gauge product ballistically, and the big 10 may well be another solution to handling the longest ranges sensibly attempted with steel shot.

Hitting with Steel Shot

On opening day of one duck season, I happened to hunt flooded timber alongside a man who was using his first pocketful of steel shot loads. There were a lot of woodies in the timber, and the shooting was fast for the first hour, during which time he burned up his whole pocketful of steel loads without cutting a feather. "Damn steel," he cursed, "it sure can't hit anything; must be bouncing off those birds." He then looked around suspiciously and reached into his waders where he had hidden a batch of his old favorite lead loads. "To hell with the law," he said. "I'm going to hit some ducks." Thereupon he sniggered some No. 4 lead-shot magnums into his Model 12.

A half hour later, his lead loads were gone, too, and he still hadn't folded a bird even though he'd had some excellent chances directly overhead.

All this points out that hunters don't only miss with steel loads. Indeed, hunters not only miss a lot with steel today — they also missed copiously with lead yesterday. For if the truth were out, we would know that most hunters are poor wingshots. They miss with everything. The change to steel has merely given them a convenient scapegoat. Like the hunter I met that opening day, they can't hit a very high percentage even with the lead-shot loads they sneak into the swamps and marshes! Thus, don't be misled into believing bad things about the scoring qualities of steel shot loads from the complaints of weekend hunters.

In the beginning, it was widely theorized that steel shot loads required different forward allowances than lead loads. The rule of thumb was that 1) steel shot needed less forward allowance than lead shot inside about 25 yards because steel shot started faster and, inside that short range, held its speed quite well due to retained aerodynamic form; that 2) between roughly 25 and 40 to 45 yards, steel shot required approximately the same forward allowance as lead shot, but that 3) beyond 40 to 45 yards steel needed increasingly longer leads since it slowed so abruptly.

That reasoning, of course, was done relative to identical shot sizes in both metals, namely, matching steel 4s with lead 4s, steel 2s with lead 2s, etc. For this reason, hunters have tried all sorts of funny aiming and leading tactics to compensate for the supposed changes in exterior ballistics and forward allowances. Many speak of "aiming just a little more ahead" at long range or "holding on the bill" at short range. Unfortunately, the only thing that this sort of talk has done is cause shotgunners to be too conscious of leads. Never truly good, smooth swingers anyway, hunters have taken giant strides backward in an attempt to hit with steel by trying for greater precision. Slow gun work and glances back at the gun for careful alignment have ruined overall technique.

SHOTGUNNING TRENDS IN TRANSITION

Those who fancy side-by-sides can again take their favorite form of the smoothbore waterfowling. This Parker Reproduction 12-gauge Magnum is made for steel shot using chromed bores and brazed barrels.

THE STEEL SHOT SOLUTION: THE "RULE OF TWO"

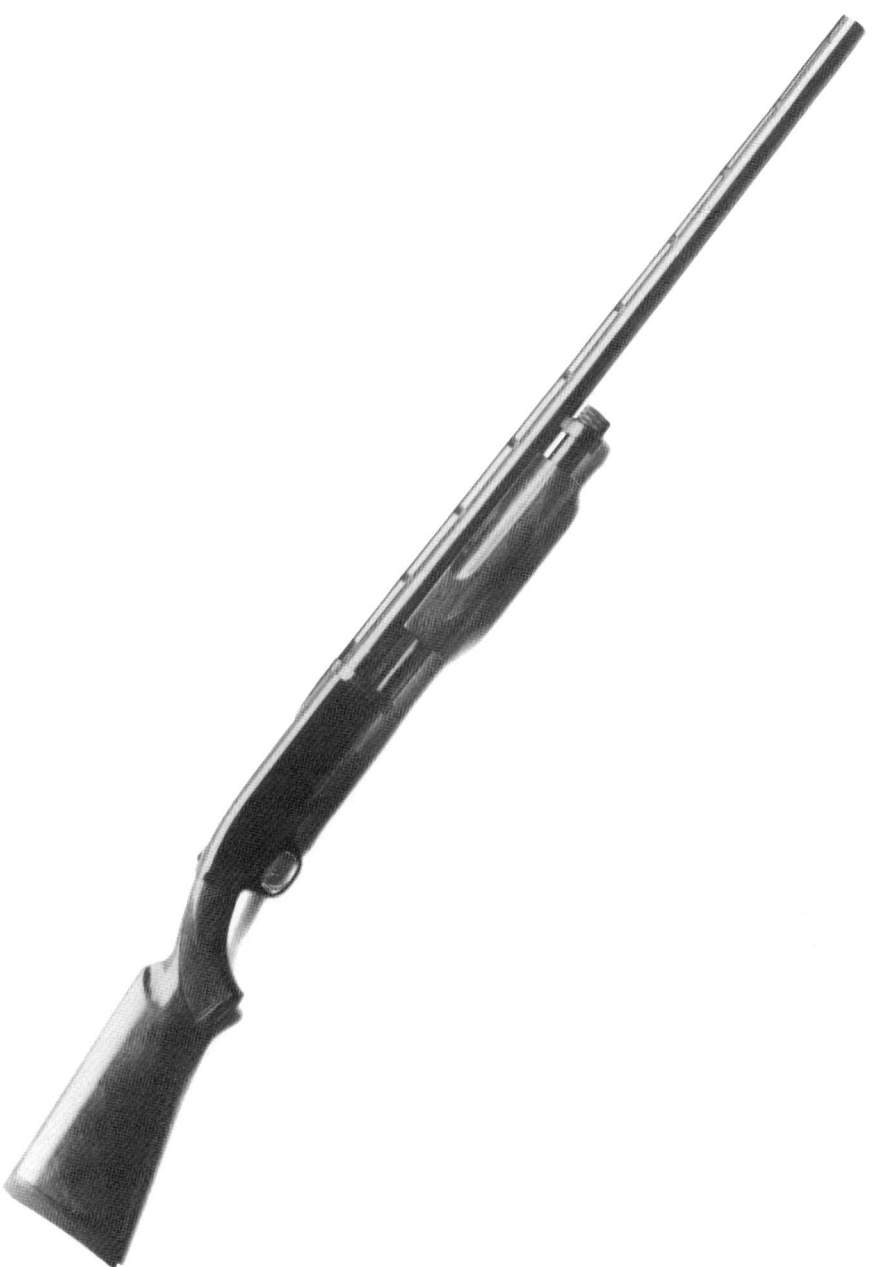

Because steel-shot loads are lighter than lead-shot loads, the 10-gauge Magnum can be made equally lighter for easier handling and carrying. The Browning BPS 10-gauge pump-gun is the first example of what may become a longer line of more manageable 10 gauges.

SHOTGUNNING TRENDS IN TRANSITION

The key to hitting with steel shot is the same as it always has been with lead shot: Apply all the fundamentals smoothly — eye on the target, not the gun — and crisply use an aggressive stroke. Trying to measure off minor differences in forward allowances is a major mistake. The difference between steel and lead shot *is* minor when one intelligently employs the Rule of Two. Although lead 4s may outrace steel 4s beyond 40 yards, the Rule of Two says that steel 2s are the equivalent of lead 4s; and when steel 2s are matched against lead 4s, the downrange disparity in leads tends to evaporate. So, too, do the forward allowance differentials fade when other steel sizes are two numbers larger than the lead pellets in question. Following are some downrange data churned up by the Remington computer for the below-listed Remington steel shot loads vis-a-vis Remington lead shot loads:

Comparative Forward Allowances
(assuming lead pellets remain round)

load	3-foot velocity (fps)	lead in feet at 30 yards	40 yards	50 yards
Remington 12 gauge, 3 inches, *steel* shot: 1¼ ounces No. 2.	1,375	4.8	7.0	9.5
Remington 12 gauge, 2¾ inches, *lead* shot: 1¼ ounces No. 4.	1,330	4.9	7.0	9.4
Remington 12 gauge, 2¾ inches, *steel* shot: 1⅛ ounces BB.	1,365	4.7	6.7	9.0
Remington 12 gauge, 2¾ inches, *lead* shot: 1¼ ounces No. 2.	1,330	4.6	6.5	8.6
Remington 20 gauge, 3 inches, *steel* shot: 1 ounce No. 2.	1,330	4.9	7.2	9.7
Remington 20 gauge, 3 inches, *lead* shot: 1¼ ounces No. 4.	1,330	5.3	7.6	9.9

Note in each comparison how the forward allowances are very minor when the Rule of Two is employed, and that the mathematical differences are absorbed easily by a 30-inch pattern's width and height. Steel BBs approximate the necessary leads for lead 2s, while steel 2s approximate the leads for lead 4s.

Thus, the solution to hitting with steel shot loads is to employ the Rule of Two and then forget that there's any difference between steel and lead. Swing as you always have, and if you miss, blame yourself for having faulty technique, not the loads for having different ballistics!

PART 3
THE GAMES

Chapter 13

Sporting Clays: Is It Really a Hunter's Game?

IT WAS IN the 1920s when two clay target games took form: one was American skeet shooting; the other was British Sporting Clays. Although both were developed to simulate the flights of game birds, there were major differences between them. Skeet was started as an informal practice routine, providing right and left angles on incomers, crossing shots and outgoers over a fixed distance of 20 to 25 yards. The originators of skeet, including the Davies family and William H. Foster, who also wrote the classic *New England Grouse Shooting*, had absolutely no intention of creating a competitive sport; they were solely interested in practicing shots they had missed afield. Amazingly, skeet's popularity grew and it became a tournament sport which, because of its short range and known target flights, made high scores inevitable. This has become especially true since skeet rules were relaxed to permit a pre-mounted gun and an instant target release. Skeet, as fired under tournament rules, has lost most of its value to the hunter.

When the British staged their first Sporting Clays events in the late 1920s, however, they took a different tack. They didn't equate their game with informal practice; it was planned as a tough, competitive sport for about that time British laws mandated an end to live pigeon shooting, and the British competitors were seeking a new tournament format. Thus, they devised setups for realistic hunting ranges and flight angles, and they threw extremely fast targets to track the courses flown by game birds. Whenever possible, they utilized the kind of cover and setting in which a given species would be hunted, resulting in shooting stations that could be spread about the countryside. History relates that the inaugural Sporting Clays match of the late 1920s covered 30 targets with 10 shots being fired at each of three stands. One stand threw targets that represented a duck crossing at a right angle and well out; another copied the low flight of a driven red grouse or grey partridge; and a third duplicated the towering, incoming high pheasants so famous in British wing-gunning. From these meager beginnings, Sporting Clays has progressed to become *the* national scattergun sport in the United Kingdom with,

SHOTGUNNING TRENDS IN TRANSITION

at this writing, a reported estimate of roughly 150,000 participants, 500 Sporting Clays layouts, and more than 20,000 shooters who regularly participate in registered tournaments. If one considers the size of the British Isles, he'll find it hard to believe the tally of layouts in such a smallish land. But the data are verifiable and they attest to the lure of Sporting Clays.

Now Sporting Clays has come to America. Its progress was slow at first. One of the initial attempts was held at the Remington Farms near Chestertown, Maryland, in November 1981 when Remington made an effort to get the game moving under the name of Hunter's Clays rather than Sporting Clays. An informal competition was held between members of the Remington staff and visiting gun writers. The same year, Remington published a booklet covering the aspects of the game which was distributed free. Progress was slow, and a fledgling organization known as the United States Sporting Clays Association (USSCA) was founded.

In the last few years, however, the game has grown steadily and, in some respects, explosively. The first USSCA national championships were held in 1988 with an attendance of 150 shooters, but just one year later the nationals attracted 471 shooters and outgrew the facilities. Sporting layouts have popped up about the countryside as shooters find them entertaining alternatives for static skeet and trap.

Unfortunately, American hunters often expect Sporting Clays to be some sort of "walk" in which targets spring up to surprise them, such as happened on the old quail walks and grouse walks of the 1960s. But Sporting isn't a walk-along game *à la* the actual hunting field; targets aren't surprises. In Sporting Clays, the shooter knows exactly what the targets will be at any specific stand. The gunners do indeed shoot from a stand, which is often an enclosure known as a safety cage. They can observe the action while other shooters take their turn ahead of them or when the trapper throws a sample. For example, if it's a springing teal stand, the targets will be thrown upward sharply allowing the shooter to basically predict their flight lines before stepping up. If it's a running hare, the shooter again has a chance to observe its route along the ground before loading up.

What makes Sporting Clays so tough if the targets fly routes known to the shooter beforehand? The game is made testy by six factors: 1) by speed, which is considerably faster than typical American skeet and trap clays; 2) by a stateside rule demanding a lowered gun until the target is seen; 3) by a variable three-second delay in the release of the target(s); 4) by the terrain and foliage of the layout; 5) by optical illusions created by target angles and target sizes; and 6) by the variations, which occur from stand to stand and layout to layout. The essence of Sporting Clays, then, isn't predicated upon surprise flushes, but upon constantly changing targets, flights, speeds, backgrounds and foregrounds, and gun-handling.

The stands in Sporting Clays can be whatever a given club desires as long as they represent legitimate field-type challenges. The USSCA rules recommend no less than three different stands per layout. After fulfilling those basics, the creativity

SPORTING CLAYS: IS IT REALLY A HUNTER'S GAME?

Like a ruffed grouse, a target flashes through an opening in the woods. Sporting Clays has the potential to attract hunters if the game's organizers develop the game patiently with grass-roots participation.

and available land area determines any club's final course. Some clubs emphasize doubles over close or moderate ranges; others may employ long-range shooting, sometimes at singles (although British Sporting is based heavily on doubles). Some stands are pushovers; others appear impossible. Innovations pop up, such as using a pit from which one shoots like a goose hunter. Or there can be a stand in a boat to add realism and wiggle-wobble as clays come whistling in like bluebills. Or hunters can be placed atop the trap house as targets mimicking rabbits or low-flying partridge are sent skimming along the ground. At some installations there are 120-foot towers which launch high birds. At other clubs, doubles snap across small openings and disappear quickly into cover unless a gunner moves swiftly. It is indeed, the variety of stands that makes Sporting Clays the spice of shotgunning life.

The targets used in Sporting Clays also make life more interesting. There are currently five sizes and types made especially for Sporting, none of which exactly duplicates the standard American skeet/trap target. Sporting targets include the (1) standard target, (2) mini, (3) midi, (4) battue, and (5) rabbit.

The standard Sporting Clays target closely resembles the American skeet/trap target dimensionally, having a diameter of about 4¼ inches (110 mm) and a height of approximately one inch. This Sporting target, however, is moulded harder than the standard Yankee skeet/trap target, because it must withstand snappier launching speeds. Moreover, having greater sectional density than the American skeet/trap clays, the Sporting target retains velocity better. According to current rules, this standard-sized Sporting target must be thrown at least 70 percent of the time in sanctioned competitions. Most of the time it is a blaze orange color so it will stand out against a leafy background.

At the opposite extreme from the standard Sporting target is the mini, which is roughly half the size of a standard saucer. A mini has the same dome-type configuration as the larger standard clay, but it doesn't retain its speed as well. Minis are foolers as they can present optical illusions. When thrown high against the sky, they look terribly small causing shooters to misjudge distance and lead. Likewise, they can present the image of a terribly fast bird while actually slowing. Should they come out against a foliage background, minis are difficult to pick up. From what I have observed, minis are normally colored black rather than orange.

Midis, as their name tends to imply, are mid-sized targets. Shaped like standard targets, they have a diameter of about 3½ inches (90 mm). They start quickly and retain their speed better than minis, but midis are deceptive because they appear to be standard clays at long range.

Battues are the oddballs of Sporting Clays. Although roughly the same diameter as a standard target, battues are nearly as flat as a pancake. Only a minor dome rises above their thin edges and the resulting aerodynamics prompt erratic flights. The thin battue also offers little edge profile to the pattern. That can influence

SPORTING CLAYS: IS IT REALLY A HUNTER'S GAME?

Sporting Clays offers some weird target angles such as this sharply rising clay referred to as the springing teal.

SHOTGUNNING TRENDS IN TRANSITION

Sporting Clays uses at least five different-sized targets. Starting at the trigger guard and running clockwise they are, the thick-rimmed rabbit, the midi, the mini, the standard target, and the thin-edged battue leaning against it. The gun is a Winchester Model 6500 Sporting, sold mainly in the United Kingdom.

SPORTING CLAYS: IS IT REALLY A HUNTER'S GAME?

a savvy shooter's timing, for he will attempt to make his shot when the battue shows him the bottom, thus giving the pattern increased striking area. Windy days exacerbate the battue's erratic flight. To a certain degree, battues are foolish targets. Because they are harder than other clays, they occasionally don't break despite a fair edge hit. I believe they are expensive targets that unnecessarily increase the price of a tournament. There is no rule requiring the use of the battue and, in general, nothing is lost when they aren't included.

Rabbit clays also are about the size of standard clays, but they are moulded hard with heavy rims to handle the impact as they fly off the trap arm and collide with the ground. The British have engineered a special trap machine for this target; its throwing arm extends downward, perpendicular to the ground, so that the released target rolls on its edge like a bouncing rubber tire. On a cleverly devised course, the rabbit stand includes some brush obstructions and bumps to obscure the target and to make it roll and bound irregularly. Clubs do not need machines to throw the rabbit. Some of the smaller British clubs hand-roll them down steep banks and have considerable fun using that method.

These targets are best thrown on the specially made Sporting Clays trap machines whose powerful springs lay those clays well out and spin them briskly past stands. In general, traps made for American skeet and trap lack this power. Similarly, the various ground-mounted practice traps available in the U.S. are not equipped with strong-enough springs for optimum Sporting Clays performances.

Sporting Guns and Loads

Theoretically, Sporting Clays was devised to simulate field shooting. Hence, one would think that basic hunting guns would suffice, and in some instances, they do. There is absolutely nothing wrong with starting one's career in Sporting Clays with a pet bird gun to discover what the sport is like. A 12, 16 or 20-gauge repeater, or double with at least one ounce of No. 8 shot will adequately handle the initial rounds. If a hunter has no tournament aspirations, his field guns will perform splendidly at any time, for as a practice game, Sporting Clays helps familiarize a shooter with bird guns. The sport can be a lot of fun even if you aren't the competitive type.

But Sporting Clays has a long history of tournament competitions and this is what attracts sophisticated shotgunners more than the idea of keeping in shape for next fall's pheasants, ducks and grouse. As always, such advanced shotgunners opt for specialized equipment that may score another target or two to give them a competitive advantage. After a typical hunter has been in Sporting Clays for a while, he quickly learns that pumpguns and 20-gauge side-by-sides do not fare especially well against bona fide Sporting Clays models or slick autoloaders.

In fact, when it comes to tournament competitions, pumpguns, smallbores and side-by-sides simply haven't fared well. After touring their first Sporting Clays course, Americans who conclude that they need a light, fast-starting piece are fundamentally wrong. Lightweight guns and short-barreled "pokers" aren't winners in Sporting. They are whippy, jerky and contribute nothing to a positive follow-through. Even the British do not use their traditional side-by-side game guns in Sporting Clays as they tend to be inferior in competition. Instead, they occasionally establish a separate event for the side-by-sides. Thus, the feathery gun with lopped-off barrels, which seems fine for woodcock, bobwhite and some ruffed grouse, is a loser in Sporting Clays.

Champion Sporting Clays shooters place emphasis on a gun's smoothness of swing and positive follow-through rather than on its jumpy start. It is, after all, the stroke that scores a target, not the leap into action. The guns that win in Sporting Clays have a mixture of features combining more weight *and* length than many American upland hunters deem advisable, but they also have the pointing qualities and responsiveness of a proven International skeet gun. The weight and length are utilized for smoothing the swing and generating the momentum which flows into a follow-through; the pointing qualities and responsiveness are desirable for the fastest possible start without any sacrifice in weight or length. The point is that proven British performers emphasize swing and follow-through in their guns' dynamics, whereas Americans enjoying the game for the first time often become overenthusiastic about light guns and short tubes that produce lightninglike starts. Often a gun that literally jumps into action is too fast for most shooters and it doesn't replace poor technique.

Champions appear to favor over/unders with barrels no shorter than 28 inches. They do not want heavily walled barrels that sag, but prefer barrels which deliver a tad of forward inertia to transform into momentum without retarding the start and pivot. On autoloaders, the 26-inch barrel has sufficed because the receiver gives added gun length, but the best autoloader on the circuit at this time, the Beretta Model 303 Sporter, comes with a 28-inch barrel. What surprises most Americans who are just entering Sporting Clays is that the British have gravitated to 30-inch-barreled over/unders, and some have experimented with 32-inch guns. The guns made primarily for Sporting Clays, such as the Beretta over/unders, the Winchester and Classic Doubles stackbarrels, and now the Browning GTI and Lightning models, are generally responsive even with their 30-inch tubes.

The Winchester 5500/6500 guns were given somewhat thin-walled barrels to lessen the muzzle hang and to provide good pivoting action plus follow-through. It is interesting that most Americans never realized that Winchester was making this specialized gun for the British and European Sporting crowd.

Currently Sporting Clays is a 12-gauge sport, but there is a chance that Americans, being accustomed to shooting skeet with four gauges, will one day introduce smallbore Sporting events. The first probably will be a 20-gauge event. For this, a 30-inch-barreled 20 would be ideal to eliminate the inherent whippiness in the smaller gauges. Since there is currently no such gun on the market, I would

SPORTING CLAYS: IS IT REALLY A HUNTER'S GAME?

Winners at Sporting Clays tend to favor over/unders with autoloaders a distant second. There has been a trend toward long barrels on Sporting Clays guns — 30 inches not uncommon in the United Kingdom for over/unders. Such barrels smooth out swings and promote positive follow-throughs on passing targets such as this.

SHOTGUNNING TRENDS IN TRANSITION

select the Ruger 20-gauge over/under with 28-inch barrels. The Ruger has considerable weight for a 20, and its 28-inch barrels are manageable and swing smoothly. A second choice for the impending 20-gauge event would be a weighted autoloader, such as the Remington Model 1100 with a 28-inch barrel, and the weight set Remington manufactures for skeet-grade 1100s.

Comb height on Sporting guns is subject to individual fit and tastes, of course, but high-shooting shotguns are taboo in Sporting, as many stands feature downward slanting targets. The gun should shoot flat, and one's cheek should easily fit the comb without any need to hunch or scrunch. A high-patterning gun is anathema in Sporting Clays.

Just as a golfer changes clubs as he travels from tee to green, so can a Sporting Clays shooter change barrels or choke tubes for each stand. But thoroughly experienced Sporting Clays shooters don't often switch tubes, if at all. They tend to use the least amount of choke possible, usually employing unbelievably open chokes on the longest Sporting ranges. The improved cylinder tube is a favorite. Another popular tube is one the British call a quarter choke. That one has a 10-point constriction in the 12 bore.

World Champion A. J. "Smoker" Smith of England uses improved cylinder tubes in both barrels of his Winchester Model 6500 over/under. When asked how he keeps them in place during all that shooting, he replied that he installed them with water — meaning he rusted them into place. The point is that one's swing is more important than a couple of inches (more or less) pattern.

A common tandem in Sporting is skeet choke in the first barrel and IC in the second. Seldom in Sporting Clays would one need modified choke. Indeed, the targets thrown from 120-foot towers can be easily and consistently broken by improved cylinder patterns, as has been reported by competitors who regularly break the 120-foot-high birds, true 40-yard targets, with nothing more than skeet choke.

The success and popularity of these open degrees of choke rests upon the fact that in Sporting Clays one only needs to break off a visible chip to score the target, whereas a hunter requires more choke because multiple hits are necessary for a clean kill. Thus, chokes used by Sporting shooters have little in common with actual field hunting needs. As a rule of thumb, one can effectively use approximately two degrees less choke for any given range in Sporting than for field hunting. Clay targets don't bleed; therefore, it is not inhumane to make chippy hits that would merely cripple game birds.

Sporting Clays limits ammunition to $1^1/_8$ ounces, and the standard 12-gauge target loads handle that nicely. (There is a second international Sporting Clays format (FITASC) which permits $1^1/_4$-ounce loads because it is a tougher course of fire.) Initially, the three drams equivalent trap load with $7^1/_2$s or 8s was deemed the best, but those who use over/unders have found that the new lite loads with

SPORTING CLAYS: IS IT REALLY A HUNTER'S GAME?

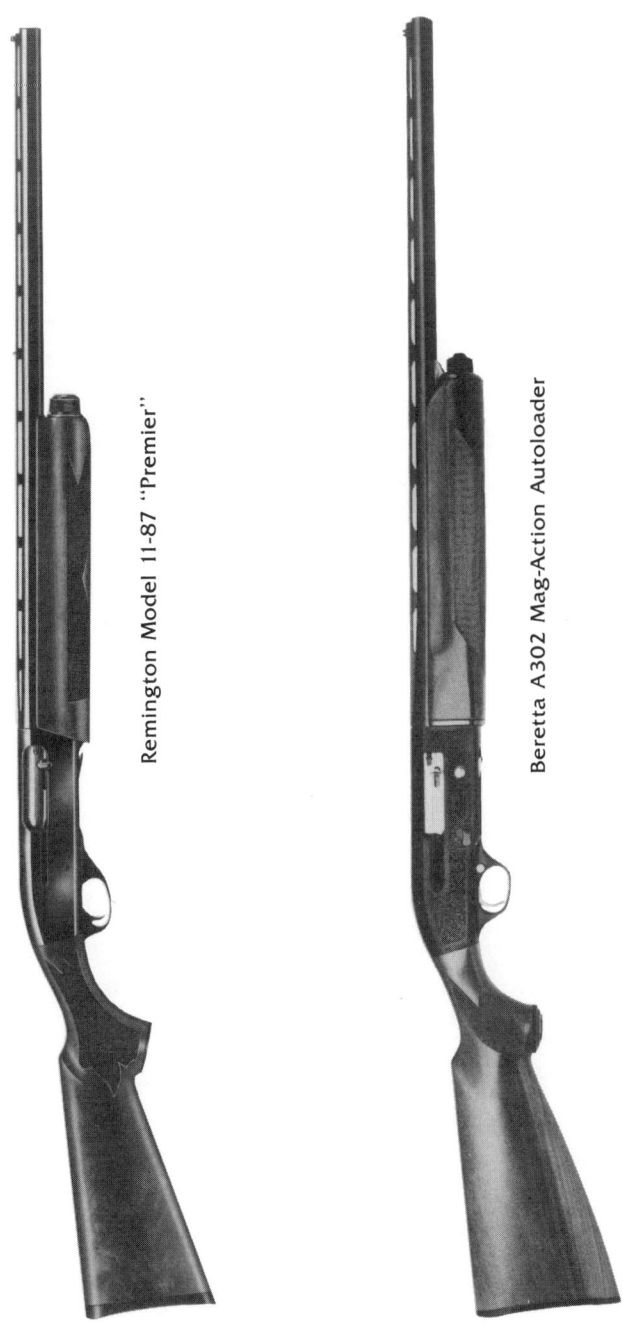

Despite the penchant for break-actions in England and Europe, the author believes that soft-recoiling autoloaders, such as the Remington Model 11-87 and Berettas will become increasingly more visible in stateside Sporting Clays.

Going up for a "tall" clay with the Winchester Model 6500 Sporter and 30-inch barrels. Although little known stateside, this gun was one of the early specialized models for Sporting Clays and is a winner in the United Kingdom.

velocities below 1,145 fps still get the job done without abusive recoil. The Winchester Super-Lite received considerable attention at the 1989 USSCA nationals. The lite loads appear best in 30-inch-barreled over/unders that can generate the round's full velocity.

In general, however, any shooter who takes legitimate $1^1/_8$-ounce trap loads of No. 8 shot to a Sporting Clays layout has the best all-around load available. Even when minis are thrown high, a properly placed pattern of 8s invariably finds the clay.

Gun Handling

The rule which makes a Sporting Clays shooter start with a lowered gun is what gives the game much of its zest and realism. It is what American shotgun shooting has lacked since skeet changed to "modern" rules that permitted a gun-up start. Faulty gun handling from a lowered position accounts for myriad misses in Sporting. If Sporting Clays allowed the gun-up start (as do skeet and trap), much of its appeal would be lost and scores could easily approach perfection. (To improve your overall shotgun handling, see Chapter 21 which details effective gun-mounting technique for optimum eye-hand coordination.) Unfortunately, the British rules for Sporting *do* permit a pre-mounted gun, but to do so is considered poor form, and few do it except on certain stations. As I understand it, there is a group in England that strongly opposes the pre-mounted gun and is campaigning against it to make all of Sporting a low-gun game. More power to them — and to those who fight to keep American Sporting low-gun!

The Future: A Hunter's Game?

When Sporting Clays first broke upon the United States shotgunning scene, it was touted as the hunter's game — variable targets in natural cover flying like upland birds and waterfowl or bouncing along like a crazy hare. To varying degrees, many hunters who never shot skeet or trap did come out of the woodwork. There has been an increase in clay target shooting's popularity stateside, thanks to the introduction of Sporting Clays. But the question remains: Will the game continue to grow? In many respects, the administration of the game has adopted a trickle-down policy which emphasizes the larger, more prestigious and more expensive tournaments while allowing rank and file shooters — the "hunters" of moderate means and abilities — to amble along independently. Administrative emphasis has been upon the sophisticated shooters, who are certainly responding, as witnessed by the record crowd at the 1989 USSCA nationals and by the number of layouts being developed across the United States.

Remember, however, that skeet was also a fascinating, fast-growth game back in the 1920s and 1930s. There were skeet fields everywhere, and then — flop! Skeet managed to shoot itself in the foot with institution of high entry fees and ridiculously easy scoring. Skeet's administrators removed the game from the hunters who were its backbone. Today, registered skeet is an insignificant part of American shotgunning. Will organized Sporting Clays ruin itself by ignoring the greater mass of hunters who could support it? Only the future will tell, but that is a possibility.

As this book nears completion there is a competition for dominance taking place between the United States Sporting Clays Association and the National Skeet Shooting Association. Recently (summer 1989) the NSSA has spun off a separate Sporting Clays division which publishes a bimonthly magazine. It hopes to revitalize the NSSA's meager coffers with registration monies from Sporting Clays events. Meanwhile, the USSCA's leadership, which has come under fire from member clubs and individuals, has had to revamp some of its thinking to compete with NSSA for shooter favor (and money).

The advantage could fall either way. Shooters will benefit as the two organizations compete for members, but only time will tell which one amasses the major following. The strength appears to lie with USSCA, because it is recognized by the international family of Sporting Clays shooters and has become the sole registrar of U.S. FITASC events. But the NSSA has a somewhat greater membership already in tow, and if it sponsors interesting tournaments it could begin to dominate the U.S. game. My one objection to the NSSA's role in Sporting Clays is that it has always been noted for charging excessively high prices and for making games ultra-easy for ego-gratifying scores. The NSSA could weaken and wreck a proud, tough game. Shooters will have to keep an eye on that organization.

The question remains whether the typical hunter will enthusiastically support the game. Historically hunters have not been dedicated shooters. They may try a game a time or two, but will they become active on a long-term basis? More than a few typical hunters have found their skills sadly lacking, and, after breaking something like 15x50 on a tough Sporting course, they've slipped away forever. Sporting Clays, shot as the fast, tough game it must continue to be, may simply be too difficult for most hunters. If those low-scoring beginners take no pride in improving their techniques, the broad base of support is gone. That leaves only the sophisticated shooters, who do in fact support the game. Unless typical hunters begin to take hold in Sporting Clays, then the question is moot as to whether it truly is the hunter's game.

Thus, three factors currently leave the future of Sporting Clays in doubt: 1) the trickle-down policies of the USSCA which emphasize major tournaments while slighting smaller clubs; 2) the NSSA's quest for monies and its tendencies to cheapen games; and 3) the still-unknown support from typical hunters. My advice to beginning Sporting Clays clubs would be to remain independent for a couple of seasons and observe the mounting competition between the USSCA and the NSSA to determine which organization better assists the smaller clubs. Hold separate, unregistered local tournaments at modest prices to encourage participation and hope that a strong, sensible, concerned national organization will emerge as USSCA and NSSA fight it out. A lot of chips are on the table and you don't want to bet on the wrong hand.

It's a great sport, this Sporting Clays — let's hope the organizers keep it that way!

Chapter 14

Registered Skeet: Some Call It "Modern"

IF SKEET shooting ever had a friend and a free publicist, it was Bob Nichols. His *Shotgunner* not only mentioned skeet continuously, but 10 years earlier (1939) he wrote a book devoted entirely to the then-new game, *Skeet and How to Shoot It*. From his post as shooting editor of *Field & Stream*, he kept skeet before the public's eye.

Other publications also provided substantial space to skeet, which was then the most exciting thing in sport shooting. Magazines like *The National Sportsman*, *Hunting & Fishing*, and even *Sports Afield*, carried monthly columns or features about skeet. Additionally, skeet was boosted by the glamour of Hollywood stars, many of whom flocked to shoot skeet rather than golf. Some movie idols even had private skeet ranges built on their palatial estates. Skeet fields popped up all over the United States, and when World War II came along skeet was chosen as the method for training aerial gunners. Thus, having caught on so broadly, skeet seemed poised for post-war greatness as a sport that every shotgun fancier and bird hunter would love.

Instead, however, skeet hasn't come close to reaching its potential. Its popularity among tournament shooters lags far behind trapshooting, and it doesn't attract hunters. Why hasn't skeet flourished?

The fact is that there are two different types of skeet shooters today — practice shooters and tournament gunners. Practice skeet actually isn't doing that badly. Gun clubs that have skeet setups still do a lively business in a practice mode — many practice shooters indeed being bird hunters at heart. The weekly turnout may not be as great as it is for trap leagues or registered trapshoots, but those who have gotten into skeet shooting for personal reasons other than blood-in-the-eye competitions thoroughly enjoy the sport. I've become one of them, shooting perhaps a hundred shells on skeet a week some summers, but never entering a registered skeet shoot.

Registered skeet shooting is no longer a hunter's game, no longer a gun handler's challenge. The sport was stolen from hunters by city tournament shooters who operate under the guise of the National Skeet Shooting Association (NSSA), and under their leadership the game fell from grace in the 1950s when rule changes abolished the low-gun starting position and three-second variable delay target release. Once skeet went to the pre-mounted gun and instant target release, it became nothing more than short-range trap on grooved targets; a game of timing rather than a game of gun handling and field-style swinging. In recent years, this corrupted form of skeet has become known as "modern" skeet.

Modern skeet is a precision shooter's game. The rule changes which permit a pre-mounted gun and mandate an instant target release have eliminated most opportunities for human error. Serious competitors find it extremely simple to learn their mechanical and timed moves for enough perfect scores to gag a computer. Tournament skeet shooters' movements have the monotony of a demented metronome. These liberalized skeet rules which generate perfect scores occurred after Nichols had written both *The Shotgunner* and *Skeet and How to Shoot It*, but they may be making him extremely uncomfortable in his grave. In *Skeet and How to Shoot It*, he had written that "the only type of shotgun shooting worth talking about [is] — shooting in the field (or at skeet) where the shooting function begins from scratch and includes everything, all the way up from the mounting of the gun to the crash of the shot."

To Nichols and so many others like him, then, skeet was and is nothing without the lowered gun. It apparently remains so today, but ego-bent tournament skeeters are so intent upon breaking season averages of 99.99 percent that they don't realize the harm they've done to a once-splendid sport.

Perhaps pressure from Sporting Clays, a game that simulates field shooting and requires a lowered gun, will one day force the National Skeet Shooting Association to take another look at itself and what the game has become under the rule changes of the 1950s. With a lowered gun and delayed targets, skeet can be as challenging and entertaining — plus less expensive — than Sporting Clays. Shooters can accomplish as much in one round of skeet with a lowered gun as they can in Sporting Clays. The main difference between low-gun skeet and Sporting Clays is that Sporting Clays changes the background to make a shooter think he's in the field. But a sharply breaking high-2 or low-5 on a skeet layout can be just as tough.

Meanwhile, other factors besides the groove-shooting aspect mitigates against the resurgence of skeet, including high tournament fees and equally expensive equipment concepts that make perfection so easy, so simple and so boring.

The Equipment Revolution

From the 1920s well into the 1960s, the types of guns used in skeet formed an interesting mosaic. Pumps, autoloaders, over/unders, side-by-sides — they all

REGISTERED SKEET: SOME CALL IT "MODERN"

Registered skeet has become a highly stylized game, one based on a short, grooved swing unlike the strokes hunters would make afield. The shooter here is fully prepared for his swing using the pre-mounted gun position which is legal in tournament skeet but which has made perfect scoring ridiculously easy. All the shooter needs to do is time his short stroke for a perfect score.

were present. Side-by-sides were the first to disappear, followed slowly by the pumpguns, while over/unders were relatively late bloomers.

One would think that low-gun skeet, which simulated the gun handling of upland hunting, would have been the perfect game for side-by-sides. Responsive pieces, side-by-sides should have swept into action spiritedly to sweep the sky clean of clays before they reached the crossing point. To an extent, the side-by-sides did get a play from pre-World War II skeet shooters plus a little post-war follow-up attention. Houses like Winchester, Parker, L. C. Smith, Iver Johnson, and A. H. Fox turned out skeet-grade doubles. The Winchester Model 21's stock and forend designs, in fact, were said to have been influenced by skeet's requirements. Iver Johnson turned out a straight-gripped little number called "The Skeeter," and A. H. Fox also made a few skeet guns with beavertailed forends and single trigger. The famous house of Parker did not come up with a true skeet grade double until after Remington had purchased the company in 1934; however, some skeet shooters employed field-grade Parkers prior to that date.

A most interesting episode in the side-by-side's skeet venture arose when the L. C. Smith doubles were made in a series of special skeet grades that met no public acceptance whatsoever. In 1939, a Skeet Special was introduced by L. C. Smith (then Hunter Arms) for $47. It offered optional barrel lengths of 26, 27 or 28 inches and was available in 12, 16, 20 and .410 bore. After 1941, the .410 model was deleted from the listing, but the remaining gauges stayed in the catalog until 1944, at that time priced at $100. Apparently based on the Featherweight L. C. Smith frame, the Skeet Special had a single trigger, beavertail forend and No. 1 and No. 2 skeet chokes. The engraving pattern was simply a shallow-cut, amateurish replica of the NSSA logo — a flying bobwhite with a clay target body — on the left sideplate. About five years after the Skeet Special was dropped, another skeet double appeared, the L. C. Smith Premier Skeet. It followed the former Skeet Special in many respects, except that it was somewhat better engraved (although still far from expert). Both skeet-grade Smiths sold poorly. The earlier Skeet Special moved only 770 copies between 1939 and 1944; the Premier Skeet sales were also bad, just 507 between 1949 and 1950. Talk about handwriting on the wall!

Why did the side-by-side fail in skeet? Popular claims were that the broad muzzles gave poor alignment. While I disagree that side-by-sides hinder alignment *for field shooting*, I tend to agree that they leave something to be desired for skeet. Shot with the lowered gun start, skeet was a fast-breaking game, and it is possible that the shooter's eyes could have had problems with the broad muzzles when the targets were viewed with peripheral vision under pressure. But more importantly, the side-by-side didn't permit optimum target visibility on low-starting clays, and there are plenty of those in skeet. The Station 8 low house, in particular, has always struck me as difficult with a side-by-side practically blotting out the sharply rising target.

REGISTERED SKEET: SOME CALL IT "MODERN"

(Photo by Gerald F. Moran)

An L. C. Smith Skeet Special showing the NSSA quail-and-target logo. Side-by-sides never did make the grade in skeet despite their vaunted handling qualities even when skeet was a low-gun game.

Visual factors aside, it also is likely that side-by-sides failed in skeet because they were too lively. As skeet developed, the knowledgeable shooters swung toward heavier guns with steel Cutts Compensators up front for smoothness and a forced follow-through. The side-by-sides put a premium on fast starting, but experience soon taught that skeeters didn't have to leap out of their socks to catch targets; they could intercept targets before the crossing point even with 8 to 8½-pound autoloaders and pumpguns. Side-by-sides may have started too fast and put too great a demand on timing; and since one error is enough to lose a skeet championship, the side-by-side was ignored. But those skeet-grade doubles of yesteryear certainly do make great upland guns today, and they're carrying premium prices on the collectors' market.

About the only noteworthy skeet win for a side-by-side was Dick Shaughnessy's 1936 national all-bore championship with 248x250 from a 16-gauge Winchester Model 21. Today, 248x250 wouldn't even place at the nationals unless the event were fired in a two-day typhoon — and it still probably wouldn't win, but merely be a place or show score!

Gradually, serious skeet shooters settled upon pumpguns, autoloaders and an occasional over/under. The 1940s, 1950s and early 1960s were the heyday of pumpguns. Any visit to a major tournament produces rack after rack of Winchester Model 12s, Remington Model 31s and 870s, and Winchester Model 42s. Most of the Model 12s and Model 31s had bulbous Cutts Compensators, as did many of the 26-inch-barreled Model 42s. Although the Ithaca Model 37 was offered in skeet grade, and although it was often seen with superb American black walnut, it never caught on with skeet shooters because of the awkward bottom loading and ejecting feature.

The favorite .410 was a 28-inch-barreled Winchester Model 42. Many of the persnickety competitors preferred a 2½-inch chamber to prevent the pattern disruption possible in a three-inch chamber with the scant wad column of the period. Savvy shooters also slipped lead slugs into the Model 42's tubular magazine to enhance the weight-forward characteristic that was becoming so desirable in skeet guns. In a few instances, gunsmiths slid a 20-gauge Model 12 barrel over the Model 42's slender .410 tube as another way of bulking up the sub-smallbore. More than a few important championships went to pumpgunners.

The pumpgun is now a totally uncommon sight at skeet tournaments. The prevailing theory is that pumping adds another element for potential human or mechanical error, and in this era of perfectionist skeet, nobody needs more opportunity to miss under tournament conditions. About the only time that pumpguns are seen on skeet fields today is when hunters show up for their first-ever try at the game or for their once-a-year practice session. The demand for skeet-grade pumps has fallen off so markedly that Remington has dropped the Model 870 in that persuasion.

As they have been from the beginning, autoloaders are still a dominant factor in skeet. At first the long-recoiling Browning Auto-5 and Remington Model 11

REGISTERED SKEET: SOME CALL IT "MODERN"

The Browning or Browning-type autoloader with long-recoil system and a Cutts Compensator was a foremost skeet gun in the early days of tournament shooting. This one is the Savage Model 720-C. Many such guns were without ribs.

prevailed. To mitigate against the abusive barrel shuffling, most of these autoloaders had Cutts Compensators attached. Often the guns didn't have ribs; the Cutts hung stark-naked against the sky. But scores didn't change, as the bold Cutts apparently acted like a muzzle bandage to help the shooters establish pointing alignment quickly from the low-gun position.

One of the most popular designs was the Remington Model 11 "Sportsman," which had a three-shot capacity and a beavertail forend. In the late 1930s, Savage also brought out a three-shot, skeet-grade auto based on the Browning long-recoil system, and it had a beavertail forearm plus a factory-installed Cutts Compensator for an overall barrel length of 24½ inches. Winchester's ill-fated Model 40, perhaps the first new design to be influenced by skeet shooting, was made in a skeet grade with dense burl walnut and a factory-attached Cutts to make a 24-inch barrel length. Finally, in 1948, Remington introduced the Model 11-48, which was an ultra-streamlined autoloader that continued in the long-recoil tradition, but eventually it was made in all skeet sizes. The 28-gauge Model 11-48 was introduced in 1952, followed by the .410 in 1954. Both of these smallbore Model 11-48s saw considerable tournament action and weren't dropped until 1969. Unfortunately, both the 28-gauge and .410-bore Model 11-48s were light and had to be doctored for a weight-forward effect.

On the heels of their 1940 debacle, Winchester launched the Model 50 skeet gun in 1954. Utilizing the inertia-block principle discussed in an earlier chapter, the Model 50 was extremely light in recoil and had the feel of the famous Model 12 pumpgun. It, too, failed to generate a following, probably because blowback debris from extensive firing in skeet caused the slipping chamber to hang up.

The big breakthrough in skeet-grade autoloaders came in 1956 when Remington introduced the gas-operated Model 58. Almost overnight the old Browning-type autoloaders fell by the wayside as skeet shooters took advantage of the soft-recoiling gas guns. Despite continued advances in gas-operated shotguns, the Model 58 remains a fine example of pointability in semiautos.

The Model 58 had no serious challengers until 1963, when Remington itself went the added step and announced the Model 1100, which was to become the greatest autoloading tournament shotgun in history. Made in all four skeet sizes, the Model 1100 continues to win. The 12-gauge Model 1100 has now been superseded by an upgraded version, the Model 11-87 "Premier," but in 20 and 28 gauge and .410 bore the basic Model 1100 lives on splendidly. Tournament shooters are an open-minded group, and they'll switch guns if somebody can prove another design is better, but thus far nothing has outdone the records set by Model 1100s. With a Pro-Ported barrel to mitigate against muzzle jump, the Model 1100 and the Model 11-87 are perfect for skeet doubles, hanging close to the target and engendering a rapid recoil recovery time.

Practically everyone knew that the autoloader was a natural for skeet provided some of the recoil sting could be removed. What most observers didn't foresee was the way over/unders would one day take over the game in the smaller gauges. In early low-gun skeet, the Remington Model 32 received scattered attention, and the Belgian-made Browning Superposed tagged along. But over/unders dealt out more recoil abuse than many shooters enjoyed, and those who fired hundreds of shells per day opted for a repeater and the subduing effect of a Cutts Compensator. The over/under still had a long way to go in the 1930s.

Multiple barrel sets for over/unders were made popular by Simmons of Kansas City in the 1950s and 1960s. Simmons could build .410-bore, 28 and 20-gauge barrel assemblies for the Model 32 and Superposed receivers, thereby giving a shooter a chance to compete in all skeet events with one gun action. Theoretically, this sounds perfect, especially if the barrels were all made to one weight for the same gun dynamic. Multiple barrel sets, however, have never fully achieved their potential. Even though all four barrel sets may scale the same, the guns don't feel the same from barrel to barrel. This may be a matter of bulk rather than basic weight. Whatever the cause, hard-core skeet shooters simply do not shoot as well with the .410-bore barrel sets as they do with the concept that has revolutionized skeet shooting — the tubed stackbarrel!

The Insert Revolution

The turning point for over/unders in skeet came at the 1960 world championships when Claude Purbaugh of Monrovia, California, demonstrated the practicality of slipping full-length smallbore inserts into 12-gauge over/unders. The inserts, or tubes, were simply mini-barrels which were made to fit the 12-gauge barrel from breech to muzzle; they had their own chambers and were adjusted at the muzzle end to fit snugly in the individual 12 gauge's choke constriction with no vibrations. The breech ends of the tubes had their own extractors which coupled with the gun's original extractor mechanism or fitted directly on the existing extractor for positive unloading. All this was made possible, by the advent of high-strength specialty steels, primarily aircraft steels, that could be drawn relatively thin to fit a 12-gauge bore and still safely withstand shotshell pressures.

The idea of tubed over/unders had substantial appeal from the start. The inserts were less expensive than extra sets of barrels, and they let a shooter stay with only one gun throughout a tournament for a better "groove." Another asset seemed to be the extra weight. A pair of inserts increased the gun's overall weight by 12 ounces to a pound, depending on the actual barrel length and type of insert, and that weight-forward condition promised a forced follow-through.

For a number of seasons, however, the increased weight of a tubed over/under plagued the concept. Shooters who tried the inserts and continued to use their normal technique and hold points did not fare well. Many of them shot scores below their former levels and they cocked a skeptical eyebrow at the concept

SHOTGUNNING TRENDS IN TRANSITION

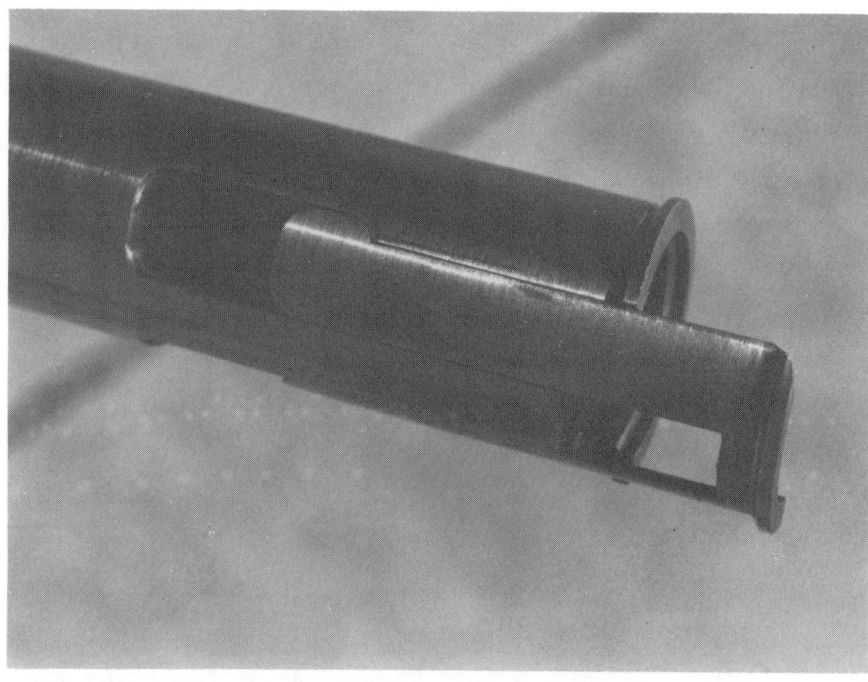

The smallbore inserts are made of high-strength aircraft metals with integral extractors, such as these found on Kolar tubes to fit on the gun's original extractors.

REGISTERED SKEET: SOME CALL IT "MODERN"

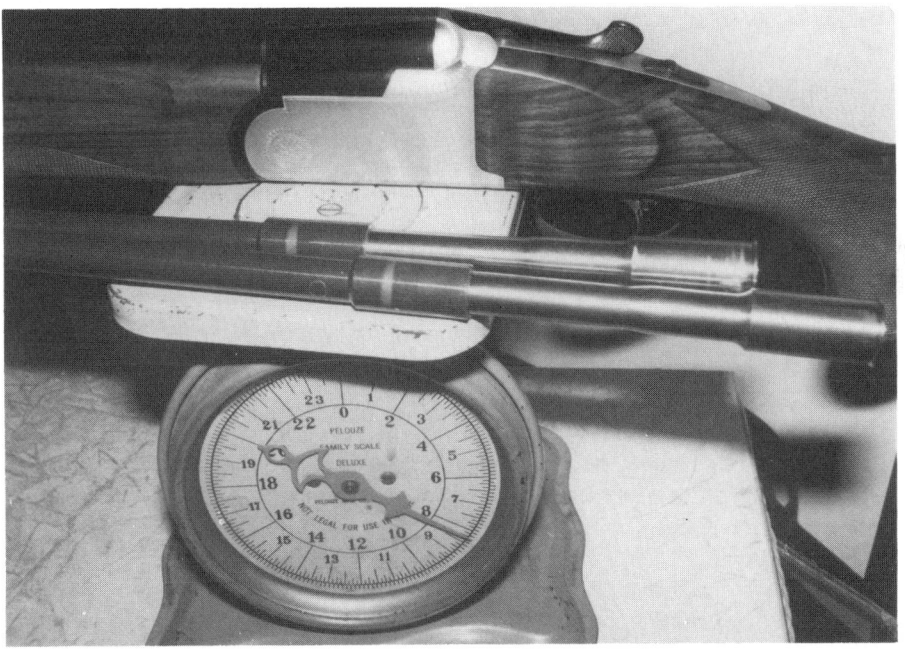

Smallbore inserts are made to fit full-length in a 12-gauge over/under. In place, they add about a pound to the gun's forward weight and generate a positive follow-through after a smooth swing.

as their averages fell. Something was wrong here! Initially, it seemed that the tubes were too much of a good thing; shooters simply couldn't start the tubed over/unders like they could guns weighing a pound less up front. Thus, the tubed over/under didn't immediately set the skeet world ablaze.

But the tubed over/under refused to die. Shooters kept trying them, and eventually solved the dilemma of how to make consistently timed starts with the heavy inserts in place. The answer was found in altered hold points. Traditionally, skeet shooters were taught to make their starting hold point roughly 10 to 12 feet out from the skeet houses; practically every manual I have in my collection recommends that distance.

(For those readers who are not conversant in skeet parlance, it must be observed that pointing the gun directly at the skeet houses always has been deemed a mistake. The target's first 10 feet of flight are a mere blur as the eyes do not pick up the saucer sharply. Therefore, to point back "into the hole" leaves the gun and the gunner well-behind a speedy clay. Shooters long ago learned that using a starting hold point 10 to 12 feet or so out from the skeet house put them in good position to see the target more clearly after its emergence streak and, with untubed guns, to catch it by the center of the field for excellent timing, vision and swing.)

Unfortunately, however, starting 10 to 12 feet out from the house with a heavily weighted over/under tended to leave a shooter behind the target, and the process of muscling such a weight-forward gun proved too much for many shooters. With that extra pound of inserts riding in the bores, they began to find skeet more work than pleasure.

By the late 1970s, though, the dilemma was solved. Instead of continuing to start their tubed over/unders 10 to 12 feet out from the house, shooters shifted their hold points further out. Eighteen feet seems to be a nominal distance these days, give or take a mite for each individual shooter. This new extended hold point gives the shooter more time to get the gun moving before the target dashes past the muzzles to be chased.

With the tubed over/under now started about 18 feet from the skeet houses, the shooter has ample time to pick up the target in his peripheral vision, zoom down into at least secondary vision before the target reaches the gun, and start smoothly into a sustained lead. The shooter's eyes focus onto the target's primary zone as the swing develops, and the gun's momentum provides the positive (forced) follow-through it always promised. Starting the tubed over/under from an 18-foot hold point is almost effortless, whereas using the same tubed over/under with a 10 to 12-foot hold point is agonizing work. As one champion put it, "Once you've got a tubed over/under rolling, you can't stop it!"

But while progress is inevitable, the high scoring capabilities of the tubed over/unders have almost turned the game of skeet shooting into a farce. Four-gauge tournaments are being won with overall scores of 400x400, and one competitor has put three such perfect tournaments together for a 1200x1200 record. Once it was a miracle to shoot 100x100 with a .410, but now it's a common occurrence to see several gunners shooting off 100s in the .410 at well-attended events. Indeed, the reason skeetmen didn't score well with the .410 a generation ago wasn't because the .410 couldn't pattern effectively; the problem was that the basic .410 is a scaled-down gun which doesn't have the weight or bulk for optimum smoothness, follow-through and consistency. The tubed over/under changed all that, giving the .410 much the same swing characteristics as the 12 gauge, and shooters now swing the same groove in the sub-smallbore event as they do in the 12-gauge contest.

Although the high scores generated by tubed over/unders make skeet shooters giddy about their high averages, such ultra-efficient equipment has turned skeet into a game of marathon proportions. The appeal that skeet had when field-style guns were fitted to the game has been lost; the novelty is gone; the chances for human error are reduced. There is little relationship between the stroke applied by a high-gun skeeter using a pre-shouldered, tubed over/under and that required for actual field shooting. The game of skeet as shot in NSSA tournaments has become sterile and ultra-mechanical. It is mainly an equipment game: If one doesn't invest in an expensive tube set, his chances of winning in the smaller gauges diminish significantly, especially at major tournaments. All those factors have driven people from skeet; even practice shooters are critical of the game because of what they see and hear about tournament scoring. Moreover, those competitors who average 99.99 percent over the course of a season are admired only by the few others in that small coterie called registered skeet. Typical field shooters scoff at such accomplishments because they represent groove shooting in its easiest and most mechanical form yet contrived by shotgunners. Tournament skeet simply isn't going to grow as long as an average person must spend $5,000 on a tubed over/under just to get into a prolonged shoot-off!

Does Skeet Have a Future?

Books and magazines from the 1930s and 1940s show crowds of spectators watching skeet tournaments. It was apparently enjoyable for non-shooters to watch the squads line up and to see each man step up in turn. Some perfect scores were shot in those days, to be sure, and there were obviously shoot-offs, but the competitors had to work for their 99s and 100s. They watched for a target that could appear at any time within a three-second span and then could mount the lowered gun only after the target was airborne. There was more chance for human error. The variable target release and lowered gun made the game of skeet entertaining.

Today, many skeet tournaments don't draw more than a small handful of shooters, let alone a crowd of spectators. If one scans the pages of *The Skeet Review*, he will see that some NSSA registered events have only one or two entrants! Of

SHOTGUNNING TRENDS IN TRANSITION

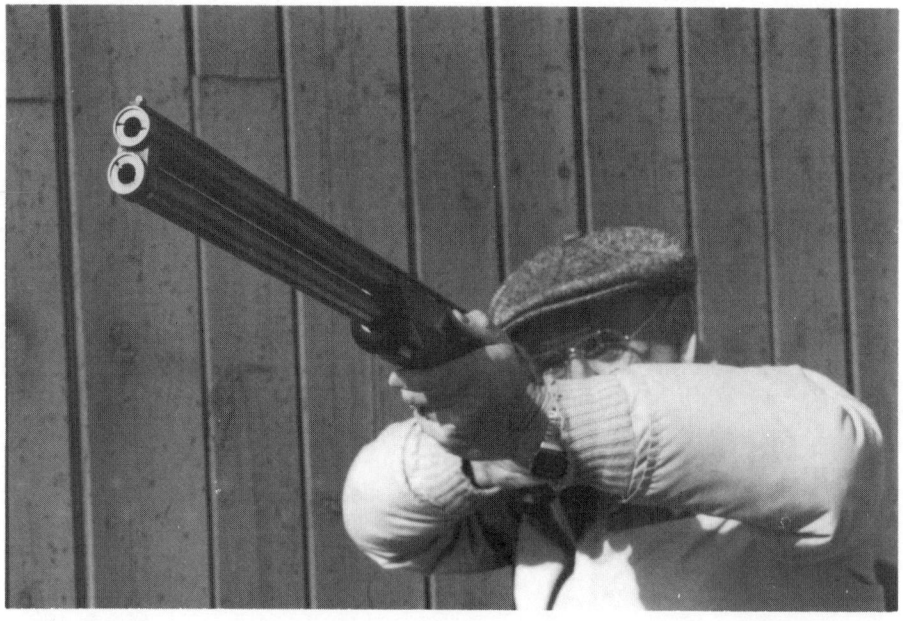

The gun that revolutionized skeet shooting — a tubed over/under, shown here with the .410 tubes that have made perfection so much easier than the original scaled-down .410 skeet guns of yesteryear.

REGISTERED SKEET: SOME CALL IT "MODERN"

Starting a round of American high-gun skeet. It's a fun game, still the best teacher of a good shotgun swing. But current rules have cheapened it, and hunters are urged to try it with a lowered gun to simulate field conditions.

course, skeet is no longer the novelty it once was, and non-shooters have many more activities available to them. But one would expect that a nation with over 16 million licensed hunters could attract more than 20,000 registered participants to a game well within the parameters of sport shooting. Except when the national economy is riding high, skeet shooting goes nowhere; even the gains that tournament skeet registers when employment and income figures are high don't amount to much. Meanwhile, the United Kingdom has 150,000 participants in Sporting Clays and Italy has 1½ million in trap. Thus, there is reason to ponder the future of skeet as it now exists.

Skeet shooting might make a comeback if independent clubs ignore the trend set by NSSA leadership, and shooters who dote solely on perfect scores no matter how easily such 100s are attained. But it must become less expensive and be made more appealing and challenging. The current skeet shooting obsession with longer and longer strings of consecutive hits and higher and higher seasonal averages means nothing to the typical hunter or casual shooter.

The "country club" entry fees of skeet tournaments also impede the game. Cost has always stymied skeet, as club managers try to extract a year's profit from one tournament. Whereas trapshooters currently pay $15 or less per 100 registered tournament targets, skeet fees often range between $25 and $35 per 100 targets. And what does one win for his $35 plus shells, travel, meals and lodging? A silly little pewter candy dish or a useless "stump sitter" trophy. Thus, if a skeet shoot involves all four gauges, plus the new game of doubles at all stations, a shooter can pay $125 to $175 just to get squadded. Not many people can, or are willing to, spend that much on a game where the experts break 400x400 and where nothing is gleaned for field shooting. True, skeet shooting is a marksmanship contest, not a pheasant hunt, but people who are outside of skeet don't think that way. Skeet must make some concessions if it wishes to expand.

It is extremely doubtful, however, that skeet will lower the gun as long as the NSSA's board of directors is comprised of the same shooters who feed their egos on 100-straights. Like the trapshooters who voted against extending their handicap distances from 27 to 30 yards, skeet shooters don't want things made more difficult, either. So change becomes a political matter, and it seems that those who now control registered skeet would sooner have a small, insignificant sport than sacrifice a point in their seasonal averages.

Having ruined one sport, the NSSA is now becoming involved with Sporting Clays as it scrambles to collect fees to remain in business. Frankly, I like the NSSA organization, but one can only hope that, if the group does become firmly established in Sporting Clays, it doesn't cheapen that game, too!

Except for attracting an occasional millionaire and a few people who suddenly become obsessed with breaking serial 100-straights at the sacrifice of everything else, registered skeet will remain a terribly small clique. It has a dim and darkening

REGISTERED SKEET: SOME CALL IT "MODERN"

future unless radical changes occur soon to re-establish the testy challenges that once made it so popular. The biggest joke of all was demonstrated at the 1988 skeet nationals at Savannah, Georgia, when, in one day's shooting, 106 entrants broke 125x125 and began a prolonged shoot-off that may still be going on.

Whatever happened to registered skeet? Nobody really seems to care! But don't forget the skeet practice field with a lowered gun, as that's the best practice a hunter can get. Ditto for a beginner.

Chapter 15

Trapshooting: The Old Grey Mare...

AMONG THE various American shooting sports that have been organized under official rules and governing bodies, trapshooting undoubtedly is the largest and most active. Although there are some rifle and handgun groups that boast substantial memberships, there has always been something anemic about their actual number of tournaments and membership participation.

Indeed, there are millions of rifle and handgun owners, but very few of them ever "put it on the line" in actual competition. Last summer, for example, my local club hosted the county trapshooting championship, and 120 shooters showed up. Shortly thereafter, a nearby club held a novel tournament for handguns that would be used for deer hunting. In view of the many hunters who enthusiastically bought such handguns, one would have anticipated a horde of entries. *Nine* showed up, a paltry count by any standard.

Meanwhile, trapshooters continue to turn out for weekend events in numbers that make handgun and rifle competitions look like amateur night. At this writing, the Amateur Trapshooting Association (ATA) has approximately 97,000 members, and nearly 40,000 are regular participants in registered events. (Don't let the term "registered shooting" scare you. It only means the scores are punched into the ATA's computer so each member is properly classified and handicapped according to his or her official average.)

In 1987, there were 5,406 ATA registered shoots. Moreover, when the Grand American Handicap is held each August at the ATA's home grounds in Vandalia, Ohio, anywhere from 3,000 to 4,000 shooters will go "down the line" each day. Until the recent craze for marathon running developed, the Grand American Handicap trapshoot was the largest one-day participant event in U.S. sports. To handle such a crowd each day, the ATA's home field has, as of this writing, 88 traps in line, a layout that stretches for at least a mile! When one adds up all the practice shooting, non-registered events, merchandise shoots and local leagues that

SHOTGUNNING TRENDS IN TRANSITION

Trapshooting has changed through the years, becoming an easier game due to alterations in the trap machine settings which no longer give hard, sharp angles. Most clubs now use the two-hole trap setting for gentle angles such as this.

burn up trap fodder, he must conclude that trapshooting is entrenched and enjoyed by a tremendous number of people.

But as popular as trapshooting may be, the game has gone through a period of change. Among the shooting games it is comparable to the old grey mare that "ain't what she used to be!" If the old-timers who laid the foundations for the game returned, they would certainly recognize it as trapshooting because the basic layout hasn't changed, but practically everything else has.

Continuing the tradition, trapshooting American style has three events: 16-yard, handicap and doubles. At one time, the maximum handicap distance was 25 yards, but it has been moved back to 27 yards. The sad fact is that even a 27-yard handicap isn't far enough to offset the talent of many young and/or experienced shooters whose athletic ability and/or continuous shooting make them threats to winning any handicap event. Likewise, the modern shotshells teamed with highly specialized trap guns and refined barrels for ultra-tight patterns enable a long-yardage shooter to break more targets today from 27 yards than the old-timers did from 25 yards with their lower-combed guns and dicey shotshells (*sans* high antimony content and plastic wads). To compensate for poor patterning, the early trapmen were allowed 1¼-ounce shot charges of nos. 7, 7½, 8 or 9 shot, whereas today No. 7s are illegal and the heaviest load one can legally chamber is 1⅛ ounces.

The basic theory behind trap handicap shooting was to place everyone at a yardage that would put them all on a given level of performance. It's comparable to weighting down horses so they all must carry the same weight through a given race. In the pre-plastic era, trap handicapping did work reasonably well because poor patterning helped the maximum-yardage shooters miss a few. But with today's talent level and gun/load performances, such misses don't occur. If a competitor can point them properly from 27 yards, he'll break every target.

As a result of this heightened gun/load patterning ability, the top 16-yard shooters, who were supposed to be handicapped to give the lower-scoring gunner a chance, have continued to dominate the game despite the 27-yard distance. Talent prevails due to technological advances and product perfection. Indeed, it is virtually impossible to find shotshells that have ever been held to a higher level of performance and quality control than those made by Remington-Peters, Federal Cartridge Corporation and Winchester.

As a result of this ability to break winning scores practically from the gun club's parking lot, this same nucleus of talented, tournament-hardened shooters that dominates 16-yard championships now also terrorizes handicap events. In the 1987 ATA listing of official averages, for example, there were 74 27-yarders among the top 80 handicap averages.

The point I am making, of course, is that the 27-yard stripe is no longer a true handicap. Unless winds upset the targets, the 27-yarders invariably will win against people shooting from much shorter distance *because they have the talent*.

Theoretically, it may be easier to break 100x100 from 21 yards than it is from 27 yards, but shooters who populate the shorter distances simply aren't athletically skilled enough to take advantage of their lesser handicap yardage. To win in trap handicap today normally means breaking at least 98x100 and generally 99x100 or 100x100, but the short-yardage shooters can't handle that. They are plagued by shortcomings in coordination, timing or nerves. The high-scoring 27-yarder with the proverbial ice water in his veins, can sit back on the 27-yard line all day and center clays, but when a typical short-yardage gunner gets close to a perfect score he tends to "choke" and miss just enough to lose. Indeed, if there is one thing that tournament shooters must realize, it is that the major difference in clay target competition is between those who can overcome the pressures to break perfect "100s" and those who cave in and only post 99s.

If the records have proven anything during the past 15 years or so, it is that trap's handicap system is a modern failure. The man who doesn't have the coordination and/or the mental game to break 100x100 from 16 yards is certainly no match for the current breed of talented, money-hungry shooters in handicap using the present system. Yet, the game of trapshooting has many "suckers" who, blindly believing that handicap distances will even things out, bet high sums in hopes of winning the fabled pot of gold. It's called "feeding the kitty" by some, but it's known as placing sucker bets by more realistic shooters. Hope springs eternal, and shooters who can't break 25x25 from 16 yards with regularity continue feeding the barracuda.

The Sleaze Factor

The presence of added monies and rich purses has brought an element of sleaze into trapshooting. Unlike professional golfers, who have the ethics to call shots on themselves for mistakes made when no one else is watching, some trapshooters are in the game only for the money. They will cheat in whatever way they can. This is especially true in the handicap events, where "sandbagging" is a common practice. Instead of shooting to the best of their ability in each event, many gunners purposely miss extra targets on the last field or two if they realize their scores aren't high enough to win. For in handicap trapshooting, under ATA rules, any score of 96x100 or better earns at least another ½-yard of handicap distance (although 96s often will not win anything). Hence, the popular question among trapshooters: "Why should I take more yardage if I'm not taking home some money?" Potential 96s soon become 90s, which may reduce the shooter's handicap and bring him forward for easier scoring. Indeed, there are many trapshooters whose averages do not reflect their true ability; they are sandbagging, waiting for that "hot" day when they can cop the cash.

Another trick among trapshooters has been exchanging membership and classification cards so that a good shooter has the yardage of a lower class shooter. This has happened any number of times. For example, let's say there's a high stakes trap tournament in Las Vegas and a pair of shooters from New Jersey want to get their mitts on that purse. One of them is a hot 27-yarder; the other is a 22-yard handicap shooter who can't make the flight. The 22-yarder gives his cards to the 27-yarder, who then flies out to Las Vegas and enters from the 22-yard stripe under the wrong name. Nobody knows him, so he gets away with it. If he's still hot, he can break a score that puts him in the money, and later split the winnings.

The problem with trapshooting, of course, is that it dangles tantalizing purses before a lot of small-minded people who forget the enjoyable sporting aspects of the game and think only of the money. Trapmen like to say, "My shooting has to pay for itself," but that's usually a joke, as very few typical trapshooters ever win any significant sums. A paltry $100 here and there would hardly cover a career in trap.

This same idea of making a sport pay for itself has not infected skeet shooting, which is one of its tremendous strengths. It keeps the game basically a sport, ethically engaged in, by people who shoot for pleasure rather than fortune.

Needless to say, handicap trap will never be a perfect game because of the prevalence of various forms of cheating. If everyone shot honest scores to the extent of their ability, an added-target handicap system would be far more equitable, because it would bring the low-scoring shooter (the one who can't get his nervous system over the hump to break perfect scores) to the 99x100 or 100x100 level and thus challenge the talented 27-yarders. However, since sandbagging is rampant, the added-target method simply won't work.

In 1983, a motion was made to extend the handicap distance another three yards, moving it from 27 back to 30 yards. Trapshooters rejected the proposal. I happened to be at that meeting in Vandalia when it was almost unanimously voted down. As one would expect, the 27-yarders were positively against it. They had numerous reasons — gun clubs couldn't afford it; there was no room for an expansion at many clubs; it was beyond the patterning range of the $1^1/_8$-ounce load. All the excuses were shams for the real reason: It would have prevented the continual domination of handicap by talented, money-grubbing shooters. At the Vandalia hearing, one of the 27-yarders who opposed the 30-yard handicap extension was a young man who had quit his job to make a living at tournament trap. He made the ridiculous remark that the handicap distance shouldn't be lengthened because nobody was making a *decent* living from the 27-yard line!

What was truly amazing was that the rank-and-file ATA membership also was opposed to a 30-yard handicap. It appears that the 27-yard line and innumerable 100-straights are an obsession among ATA members. Their dreams must be to break endless (albeit easy) perfect scores and to make the 27-yard handicap line (at which time they'll receive a pin to commemorate the occasion). For many people, that 27-yard lapel pin is an end unto itself. As long as the 27-yard handicap line is the ranking symbol of greatness, the ordinary trapshooter has no one but himself to blame for the domination by long-yardage handicappers. By voting in the 30-yard line, trap handicap might once again become a competitive sport among all shooters, but today it's only a matter of which 27-yarder will win.

Easier Targets

One change that has made ATA trapshooting a relatively easy, high-scoring game is the way traps are set and targets thrown. Trap clays are now being thrown shorter distances, slower and at greatly reduced angles. At one time, the nominal flight of a trap target could be 48 to 52 yards, and clubs didn't hesitate to throw them the full distance, but current rules have dropped back to a 48 to 50-yard flight. Although ATA rules recommend a 50-yard carry, many clubs merely lollipop them 48 yards and let shooters tear up high scores.

Another change in trap settings is widespread employment of the two-hole machine adjustment. This has lopped some of the sharpness from the extreme right and left angles, and it has played directly into the hands of talented gunners whose only problem upon occasion was a sharp right or wicked left from a three or four-hole machine adjustment. With trap machines set in the second hole, however, there is no longer anything like a "screaming right" target. There are still rights and lefts, but they are gentle and much easier to handle.

Indeed, at one time trapshooters claimed their game was harder than skeet because "in trapshooting you don't know where the targets are going due to trap rotation." That statement has little merit now, for the two-hole trap adjustment has greatly reduced the field of distribution ahead of a trap house, and a shooter doesn't have to move his gun very far to pick up any or all targets. When trapshooters tire of breaking endless strings of 25s, they can revitalize their game by returning to the four-hole machine setting and cranking the spring for a 55 to 60-yard flight as in skeet.

Another change in trapshooting is that competitors can reject any targets they don't like and blame it on the puller as a "slow" or "fast pull." To the game's detriment, this procedure generally has been permitted by tournament managers. Unfortunately, the shooters who reject the most targets are all-Americans, Class AA gunners and prima donnas on the 27-yard handicap line. Few high-scoring champions like the widest angles even though they aren't sharp with today's two-hole settings. When they see the wide angles come up, the champions apparently "choke"; at least they don't shoot. They lower their gun and call, "Too slow." And they get away with it.

Another reason these chokers turn down the harder angles is because they try to "read" the traps and, when they miss their read, they find themselves out of position, both mentally and visually. They then reject that out-of-location target as too fast or too slow rather than take a chance.

TRAPSHOOTING: THE OLD GREY MARE...

Trapshooting is America's most popular and affordable clay target sport, and will probably remain so.

SHOTGUNNING TRENDS IN TRANSITION

Perhaps registered trapshooting needs more tough "super" referees to work alongside the teenagers who inevitably work the scoring and pulling jobs at major tournaments so that rules will be enforced! At Vandalia, Ohio, I once followed a young man who was one of the hottest trapshooters. An athlete, he had been setting records galore. While I watched, he turned down five targets as too fast or too slow, and the high school girl pulling allowed him to get away with it although nobody else in the squad turned down even one target. Is it likely that the hotshot was the only one getting poor pulls? Hardly. He was reading the trap and positioning his eyes for only one quadrant of the field. When he didn't get a target in that quadrant he turned the pull down for one more to his liking. I submit that anyone can break hundreds in trap if they can pick and choose among targets.

There are some people who question whether modern trap machines, which are equipped with so-called "interrupters," can be read successfully. Perhaps this feat can't be done perfectly, but it can be done by many intense competitors. I once sat directly behind the firing line at Vandalia for a shoot-off among all-Americans who were right-handed shooters. A guru sitting alongside me said, "Watch to see how many hard right-angle targets these guys get." I watched closely through three shoot-off rounds and saw only one right-angle clay, which was immediately turned down as a "fast pull"! Moreover, in one issue of the now-defunct *American Shotgunner* magazine, an all-American trapshooter was so bold as to write a column on how to read interrupted trap machines. I rest my case.

Modern trapshooting has its woes, so why does it remain so popular? I believe trap will continue to be the largest participant shooting sport in America because it is simple to learn and easy to handle for respectable scores. One really doesn't have to be an athlete to become a good trap shot. It doesn't hurt to have nerves of steel and optimum eye-hand coordination, of course, but many non-athletic people can master trap if they obtain sound instructions and apply the fundamentals. The reason some people remain poor trapshooters — just as they remain duffers in golf and hackers in tennis — is because they don't receive proper instruction or, after having been coached, don't apply what they have learned. Low-scoring trapshooters often have enormous egos and believe they are naturally great with a gun. In reality their self-taught method holds them back.

Yet, trapshooting holds out hope, and that's what brings people back. Even the lowest-scoring shooter in a local league hits all of the angles at one time or another, and he reasons that if he can hit anything that comes out of the trap house he will, eventually, put it all together for perfection — it's just a matter of time. For most shooters, however, that becomes a long, drawn-out affair. Self-taught shotgunners seldom go very far unless they dig deeply into theory and, by insight, learn to apply the proper details and fundamentals. Even great athletes from other sports — baseball, basketball, track, bowling and tennis — do poorly when they initially try shotgunning, because they haven't learned sound technique. However, since today's trapshooting has become so terribly easy with slow, lofted targets flying minimal angles, even awkward techniques can score enough targets to keep a poor shot happy.

The name of the game is no longer a challenge to hit difficult targets. Trapshooting has become a game which makes high scores easy for a purpose: It keeps shooters coming back. And when shooters return, it means money in the till for club operators. If a present-day trap club threw difficult targets which made shooters miss so they wouldn't run their scores in the high 90s or 100x100s, that club would quickly lose popularity. The current shooter is obsessed with perfection no matter how easily it is attained, and trap is a primary example of that switch. Interestingly enough, however, few trapmen who run endless strings of 25s ever generate enough gumption to attempt Olympic trap with its radical angles and hard, swift targets that fly over the horizon. Why not? They can't run 25s, 50s and 100s! Perfection, like alcohol and drugs, seems to be an addiction for trapshooters — they can't break the habit.

Equipment Changes

Not only have target flights and shooter attitudes changed in trapshooting, but so has the equipment. It is constantly being upgraded and becoming more sophisticated. The trend has been toward lighter recoil, faster timing and better pattern control.

Back in the early days of organized trapshooting, it wasn't unusual to see events won by shooters using field-grade guns. In *The Shotgunner* Bob Nichols reported that a 16-yard class championship was won at the 1938 Grand American tournament in Vandalia by a Missouri gunner using the then-new Winchester Model 37 "Steelbilt" single shot, a basic knockabout break-action that sold for no more than $10. There still are some instances of trapmen using field-stocked guns to good effect. My friend and neighbor, Claude Kolbe, won the 1981 Grand American Handicap with 100-straight and a shoot-off victory using his Remington Model 1100 hunting gun with 30-inch barrel. Claude didn't like the way his trap gun's high comb was beating him under the eye, so he switched to the field stock and made off with the most prestigious prize in American trapshooting.

Even on early trap grades, combs tended to be lower than on today's field guns. The Winchester Model 97 hammer pump, made in the Black Diamond trap grade, had a terribly low comb for trapshooting. Likewise, trap grade doubles and singles from Parker, L. C. Smith, A. H. Fox, Ithaca and Baker invariably have comb and heel drops on the low side. I have long had an interest in the Parker SC for my periodic trapshooting, but every sample I've come upon has had such a low comb that I invariably find myself looking directly into the opening lever or my thumb rather than over the rib. Those Parkers I've handled with higher combs got that way by custom splicing, something that I reject as non-original. But every time I mount one of those crooked-stocked old trap guns, I shudder at the thought of firing 200-target events with them using 1¼-ounce loads! The accumulative recoil effect must have been awful!

The days of low-combed trap guns are behind us, of course. Unfortunately, some gunmakers now go to the opposite extreme and design them with excessively high comb lines which leave trapshooters complaining they, "Can't get down on it!"

On a purely theoretical basis, trap guns should have high combs so that, when properly mounted and cheeked, they will pattern slightly high for built-in vertical lead on rising trap targets.

The high comb does exactly what the rear sight of a rifle or handgun does when it's elevated: It produces high shooting, because the shotgunner's eye serves as a rear sight. However, enough is enough. A high-patterning gun scores well, even effortlessly, when conditions are perfect and the targets rise uniformly. Many handicap shooters enjoy high pattern placement so that they don't have to swing upward with the target. Those who are truly fast shooters just move over to the emerging target and shoot, letting the high pattern placement do the rest, but let the wind blow and the targets vary, and the shooter suddenly has problems with a high-shooting gun. If he normally can hit a rising trap clay by pointing six inches or so below the target, what happens when the wind suddenly flattens the target flight in midswing? Or, what if the wind comes from behind a shooter all day to hold targets very low? Or, what if an incoming or quartering wind makes the targets climb variously or fly in a bouncy manner? How does one successfully find the same point six inches below every erratic target? The answer, of course, is that he doesn't. He misses.

For a short time, there was a fad among trapshooters in which barrels were bent upward for high pattern placement. These shooters generally employed conservatively dimensioned stocks for comfort and easy viewing over the rib, but they "bowed" the barrel for exaggerated pattern elevation. This fad wasn't widespread, although it did generate a lot of conversation. It also brought gunsmiths a lot of work as people who didn't know what they were doing snapped rib supports off barrels.

To make perfect use of a high-patterning gun, one must be an extremely swift and talented trapshooter, taking the target while it is rising most sharply and uniformly right out of the house. If the shotgunner is of average timing and coordination, taking the clays as they travel farther away and begin to peak out, the torqued tube only exacerbates missing as the shot string slips over the top. Thus, anybody but an athlete with lightning-like reflexes would do well to ignore radically high pattern placement. After substantial patterning, my feeling is that a pattern impacting four inches high at 35 yards is maximum for typical shooters. Most shooters would improve by keeping their head down, touching the target and swinging the line of flight for optimum pointing accuracy within the parameters of their physical ability, rather than snap-shooting with a high-patterning gun.

Trap gun designs have been modified in an effort to reduce recoil, which is praiseworthy. A lot of one-day trapshoots involved 300 targets, and that adds up to tremendous recoil energy. According to an old industry rule of thumb, a $1^1/_8$-ounce trap load with three drams equivalent of powder for about 1,200 fps from a 30-inch barrel generates roughly 18 foot-pounds of recoil energy in an 8-pound gun. Multiply that by 300 and it tallies 5,400 foot-pounds, which is nearly three tons of recoil! Anything to relieve that is important to trapshooters.

One method of reducing sensible recoil is by elevating the comb and depressing the bore axis. It is a fact of physics that the higher a bore sits relative to the comb line, the more noticeable recoil will be. The way a specific gun bucks under recoil is commonly called "kick," and guns with crooked stocks kick like the devil. Conversely, a gun that has its bore axis depressed below the comb line tends to give what is known as a "straightline" recoil effect and sets up less noticeable kick by causing the recoil energy to drive directly back into the shouldering area without the upward jolt and cheekbone rap of a high-sitting bore axis. This is why the lower barrel of an over/under normally is made to fire first: Its location below the comb line produces straightline recoil for less jump and a quicker recovery.

Thus, the straightline recoil concept brought about a new trap gun design known as the "unsingle." Essentially this gun is an over/under with the top tube removed and a high-post ventilated rib filling the gap and resembling the Golden Gate Bridge. Despite its ungainly appearance and dubious aesthetics, the unsingle has caught on and become a definite part of American trapshooting. Of course, trapshooters could get the same basic results by using an over/under, but for 16-yard and handicap many shooters want a longer barrel of 34 inches as opposed to the normal 32-inch maximum of stackbarrels, without the weight of a second tube.

The same depressed-barrel concept has been used in the more conventional single shots, pumpguns, and autoloaders by the expedient of high monte carlo combs and equally high ventilated ribs. By raising the comb and rib on any gun, the bore axis automatically is lowered to come more in line with the shouldering area for straightback recoil. While none of these modifications will win an award for artistic splendor, they do serve their intended function quite nicely. Here, again, form follows function, but unlike the slim, trim profile of the British game gun (which also derives its form from its intended function on driven game), the unsingle and/or high-combed repeaters take the opposite tack and appear homely. Since trapshooters are interested in scores, not trimness of line, they couldn't care less.

Another trap gun modification with increasing popularity these days is the overbored barrel. In clay target circles, this is known as "backboring," a term developed by Seattle barrelsmith Stan Baker, as previously discussed in Chapter 11. The topic needs no further elaboration here except to say that nowhere is backboring more sensible than in trapshooting with its steady drumfire and recoil.

To a certain degree, gunmakers have accepted the desirability of overboring on trap models. Winchester has marketed some versions of the Model 101 target-grade guns with trap barrels overbored to approximately .740-inch. As of 1988,

The "unsingle" is a specialized American trapshooting gun built on an over/under frame but utilizing only the lower barrel. This gives the shooter an easily moved single-shot piece and places the bore axis well below the comb line for a straightline recoil effect.

Remington made overboring a standard feature on Model 11-87 and Model 870TC trap guns, their bores running about .743-inch. In the past, Remington's now-obsolete Model 870 "Competition" single-shot trap gun had already been overbored to help its gas-relief system lower the recoil level. Unfortunately, this Remington single-shot, low-recoil pumpgun didn't catch on with the public, and its bleeder system demanded constant attention. But the concept of overbored barrels is rampant in trapshooting these days, as well it should be.

A low-recoil mechanism referred to as a "thrust bolt" has begun to alleviate severe recoil in trap guns. The idea was initiated by Al Ljutic and employed in his so-called "Space Gun," but it also is appearing in the new Browning recoilless trap gun. In essence, this involves an inner mechanism which, combined with a strong drive spring, absorbs much of the recoil energy. The Browning also has an overbored barrel for further recoil reduction.

Ammunition makers also have approached the recoil problem with the result being a new lower-velocity level for $1^1/_8$-ounce trap loads known as the "lite" category. At this writing, Federal Cartridge has an "Extra-Lite®," Winchester has a "Super-Lite®," and ACTIV offers an "Ultra-Lite®." The last lite load to be announced is the "Rem-Lite®," and it may be the lowest-recoil load of all.

Whereas the lowest trap-load velocity formerly had been 1,145 fps for the $2^3/_4$ drams equivalent load, the new lite loads move out somewhere around 1,125 fps to 1,135 fps, on average, from a 30-inch test barrel. I have personally chronographed them down to 1,110 fps from an unaltered Model 12 trap gun's barrel. Obviously, any reduction in velocity will produce a corresponding reduction in recoil, because recoil is an action/reaction condition. Interestingly, trapshooters have been enjoying success with these lite loads, even from the 27-yard handicap distance, although just a few seasons ago most tournament trapshooters selected hard-belting three drams equivalent loads for a minimum of 1,200 fps with $1^1/_8$ ounces of hard $7^1/_2$s for handicap, convinced that they needed every last foot-second of velocity to break targets. This change from the most robust target loads to lite rounds stands out as the most radical changes by our "new" shotgunner.

Ammunition makers who turn out lite target loads have taken different approaches to powder selection. Federal Cartridge and ACTIV Industries have tried to work a push-type recoil sensation into the concept by using powders with a moderate burning rate (such as PB) rather than using smaller charges of fast-rate propellants. The idea is that the tandem of slower-rate powder and low chamber pressures will send $1^1/_8$ ounces of shot effectively on its way, despite the lowered pressure and its concomitant lengthened recoil shove. Of course, recoil sensation is a personal matter, and what feels acceptable to me may not be to another shooter.

The point is that the so-called "lite" target loads aren't simply made by shaving powder charges. Upon cutting open Federal and ACTIV lite loads, I found $20^1/_2$ to $21^1/_2$ grains of a powder resembling IMR's PB, which is in sheer weight, rather

To mitigate against recoil, the so-called "lite" target loads (as opposed to *light* target loads) have been developed with somewhat lower velocities.

generous. The difference is the moderate burning rate of the powders employed by Federal and ACTIV, and each shooter must try them himself to determine how the recoil strikes him.

The patterning I have done with lite target loads invariably produces high core densities, which may explain why trapshooters experience such good handicap results with them; for the essence of handicap is tight patterning, and when one gets high pellet densities he can use the No. 7½ pellet for added energy without sacrificing pattern saturation of the clay. Even at a starting velocity of just 1,100 to 1,135 fps, the 7½s carry more than enough energy to 40 to 45 yards for ensured target breakage. All a shooter needs to do is fine-tune his timing to match the lower velocities, which is easy because the sight pictures are virtually identical for loads delivering 1,200 fps and others averaging just 1,125 fps.

For years, my pet project was one-ounce target loads for reduced recoil, and the ammo makers eventually brought out some excellent examples for skeet and trap. Apparently, however, the public wasn't — and still isn't — ready to accept one-ouncers for serious tournament gunning. Although many perfect scores have been run with the one-ounce 12-gauge target loading, most competitive shooters tend to believe they are sacrificing too much by cutting the shot charge by $\frac{1}{8}$ ounce. "I'll use one ounce of shot when everybody else uses one ounce," is the normal remark among trapshooters. Skeet shooters, on the other hand, were more receptive to the concept, and many continue to use one-ounce loads in the 12-gauge gun.

The glory of a one-ounce 12-gauge load is that, regulated for velocities of 1,150 to 1,200 fps, the recoil level is very low. The factories came up with a nominal velocity of 1,185 fps for one-ounce 12-gauge target fodder, and it was extremely pleasant to use. The reason for this reduced recoil, of course, is that it simply requires less energy to get one ounce of shot moving at a given velocity than it does to move a 1⅛-ounce charge equally fast. Thus, there is less of a reaction against the gun at this speed range.

What amuses me is that, while patterning with the newer lite loads and one-ouncers through the same double-bored IM&F, I found that the two types had the same center-packing characteristics and gave about the same overall area coverage. The main difference was that the 1⅛-ounce loads had more shot to stick in the center of the pattern which, in actual squadded trapshooting, ground and reground the targets to the shooter's delight. For all practical purposes, the scoring was the same with one and 1⅛-ounce loads.

I seriously doubt that trapshooters will vote to outlaw the 1⅛-ounce load in favor of one-ouncers, even though that would be one way to break up the "big guns'" stranglehold on handicap wins. Although the one-ounce load is flawless at 16 yards and mid-range handicap, it might suffer some weaknesses from 27 yards, but if I know the typical trapshooter, I'd bet he would sooner re-introduce the former 1¼-ounce load for handicap.

SHOTGUNNING TRENDS IN TRANSITION

When it comes to guns, there are many new developments since Bob Nichols wrote *The Shotgunner*. The unsingle mentioned is just one example of the evolution. During the midcentury, for instance, autoloading shotguns were still considered taboo on trap fields. Some "humpbacked" Browning and Remington long-recoil guns were employed, but generally speaking, most trapshooters didn't like the guy standing alongside him bouncing all those empties off his back, shoulders and head. There weren't shell catchers in those days.

As the twentieth century comes to a close, we find that the late, great Remington Model 1100 changed all that opposition to autoloaders. It became one of the winningest guns in trap. The major reasons behind its acceptance, of course, were control of empties and light recoil. Shell catchers were devised by gun tinkerers to suit the Model 1100 perfectly. As a further feature, Remington placed a small hemispheric lump in the Model 1100's barrel tang to deflect empties downward. These improvements civilized the autoloader as a trap gun. In terms of recoil, the Model 1100's gas system and overall weight damped the setback by bleeding off gases and lengthening the recoil duration. The same attributes are offered by the Model 1100's successor, the Model 11-87.

Some shooters have found the autoloaders a bit heavy up front, due to the gas mechanism and/or barrel walls. One way around this "hang" is overboring. By enlarging the bore's interior diameter, one removes metal to lessen barrel weight. Sometimes this can be quite noticeable, especially if the overbore goes to radical extremes. For example, a nominal overbore takes the 12-gauge to .740 to .745-inch, which removes anywhere from .010 to .020-inch of metal. To some shooters, that might not be a noticeable improvement. In recent years, however, machinists have been going beyond those distances in radical fashion, and I have tested such major overbores with excellent results. At one point I used a 12-gauge Model 1100 barrel overbored to .775-inch, which is the nominal bore diameter of a 10 gauge, and I found it made the gun feel lighter and point somewhat faster. Ballistics of this experiment were detailed in Chapter 11 with a discussion of Stan Baker's Semi-Big Bore. It's one idea for making the weight-forward autoloaders a bit livelier.

One final point must be made relative to the weight distribution in current break-action variety trap guns. Some of these are obese, obnoxious and awkward due to heavily walled barrels. Shooters occasionally select such a gun because it promises a positive follow-through, but they quickly learn that, to their detriment, the gun starts sluggishly, is hard to point accurately, and tires the leading hand, arm and shoulder quickly. Unfortunately, however, gunmakers still follow the old routine of putting a preponderance of weight up front on target-grade break actions, believing that's necessary for optimum smoothness and a forced follow-through.

The Perazzi guns have proved that muzzles don't have to hang like plumb bobs for championship scoring. Perazzi trap guns have some of the thinnest barrel walls in the business, but they win consistently in the hottest competitions. If any target-grade break-action comes close to resembling the responsive between-the-hands

TRAPSHOOTING: THE OLD GREY MARE...

Trapshooting has done some dastardly things to nice shotguns and traditional lines, such as humiliating this Model 1100 with a "tommy gun" grip and a rib structured like a railway trestle, not to mention a radically high, swooping monte carlo. Poor gun!

weight condition of the British game gun, it is the Perazzi Mirage or MX-8 with 29½-inch barrels. Obviously there is more barrel heft in the Perazzi stackbarrels than the Purdeys and Powells, but Perazzi hasn't carried muzzle weight to such an extreme as the American designers and gunmakers.

Even the Perazzi single-shot trap guns are far more dynamic than the heavy-tubed wonders. Italian shooters tend to be fast shots, and the Perazzi models were obviously slanted toward that bias. Thus, although the weight distribution factor is a subtle one for typical trapshooters, it could be the element that helps somebody get more birds.

Trap guns are not all alike, and they shouldn't be evaluated solely by appearances. Check the gun's dynamics by assessing its weight distribution relative to your physical needs, timing and overall technique. Trap guns may not be bird or game guns, but they must move gracefully if a shooter is to excel. The game of trap may have gotten easier and the new loads may kick less, but the new shotgunner isn't going to break any more targets than his grandfather if his gun drags laboriously through its arc!

As previously noted, despite easier targets, higher scores and some cheating, trapshooting remains the most popular stateside shotgun game. Although Sporting Clays is making a pitch for members, I believe that trapshooting will more than hold its own to remain the dominant Yankee clay target sport. It is easy, accessible and affordable. It has an element of discipline about it which enhances organization and administration.

British champion Paul Bentley stated in his book, *Clay Target Shooting*, that Italy has 1½ *million* registered trapshooters (most of whom shoot Olympic trap). That makes America's 40,000 active ATA registered shooters look sick. American trapshooting has a long way to grow *if* it can control its pricing.

D. H. Eaton wrote a book in 1921 entitled *Trapshooting: The Patriot Sport*. That may have carried the interpretation a bit far, but Americans do love their trap. It may not be a patriot's sport per se, but at this time trapshooting has been the most democratic. The game may have little value as hunting practice, with its limited angles, pre-mounted gun and instant target release, but for those who accept the game's challenges, it is the greatest. So be it.

Chapter 16

The International Games Get Tougher

AS EACH NEW Olympiad comes along, nations assemble skeet and trap teams. In some nations there is spirited competition among numerous shooters for team berths, but that has not been the case in the United States where very few people practice the tougher, more demanding International forms of skeet and trap. The vast majority of American clay target enthusiasts spend their time on the domestic versions of each sport because they can run up all those high, ego-gratifying scores on big, soft, slow targets.

One of the latest stateside gun clubs to build a 15-machine International trap "trench" is in the Cincinnati area. It did so at the cost of $35,000, mistakenly predicting that the shooter-rich region would love the challenge. But today the International setup lies fallow, while the trapshooters play their normal 16-yard and handicap games or money events. It appears that American shooters do not have enough pride to strive for continuous improvement; they remain content with their serial 100-straights on lollipop clays. This is quite a contrast to Italy where that little, narrow peninsula of a country has an estimated 1½ million International-style trapshooters.

If Americans feared the toughness of International clay target shooting prior to the 1988 Olympics, they will definitely go into shock now! The World Shooting Sports governing body (UIT) has changed the rules to make International-style events even more difficult. The member nations are apparently not about to let these games be mastered the way American-style skeet and trap have been.

The biggest overall change in International rules is that the UIT voted in favor of reducing the shot charge to 28 grams from the previous 32. That means that, as of January 1, 1989, the one-ounce load became the legal weight. This is a reduction from the previous $1^1/_8$ ounces (which had been a reduction from earlier days when $1^1/_4$-ounce shot loads were standard in International trap). The lighter shot charge may not impact International skeet as much as it does trap, because skeet

SHOTGUNNING TRENDS IN TRANSITION

is a close-range game and permits the use of very fine shot (2mm, or approximately an American No. 9½) which continues to fill out a relatively wide area at 15 to 21 yards. In International trap, however, it will undoubtedly eliminate some cheap "fringe" hits and result in lower scores.

A one-ounce load of nickel-plated No. 7½s or 8s, which are the common pellet sizes for UIT trapshooting, can still fill out a 40-yard pattern that has a two-foot diameter and leave a few pellets beyond. Such a small pattern will demand greater pointing and swinging accuracy, of course, but that's what a world or Olympic champion is supposed to do. Moreover, what most American trapshooters don't realize is that their full-choked trap guns aren't delivering wide, evenly distributed patterns for 16-yard events, either. When utilizing hard, high-antimony shot, American trapshooters using honest full-choked barrels often work with little more than an effective 24 to 26-inch pattern at 16 yards. The foolish part is that Americans simply won't accept a one-ounce load in ATA trap or NSSA skeet because they're afraid of reducing their scores and no longer running 100-straight from 27 yards. Aw-w-w!

Beyond the switch from a 1¹/₈-ounce load to a one-ouncer, there are some other changes which will prevent either sport from becoming a pushover. Let's begin with skeet:

There are significant differences between American skeet as shot under NSSA rules and International skeet as fired under UIT administration. In most respects, the International game is shot the way Americans used to shoot skeet before regular tournament competitors softened the game. Rule modifications through the years, however, have made International an exceedingly difficult game.

Despite the fact that International and American skeet employ the same field dimensions and the same high-house/low-house arrangement, there are four elements in addition to the one-ounce rule that makes UIT skeet a truly challenging game and one that the highly publicized NSSA champions won't touch. These elements are:

1) The trap machines throw targets from 65 to 67 meters (American skeet recommends just a 60-yard flight, and most clubs toss only 55-yard distances).

2) The targets are released during a variable three-second delay (as was once the case stateside), whereas American clays are trapped instantly so that a gunner merely has to time his swing with his call rather than watching for a target.

3) The UIT shooter must hold a lowered gun until the target is released. The 1989 UIT rules require that the gun's stock toe be clearly visible below a permanently secured line (roughly one centimeter wide) running along the crest of the competitor's hipbone.

4) UIT rules have altered the target sequence to include a pair of tough doubles while dropping the cinch low-house 1 target and the singles from Station 7. The International round of skeet goes like this:

Station 1: High house single
Doubles

Station 2: High and low house singles
Doubles

Station 3: High and low house singles
Doubles

Station 4: High and low house singles

Station 5: High and low house singles
Doubles

Station 6: High and low house singles
Doubles

Station 7: Doubles

Station 8: High and low house singles

There is no "optional" shot in International skeet, and the International targets are slightly smaller and harder than American clays in order to withstand launching at significantly higher speeds. Thus, the typical American skeet shooter who breaks 100-straight with the instant target and pre-mounted gun will often do no better than 65 to 70 percent under UIT rules. That makes one wonder what, if anything, the NSSA champions are accomplishing with their easy, repetitive "hundreds"!

International trapshooting, also known as "bunker" or "trench," differs so markedly from American ATA trap that there is little comparison except that the targets come from ground-level machines and fly away from the firing line. In 1989, the target flight for UIT-governed events was from 70 to 80 meters, depending on the flight angle of the respective trap settings. There had been an anticipation of a reduction from 80 meters to 75 meters for the longest flights in deference to the one-ounce load, but that didn't happen. There might be a future distance reduction, though, as shooters gain experience with the one-ounce restriction. These distances of 70 to 80 meters, of course, are significantly farther than anything American trapshooters want, as it implies an ultra-fast start with the target emerging around 100 mph. (As mentioned in Chapter 15, American trapshooters set their traps for a slow release and normal flight of just 48 to 50 yards.)

International trap bunkers are deep with the roof virtually at ground level. The firing line is straight across, not radiused like an American trap line, and there are six shooters in every round, although there are only five stations. The shooter moves after every shot with shooters shifting from left to right, except for the one on Station 5, who comes off the line and walks to the left to begin anew on Station 1.

SHOTGUNNING TRENDS IN TRANSITION

Konrad Wirnhier, the West German skeet champion who won the 1972 Olympic gold medal, demonstrates the low-gun, hip-level starting position mandated by the rules of International Skeet. American skeet shooters are afraid to use this starting position because they won't break so many perfect scores.

THE INTERNATIONAL GAMES GET TOUGHER

Two shots are allowed on every target, no penalty being assessed for a break with the second pattern. In practice, most serious UIT trapmen fire the second shot immediately, even if they break the bird with their first load, to retain their timing.

But the major difference between American and UIT trap, and the reason bunker is so expensive, is that there are three solidly fixed trap machines before each of the five stations, totaling 15 traps. These traps are variously angled, throwing grass cutters to steep climbers, straightaways to wide angles. The shooters not only don't know which trap they'll get from any station, but the larger UIT competitions actually use a computer to ensure that every shooter gets the same angles overall, albeit in different sequences.

There is a tentative move afoot to add another shotgun game to the Olympics. After initial discussions it appears this will be a newly devised version of trap doubles. The doubles event can be staged on the regular bunker layout, which reduces the cost to that of new machine concepts.

The game of UIT trap doubles has not been firmed up as of this writing, but if plans proceed, it will be based upon using the No. 8 trap for a fixed straightaway from Station 3 and replacing trap No. 7 with a Rossini automatic (ball) trap. That trap is similar to the wobble trap occasionally encountered stateside (but never used by shooters who hate to handle unknown targets).

The application of the Rossini trap isn't fully established at this time. It could be designed to throw a "change of pace" target as well as one that oscillates variously. Only time will tell. In fact, by the next Olympiad a different machine might be employed. The point is that UIT trap doubles, shot with one-ounce loads on high-speed targets from a bunker, will be a tremendously challenging game. The second target may be well out by the time one gets to shooting at it, and the one-ouncer's patterns may fail at long range.

The Europeans will play a major role in whether this form of trap doubles is introduced into the Olympics. It is up for discussion, however, and the general Olympic Committee is open-minded to its addition. Watch for the next Olympics to see what develops. It is certain that no one will "run 'em" in this game as they can in ATA trap!

There is no doubt that over/unders have proved their prowess in International gunning. They are heavily favored by UIT shooters, and most modern championships are won by gunners using the vertical double. Nothing on the horizon seems capable of challenging the over/under for that dominance.

Nor can there be any doubt that the new UIT rules will ensure a dearth of participants stateside. Few people ever struggle to be world class shotgunners, just as a paltry few strive to be Olympic rowers, power lifters, discus throwers, speed walkers, figure skaters, or equestrians. Most of those sports fade between

SHOTGUNNING TRENDS IN TRANSITION

Olympiads, too. The unfortunate thing is that more talented American shotgunners who are capable of making a dent in international events, and who could gain some personal satisfaction from rising above the ranks of mediocrity, never bother to hone their skills in a harder game. Instead, they prefer to remain in the pushover Yankee games where they can beat the old folks and lesser talented shooters every weekend.

Anyone who is interested in the art and science of shotgunning, however, can't help but fantasize about mastering the International games and going for the gold. I once broke 96x100 to win an International skeet event, and that occasion stands out in my memory more than the couple of state championships and hundreds I've won and broken in NSSA events. When the going gets tough...

Chapter 17

The Best Game of All: Hunters' Skeet

ALTHOUGH the skeet field was fully evolved in the 1920s, there are many shotgun enthusiasts who haven't yet discovered it. Shortly before I wrote this chapter, I introduced a full squad of shooters to our skeet field. They were like kids with a new toy at Christmas. Where had this game been all their lives? They hit some, missed some and ribbed each other about their accomplishments on each station. Hey, this was fun! They'd be back! And they were.

It has long been my belief that the skeet field is an underrated source of shooting activity. Its potential is great. It can be as much fun as any Sporting Clays layout without anywhere near the cost in land and labor.

Unfortunately, skeet shooting has stuck to the same basic routine, and that has become stale for many regular shooters. It is also somewhat questionable as field-gunning practice for those who like the hunting side of things better than the tournament side, because the pre-mounted gun and speed-up system are geared for competition, not bird shooting.

For a number of summers, I ran a Wednesday evening league which knocked apart NSSA rules and longtime skeet conventions. It was called the Hunters' Skeet League, and it was designed to attract and hold the attention of those who didn't care what the NSSA said or did, namely, bird hunters and guys looking for shotgun fun rather than square-jawed perfection.

The theory behind Hunters' Skeet is to provide chances to use a shotgun in a field-like manner. This is easy on a skeet field, because it already offers every fundamental angle; anything else encountered afield is but an exaggeration of a skeet angle. Indeed, Sporting Clays layouts actually are skeet fields set among the trees with higher high houses (towers) and low houses hidden behind the bushes. If one is out to improve his gun handling for the field, he can develop that technique on a skeet field with ease, and do so at a lower cost than Sporting Clays.

SHOTGUNNING TRENDS IN TRANSITION

Although hunters don't exactly walk around the woods with their guns on their hips (as this shooter holds his in preparation for a Hunters' Skeet target), they don't exactly walk around with a fully shouldered gun, either. The hip-level start is close to reality, as only the toe of the stock need contact the crest of the hipbone.

THE BEST GAME OF ALL: HUNTERS' SKEET

To begin, Hunters' Skeet has a mandatory low-gun starting position *à la* International Skeet, meaning the hip-level contact. As in International Skeet targets are released in a three-second variable routine. No attempt is made to juice up the targets for fast starts, however, as actual bird hunting doesn't involve extreme speeds. A 55-yard target flight is adequate, and I would have no argument with backing that off to 50 yards for beginners, or a league to bring targets more closely in line with real game bird and waterfowl speeds. Most hunters become depressed easily when they miss fast birds.

The station-to-station routine in Hunters' Skeet, as we shoot it, is the same as that listed in Chapter 16 for International Skeet. Once again, however, there can be some variations depending on the individual club's experience in satisfying participants. For example, there is nothing wrong with eliminating Station 8 and using those two shells for a double at Station 4. Likewise, some tampering can be done with distances. Stations 2 through 6 can be moved backward by five to 10 yards for 25 to 30-yard shots. Station 8 also can be moved several yards toward Station 4 for a fast shot, albeit one that isn't so directly overhead (and as difficult for beginners).

Thus far, a sharp reader will surmise that I've mainly described International Skeet with a slower target and, if desired, some station alterations. That's basically correct. But here's where the major difference occurs, and it seems to fascinate field-oriented shotgunners:

Hunters' Skeet permits TWO shots on any singles target except Station 8! And it does not enforce an out-of-bounds rule. As long as the target is in the air, it's legal. This coincides with the field-gunner's way of doing things. Grouse and bobwhite taste the same whether they are hit by the first or second pattern. Besides helping hunters improve their second shot technique, this feature also helps mediocre shooters score more birds and look better.

It is surprising how shotgunners who always shied away from skeet will enjoy Hunters' Skeet. There are groups that will shoot together so they can follow the concept without upsetting, or being upset by, tournament-minded shooters using the pre-mounted, instant-release method. In fact, they prefer their own squad, because they would never set foot on a skeet field if they had to play the tournament shooters' game.

Hunters' Skeet — give it a serious try at your gun club! It catches on quickly as people love this sporty game once they have been exposed to it. It's time to do something new with skeet!

SHOTGUNNING TRENDS IN TRANSITION

Hunters' Skeet requires a hip-level starting position for the gun, which makes the game testy and restores some of its original flavor. This shooter is reacting to the high-house target from Station 2.

PART 4
THE GUNNER

Chapter 18

Advanced Concepts in Sports Vision and Sports Optics

ONE OF THE oldest clichés in shooting is that, "You can't hit what you can't see." Although there are times when sheer luck and a spreading pattern will accomplish more than a hunter's vision deserves, the cliché is a wise one. So is another timeworn bit of advice: "Keep your eye on the bird." The tenets of expert wingshooting dictate that a shotgunner's eyes should always — from flush to follow-through — be focused sharply on the moving target, *never* being brought back to the gun for even the slightest alignment check. In its purest form, shotgunning is a hand-to-eye action. Accuracy results from a well-fitted gun, properly mounted and swung by a pair of hands coordinating with the eyes.

To specialists in sports vision, however, there is more to optimum visual efficiency than either of the clichés implies. The same advanced concepts in eye usage and exercise that have been applied to professional and world class amateur athletics jibe perfectly with shotgunning. Wingshots use their eyes in the exact manner baseball hitters and tennis buffs employ theirs on moving objects. Thus, the transition of sports vision concepts to wingshooting is easily made.

Refinements in sports vision coaching leave the old dictum to "Keep your eye on the bird" in the dust. Things have become more sophisticated, and the entire target — be it a game bird or clay — is now considered too large to be an optimally effective focal point.

The most important contribution sports vision has made to shotgunning is the realization that we must narrow our focal point on the target. Instead of looking at the whole target, which means from the beak to the tip of the tail on game birds, or from the leading to the trailing edge of a clay target, the emphasis is now on something sports vision experts call "centering on the primary zone." The object is to get the shooter's eyes focused well up front on a moving target; the actual focus being sharply zeroed on the leading part of the target. An explanation of centering on the primary zone runs as follows:

SHOTGUNNING TRENDS IN TRANSITION

The human eye cannot focus sharply on objects both near and far. To be consistently successful and theoretically sound, a shotgunner must always focus sharply on the target and see his gun only as a fuzzy blur in peripheral vision.

Authorities in sports vision divide any scene into three different visual zones relative to any given target: the peripheral, the secondary and the primary zones.

The peripheral zone is everything around the target — brush, trees, sky, tall corn, hills, mountains, lakes or flats. In other words, it is basically the total scene a shooter sees if he doesn't narrow his focus sharply; a sort of wide-angle view with nothing emphasized. Practically all hunting shots, and many clay target situations, begin with the hunter seeing a broad, peripheral view.

Once a target appears, however, modern sports vision teaches that the peripheral zone should immediately become a fuzzy blur as the focus bites down hard on the target. That target is divided into two remaining zones, namely, the secondary and the primary. As defined by experts in this specialty, the secondary zone is the entire target. It's the whole ringneck, from the point of its beak to the tip of its tail. If we stopped right there in the use of our eyes, we would be satisfying the maxim "Keep your eye on the bird."

But sports vision is no longer satisfied with just focusing on the entire secondary zone. The technique of proper eye usage has been carried one step further. To satisfy the refinements in sports vision, a shotgunner must narrow his focus even further, zeroing into the primary zone. Essentially, the primary zone of any moving target is its leading edge. Thus, in the case of a flushing ringneck, an advanced wingshot wouldn't merely keep his eye on the bird; he would concentrate his focus more sharply on the bird's head/neck region. If he were a clay target shooter, he would not be satisfied with a total view of the saucer, but would visually clamp down on its leading edge.

Why should a shotgunner make the three-step jump in focusing from peripheral to secondary to primary zones? Because it improves the efficiency of hand-to-eye coordination, narrowing down the point of impact rather than leaving it broad. Even golfers recognize the advantage of using the primary zone; they have begun lining up putts on one precise dimple of a golf ball rather than merely lining up the total ball.

The point is that if a shooter can get his eyes up front on a moving target, he has a better chance of hitting, since his natural coordination will also work up front. Indeed, more than a few ringnecks have been missed because hunters with faulty sports vision technique were transfixed by long, quivering tail feathers and therefore focused behind the bird rather than on its primary zone.

Where does the gun come in? It should be seen as an indistinct, fuzzy blur in the peripheral zone, and the shooter should be only vaguely aware of it. The gun is, after all, just an extension of the leading hand's point; and if the shotgunner is practicing hand-to-eye coordination as he should be, the pointing accuracy will occur almost naturally.

Thus, no attempt should be made to sight with the rib, beads or matted receiver top. Bringing the focus sharply back to the gun causes a phenomenon called physiological diplopia (the doubling of the objects in the field of vision outside the point of primary focus). The result of such double imaging (which can go unnoticed by shotgunners who are unaware that diplopia exists) is cross firing.[1] Thus, the eyes must not be focused back to the gun or back and forth from bird to gun and vice versa. Once focused on the target's primary zone, the eyes must remain there! This will require substantial self-discipline for the millions of self-taught hunters who employ shotguns like rifles and are squinty-eyed, down-the-barrel "aimers." Applying the proper visual technique will require them virtually to start anew, finally putting the correct theory to practice.

The change in focus from the peripheral zone through the secondary zone to the primary point of impact should be done as smoothly as a zoom lens adjusts from wide angle to telephoto. This means most shotgunners must learn to use their eye muscles, as people in general view the world in a broad, wide-angle manner that doesn't condition the eye muscles to focus down sharply. Eye exercises are the solution because convergence, centering and retained focus on a moving mark are done by muscles similar to any other physical action. Indeed, 20/20 vision alone does nothing for a shotgunner unless his eye muscles are conditioned to establish and retain a hard focus on a flying target. When eye muscles are weak, lagging, shifting or drifting of the focus easily occur and can cause a miss.

Several experts in sports vision have developed publications and video equipment to help athletes improve their visual efficiency, and these can all be used in shotgunning.[2] Centering on a fast ball doing 90 mph as it nears home plate, or focusing on a smashing serve from a Wimbledon champion, requires the same visual-physical coordination as does a sharp right target from Station 5 in trapshooting or a Hungarian partridge flushing wildly across the stubble. Delving into the training advice offered by those authorities will help any wingshot, whether he's a dedicated, square-jawed competitor or a weekend hunter.

It would be impossible to list and explain all the possible eye exercises that pertain to wingshooting, but one exercise is particularly well-suited for the constant range changes that are encountered in moving targets. The exercise uses "binocular string." It is comprised of a 10-foot line on which three different colored balls or small fishing bobbers are affixed with two-foot spacing. One end of the string is fixed to a nail or hook, while the opposite end is drawn tight to the shooter's nose. The exercise consists of centering on each ball in turn and holding the focus for at least three seconds before shifting to the next. By forcing the eyes to focus first on the nearest ball, then switch quickly to the second and third balls, a shooter conditions his eye muscles to converge and remain fixed on a target that moves away. Then, by reversing the exercise and focusing from the rear ball to the front one, he conditions his eye muscles to handle the same continued focus on incoming targets. Moreover, the rapid switching from one ball to another enhances one's ability to relocate and center quickly. To practice precise centering on the primary zone, select a specific spot on each ball — the top, left or right edge, or center hole — and zero in on that point rather than merely focusing on the entire ball.

Eye muscles will tire rapidly when initially performing the binocular string exercise, so two minutes are enough at first. Let the eyes' strength build gradually. A hunter may not need more than two minutes of this exercise, as his eye muscles will not be stressed by frequent convergences and fixations, but a clay target marksman should increase his exercise time to at least four minutes to achieve the strength and endurance necessary for 100 to 200-target events. The exercise should be undertaken once a day until conditioning occurs; thereafter the sessions can be reduced to two or three times per week. Whether one is a field shot or a clay target marksman makes no difference, however. The binocular string exercise will improve convergence and centering on moving targets. Additional eye exercises found in books or videotapes won't hurt, either.

Like today's amazing tennis pros, the new shotgunner realizes that vision is an active process that must be learned, understood and commanded like any other muscular action. It is not a passive factor beyond human control. One isn't blessed with naturally fast-focusing eyes, but he can develop and train his focusing muscles to zoom onto the target's primary zone for maximum hand-eye coordination.

Shooting Glass Sophistication

To many shotgunners, shooting glasses are thought of simply as safety devices. Made with hardened lenses, the glasses serve to protect the eyes from stray pellets, chips of clay targets, leaking powder gases from shoddy reloads and the branches one encounters in grouse covers. Those styles with huge lenses also shield the eyes from wind to minimize tearing, and they ward off dust and debris. Those benefits are important, but there are other considerations to take into account when selecting shooting glasses.

Many shotgunners mistakenly believe that the necessary benefits can be realized with cheap sunglasses. But the role of glasses in shotgunning goes well beyond the simplicity of glare reduction and eye protection. To be perfectly blunt, sunglasses are more detrimental to good wingshooting than they are helpful. A more sophisticated understanding of the relationship between eyes and shotgunning technique must be explored.

A primary consideration behind intelligent shooting glass selection — and sunglass rejection — depends upon the necessity of having optimum brightness to enhance target sharpness. If one were to set down a basic rule of thumb regarding lens color selection for shotgun shooting glasses, it would be: *Use the brightest lens that can be worn comfortably*! Comfort means color selection just short of squinting. Of course, this guideline is just the reverse of sunglass selection, in which one selects lens colors to prevent light transmission.

The reason behind using bright lenses is visual sharpness on the target. That is a necessity for the previously discussed technique of "centering" on a moving mark to attain optimum eye-hand coordination. If one's eyes cannot focus sharply on the target's leading edge, maximum timing and coordination won't be achieved, either. Bright lenses with a high degree of light transmission assist sharp focusing by causing the pupil to contract; this provides the same sharpness and lengthened depth of field as that from a camera lens when it is set at a tiny aperture (such as f:22 when compared to the wider f:2 setting). On the other hand, dark lenses with poor light transmission cause the pupil to dilate which reduces depth of field and sharpness. Therefore, optimum eye-hand coordination occurs when the pupils contract but without squinting.

How much light are we talking about? Experts suggest that 75 to 90 percent light transmission is a working range. That eliminates the dark greens and grays which are so popular with casual hunters and shooters, because those colors provide only 20 to 30 percent light transmission. Thus, the greens and dark grays may appear "cool" on one's eyes, but they force the pupils to dilate; and as a consequence, they are not optimum even on sunny days. For improved eye-hand coordination and the sharpest vision, other colors excel.

Before explaining those brighter and better colors, however, it must be pointed out that a 92 percent light transmission is basically maximum through any shooting glass of the non-reflecting type. Even clear lenses will provide only 92 percent transmission if they reflect light. From that point on, any tint or coloration reduces the light transmission below 92 percent. In many respects, however, a clear-lensed shooting glass isn't bad for hunting. It provides the hunter with protection and some of the subtleties mentioned previously while also providing adequate light transmission on most days and natural colors. For years I hunted in the Midwest with clear lensed, prescription-ground shooting glasses of the Bausch & Lomb 62mm variety, and they worked well on the many dark, dull and cloudy days. I can think of a lot worse glasses for waterfowling, grouse hunting in thickets, and midwinter skeet and trap.

Although other colorations may result in slightly greater light transmission loss than clear lenses afford, there is something to be gained from a color such as gold. When made for a 10 to 15 percent light transmission, gold lenses add an element of brightness to a dark day that keeps the pupils contracted for sharp focusing. A current Gold-10 lens delivers 90 percent light transmission, while a Gold-15 transmits 85 percent. Both are ideally suited for drab days and/or for people whose eyes can use all the help they can get. Many champion clay target shooters wear gold lenses even on bright days to ensure sharpness via eye contraction. Unless it is an extremely brilliant day with glittery, high-pressure air, I can wear Gold-15 under sunny skies without discomfort; and despite the seeming incongruity, I score better at skeet and trap or Sporting Clays with them than with greens or grays that reduce light transmission. For grouse and quail hunting, where the action isn't against the skyline, gold is an extremely efficient color for wingshooting's requisite eye-hand coordination.

Note that I am discussing gold-colored lenses, not Kalichrome®. When I wear gold shooting glasses, I can remove them to find that my eyes see normally and colors are accurate. When I use Kalichrome, however, my eyes rebel. Upon removal of the shooting glasses, green grass will appear reddish. This may be a function of my personal vision, but I've heard the same reports from other shooters who have had problems with Kalichrome. Do not confuse the two!

When shooting (such as dove hunting) is done against the sky, a new color called Bronze I comes in handy. This is a mixture of brown and gold which allows 75 percent light transmission while still offering enough brightness to keep the focus sharp. In general, Bronze I is ideal for shooters in the South and Southwest. It also is excellent for skeet shooting throughout the nation on sunny days, as much skeet is shot against the sky. for trapshooting, which remains a relatively low-level game, Bronze isn't as popular as a lot of other concepts, but it can get the job done.

Trapshooting actually is a very specialized game when it comes to lens selection. Although there is the obvious necessity of having a high degree of light transmission for focusing acuity, a prevailing trend has been toward colors which produce contrast. In other words, the glasses make the clay saucer stand out boldly for easier clarification of the ground-figure relationship. Since current American trapshooting has gone almost universally to the blaze orange target, most shooting glass lenses have been tested for optimum contrast with that color target. Vermillion makes the blaze orange targets stand out boldly, and I have warmed to it even for Sporting Clays stands in the woods when the vermillion permits a light transmission of at least 70 percent. Less transmission darkens the overall scene. Other colors have come along to enhance contrast and these are commonly known among shooters and opticians who service shooters as Target Orange and Target-Sun. Target Orange needs no explanation as to color; it is indeed orange, and it can be made in varying degrees of darkness. Target-Sun is a combination of gray and vermillion that comes out purple, and it is also made in light, medium and dark shades. In general, both Target-Sun and Target Orange accomplish their goals and have done their share of winning in American trapshooting. Most shooters stick with the light and medium shades of orange or purple to obtain the brightness needed for sharp focusing. Were I an ardent trapshooter, I would want both Target-Sun and vermillion in my kit.

For hunters and clay target shooters who think they *must* have green lenses, the best recommendation is the so-called "high" green with a light transmission of about 70 percent. Green obviously won't give target contrast regardless of the color of the mark being thrown, but it does give normal coloration of everything while still providing generally adequate light transmission on bright days. This 70 percent transmission, however, is as low as one should go if he wants to retain a contracted pupil condition for visual sharpness. (Shotgunners wishing to learn more about the light transmission levels of various shooting lens colors can write

SHOTGUNNING TRENDS IN TRANSITION

to Allan Lehman Optical Co. (3125 N. 34th Place, Phoenix, AZ 85018). Lehman specializes in sports optics, and he has a mobile office in which he spends the summer traveling to major skeet and trap tournaments. He always has state-of-the-art information and products, whereas most local opticians don't know anything about specialized shooting "specs."

Two new concepts in shooting glasses were breaking just as this book was being completed. One is called the "blue blocker," and the second is the "Reflection Free®" lens by Silor Optical. I have spent several months using both, and they are worth considering.

The blue blockers began as an unheralded aid to those few people who were sensitive to blue light waves. For years, it was a low-volume business unaffiliated with sports. In recent years, however, blue blockers have become very popular among shooters, because they not only shield one's eyes from the blue and ultraviolet waves, but also subtly help sharpen one's vision.

Experts like Al Lehman explain that blue light rays tend to fall somewhat short of the retina, thus causing blurring. This shortfall confuses the eye while creating minor problems with the other light rays as well. Hence, overall sharpness can suffer. But when a shooter wears blue blockers, the blue rays are eliminated to clear up this problem; the other light rays entering the eye now strike the retina sharply for more precise eye-to-brain images. As technology advances, it is predicted that blue-blocking will be available for every lens color. I have never had problems with the blue rays, but I thoroughly enjoy Target-Sun (lite and medium) and vermillion (medium) with the blue blocker feature. Bronze I and Bronze II with blue blockers may also interest some shooters, especially skeet shooters who look against the sky for their targets.

Just coming on line in the U.S. is something Silor Optical calls "Reflection Free" coating. These lenses provide the greatest amount of light transmission and they are exceptional for driving, hunting and shooting on dark days when no lens coloration is wanted. They also will work well for trapshooting under the lights, although Gold-15 also is excellent under the lights. Whereas reflection-prone lenses reflect about 8 percent of the light, Reflection-Free lenses admit about 99.5 percent of available light! Moreover, Reflection-Free lenses reduce, if not eliminate, the various "ghost images" that drift about with normal lenses. The rest of the world is well ahead of the United States in its application of non-reflecting lenses.

There are other advantages besides light transmission and target contrast built into bona fide shotgunning glasses. One ultra-important feature is that they sit higher than do sunglasses. On some shooting glasses, the top of the frame and the brow bar ride above the eyebrows, which is desirable. When a wingshot gets his head down properly on the comb of a gun stock, his head almost inevitably is tilted somewhat forward, and the high-sitting frame and bar remain out of his line of vision as his eyes roll up. Sunglasses and reading glasses, on the other

ADVANCED CONCEPTS IN SPORTS VISION AND SPORTS OPTICS

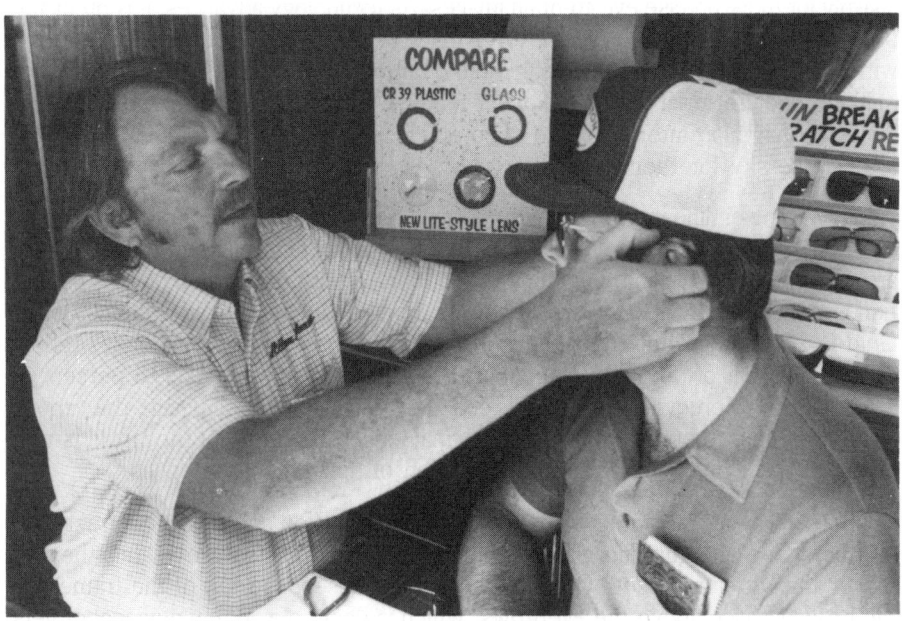

Allan Lehman, whose mobile office visits the major trap and skeet tournaments in the U.S., has done much to advance the best in sport optics, including the blue blocking concept and non-reflecting lenses. Here he fits a shooter while attending a clay target event.

hand, have frame lines and brow bars that hang low and normally contact the eyebrow level. They normally will sag down into the upper field of vision as a shotgunner settles into position. The current, stylish Hy-Wyd design emphasizes the high-sitting brow bar and is a favorite with thousands of clay target gunners. So, too, does the Decot fashion place the frame up to free the entire field of view.

Whenever possible, serious shotgunners should select glasses which place the lenses ahead of the frames. This permits space for air circulation, and minimizes fogging. Unfortunately, there are very few models that provide this feature, the Hy-Wyd being the best example. If the Bausch & Lomb shooting glasses have any shortcoming, it is that their rims enclose the lenses, thus bringing the lenses back toward the face to cause some contact and fogging directly under the brow bar. Sunglasses also tend to fit too snugly for air circulation. Many of them actually have the fashionable frames set forward so far that they push the lenses backward toward the face rather than ideally away from it.

Few sunglasses have optical centers or properly ground lenses, although both are required for optimum vision. In fact, sunglasses often have flat lenses and are sized with no concern for the individual shooter's facial dimensions. Flat lenses are especially worthless. The human eye is known as a 6-curve eye, and lenses should match that curvature. This is true whether the lens is prescription or plano. The eyes' geometry should be followed in plastic or glass lenses (the technical term being "ophthalmic" for lenses so ground).

But even curved lenses aren't the final necessary feature. Lens size should fit the individual's face so that accurate optical centers (pupillary distance) can be enjoyed. This matching of the lens size to the face is necessitated by the knowledge that each lens size tends to have a different optical center after grinding. If the finished product is to fit the individual shooter's optical centers, the starting blanks must be correctly chosen by the technician. The fellow who runs the local sport shop normally isn't an expert in fitting glasses; therefore, serious wingshots should have a professional optician make the measurements before ordering even if they don't need prescription work. Measurements can be especially vital here because, even with plano lenses, the optical centers of shooting glasses are set variously higher than they are in reading glasses to compensate for the head's forward tilting.

Once a pair of shooting glasses has been professionally fitted to a given shooter, he must make every attempt to keep them adjusted so that the eye-to-lens distance remains constant. The industry employs a 12 millimeter distance between the eye and the lens, and slippage of just a fraction of an inch can upset the power. For example, people with prescription lenses ground for myopia (nearsightedness) will lose power if the lenses slide forward, while those with correction for hyperopia (farsightedness) will gain power as the lenses slip ahead. Keeping the glasses in place relative to the 12 millimeter fitting distance means the frame needs adjustable nose pads, brow bar and wraparound temple pieces so they can be made to jibe with the individual shooter's anatomy. Without adjustable nose pads and brow bar, the frames cannot be elevated to suit the high placement of the optical centers of ground shooting glasses. Under no condition should a shotgunner relax the wraparounds to relieve pressure around his ears, as that obviously invites frame slippage and the concomitant power variables. Instead, slip-on temple covers are recommended to provide comfort on wire frames. Plastic-framed sunglasses seldom, if ever, have these adjustable features and/or adequate wraparounds to fit and hold lenses in place, which is another reason to avoid them like the plague for optimum shotgunning vision.

Maintaining shooting glasses requires periodic checks of screws and frequent cleaning. Small maintenance kits can be purchased with the proper tools for fine slot-heat screws. Use care in snugging down the screws so that the soft heads aren't abused.

When cleaning shooting glasses, realize the lenses can be "sandpapered" by microscopic dust and sand which accumulates on outdoor glasses. This is especially true of plastic lenses, which scratch easily. *Never* wipe them with a dry tissue or cloth. Always wet or flush lenses first to float away the grit. Dip them in a stream or a pond, pour water on them from a canteen, or rinse them under a faucet at the gun club. Lenses made of glass are less prone to scratching, of course, but some tender loving care won't hurt them, either.

There undoubtedly will be further improvements in sports vision and sports optics. There are already some extra-hard plastics in the works; these will be lighter and, for many prescriptions, thinner. Also of interest is a protective coating that combats ultraviolet radiation. Do not misunderstand ultraviolet protection to mean glare reduction or decreased light transmission due to darkened lenses. Ultraviolet radiation is neither glare nor brightness. You don't see it or notice it, as it is not light per se. Rather, ultraviolet is an invisible radiation that becomes a problem because it accumulates into photochemical eye damage, eventually causing such things as cataracts, macular degeneration, solar retinitis and corneal dystrophies. Opticians like Allan Lehman can have lenses coated with an anti-ultraviolet protectant without upsetting lens colors or light transmission. Anyone who spends a lot of time outdoors exposes his eyes to potentially dangerous ultraviolet radiation, of course, and having lenses coated to shield against it is the ounce of prevention that is worth more than a pound of cure. Don't consider ultraviolet protection as something that makes immediate vision more comfortable; think of it as a long-term measure against eye diseases.

Thus, the specialized fields of sports vision and sports optics have become important integral parts of modern shotgunning, providing us with eye-use techniques that refine eye-hand coordination and glasses which sharpen our vision so that optimum eye-hand coordination can take place. Hunters and casual clay target shooters who fail to take an in-depth look at these specialties will never experience the optimum degree of wingshooting finesse.

Chapter Notes

1. The subject of physiological diplopia, plus all the scientific aspects of sports vision, are treated with relevance to the shotgunner's problems in the exceptional softcover, *An Insight to Sports Featuring Trapshooting*, by Wayne F. Martin, O.D. (SportsVision, Inc., Seattle, WA. 1984). Discussion of diplopia is found on pp. 31-35.

2. Two books useful to study of sports optics are: *Easy Eye Exercises for Better Vision* by Dr. Wayne F. Martin, O.D. (Michael Windolph, Exposition Press, Hicksville, NY. 1974), and *Eye Power*, by Ann and Townsend Hoopes (Alfred A. Knopf, New York, NY. 1979).

Chapter 19

Sports Psychology Comes to Shotgunning

HE WAS A trapshooter and a mighty serious one. In fact, there was nothing he wanted to do more than go out to the club and work over 50 targets. His game had been blunted by a nasty Midwest winter, it needed sharpening, and just pounding away some reloads would have salved his case of cabin fever. But it was Tuesday evening, he had arrived home late because a fresh six-inch snowfall had snarled traffic, and he still had to shovel the walk and driveway. After that, he was scheduled to spend the remainder of the evening baby-sitting, as his wife was headed for choir practice. So much for honing the old trapshooting technique?

Not in this day and age! For after the wife had scampered off and the baby was sleeping, our trapman got down to some serious work on his game. He stretched out on a soft sofa, gave a sigh of relief, snapped on a stereo cassette player and relaxed to a tape which, although it sounded like little more than surf breaking on a rocky beach, was really loaded with subliminal commands to bombard his subconsciousness with all the right stuff. Then when he got back to actual shooting, his mental game would be intact. The tape's subliminal fare instructed him to "Keep your head down," "Start smoothly with the target," "Keep your eyes on the bird," and "Follow through," plus other important commands.

An oddball way to practice for a trapshoot? Perhaps to a casual hunter, a once-a-year clay target shooter, or a sportsfan with only superficial knowledge of training methods, but not to someone who is alert to modern sports psychology, as are many current clay target gunners. Without a doubt, it is the mental game which is being emphasized these days. Physical techniques and new equipment aside, it is still the person who must make the moves. Athletes in every specialty realize this need for a tough, motivated mental game, and the trend has continued into shooting.

If one were to skim the magazines directed toward tournament shooters — *Trap & Field*, *The Skeet Review* and *Shotgun Sports* — he would find numerous listings

SHOTGUNNING TRENDS IN TRANSITION

Specialized tapes of both the audible and subliminal varieties have been produced to enhance the shotgunner's mental game.

of such tapes. While some are subliminal, others aren't. The specialized topics they cover will surprise most hunters and casual behind-the-barn shooters. Some tapes are made to help shooters overcome mental blocks through the use of self-hypnosis, some strive to establish positive frames of mind, while others instruct shooters on how to overcome a flinch. Additional tapes "program" one's mind with advice for trap doubles, conventional skeet, or skeet doubles from all stations. And there are more.

A typical hunter may scoff at this fancy mental preparation. "All I need is my grandfather's old long-barreled pump and I'll get my ducks," he'll boast. But today's tournament shooters aren't after ducks. Indeed, some of our most active clay target competitors aren't hunters and have no intention of going after any form of game. They are marksmen — competitors who shoot for the same reason that others bowl, golf or play tennis; as a challenge and for pride in accomplishment. And since one target more or less is normally the difference between winning or losing, dedicated tournament (and money) shooters will try anything for that winning edge. If "programming" their mind by the use of subliminal tapes will produce perfect scores, so be it.

When used in its generic sense, of course, the concept of a mental game isn't new. Coaches have long stressed that, "More than half of the game is mental; you've got to concentrate!" For many people, however, the question has always been: concentrate on what? What is suddenly different is the way advanced technology and sophisticated mental training techniques have refined sports psychology and its applications so that workaday people in evening leagues can employ methods of sports psychology akin to those of the finest world class athletes. These tapes and procedures no longer leave a beginner dangling on a string, unable to straighten out his jumbled mind for improved concentration; they streamline the process with *the* vital points, and do so while you're in the comfort of your own home, baby-sitting.

But there's more to refining a mental game than merely snoozing on a sofa while some tape talks your subconscious into becoming a better shot. In effect, that's a passive method; the initiative comes from outside the shooter, and all he or she does is relax and absorb it while the little cassette spins. Putting the entire mental *and* physical games together requires additional active work which comes from within the shooter himself.

Visualizing and Imaging

Unless one has followed the course of high-level sports psychology for athletic training, he probably hasn't heard of visualizing or imaging. Essentially, both words mean the same thing. They are the practice of running through detailed mental rehearsals of physical actions to be done under pressure and specific conditions. This is an active practice/training session, as the competitor must generate the vision or image himself and carry it to such a depth that he actually feels himself

SHOTGUNNING TRENDS IN TRANSITION

going through the movement, generally visualizing in a slow-motion pace so that all components of the move fall correctly into place. Do not confuse visualizing and imaging with daydreaming or wishful thinking! It is neither. It is, as stated above, a serious, detailed run-through of the action on a purely mental basis.

Remember the petite Olympic gymnast who paced about with her chin on her chest as she waited to be called for the vault? Or recall the high-jumper who was poised, head down as if in a trance, before starting his run toward the bar? Dilettantish spectators would pass that off as simple concentration, however, anyone with an esoteric knowledge of modern athletics would know that they were visualizing. They were running their entire technique through their brains and bodies, in effect taking some jumps (experience) before starting their approaches. Visualization is not only a mental rehearsal, but, like the subliminal tapes discussed earlier, can program the body for correct execution. Whether visualizing is practiced just before a jump or weeks ahead of time makes little difference in its theoretical and practical applications; it imbues the brain and body with a *pre*-played scenario.

That visualization brings the entire body into harmony cannot be questioned. Researchers using sensitive electronic gear find that they pick up muscle impulses in sequence with the visualized action of an athlete going through the systematic mental rehearsal of a routine. Moreover, the power of visualization to improve and maintain performance is proved by the story of rifleman Robert Foster, who had been a U.S. national rifle champion and world record holder before entering the Army. Assigned to a non-combat post in Vietnam, he spent a year without any actual practice and without his tournament guns. To compensate for this lack of range work, Foster spent some time each day — perhaps 10 to 15 minutes — visualizing his shooting. Upon returning home, he went to an important match with virtually no range practice. He not only won the match, but broke his former world record in doing so! He had been able to maintain his hold-and-squeeze technique solely by in-depth visualization. Thus, psychologists have learned that visualizing some action clearly and vigorously will cause our bodies to react as if we were actually doing it.

Obviously, visualization can help shotgunners. By getting deeply inside oneself and visualizing a shotgun swing on passing mallards, skeet's high house target from Station 2, or the sharp right from trapshooting's Station 5, one can analyze technique flaws, make corrections and blend the correct moves into the whole swing program *without* firing a shot. Just think, the new champion could reach his heights by visualizing while commuting to work. And while a snowbound Midwesterner waits out winter on a soft sofa, he could visualize his way from a 95 percent shooter to a 99 percent champion.

There is room for visualization at the gun club, too. Both skeet and trap give the gunner ample time between shots and stations to visualize their next target and to make a run-through for the physical move it will necessitate. With that potential for pre-playing the shot and instructing the body how it must move, a shooter should be geared for the target and the ensuing swing. To a certain degree, skeet is a more natural proving ground for visualization than trap, because one always knows the skeet clay's exact flight; be it low-gun International skeet or the easier brand of high-gun American skeet, the next shot can always be imagined while a gunner waits his turn or reloads and adjusts his foot position between singles targets. Indeed, visualization is one good reason to load singly in skeet whenever possible, as many skeet misses come when shooters go slapdash from the high house target immediately to the low house without visualizing. This is especially true when shooters chamber two loads in a double and go through the rapid-action "Pull!" *Bang!* "Mark!" sequence with nothing but a mental blank for the low house bird. Therefore, even if one does chamber a pair of loads for skeet singles, he should always lower the gun between targets and pause a second or two so that the mental pre-play of visualization can provide him with the exact feel of the next shot. Once he has imagined the shot and felt his body develop the movement, he can remount for a fresh start.

Trapshooters like to argue that one cannot visualize in their game, that trap is so much tougher than skeet because one never knows where the target is going. The fact is, however, that trapshooting remains pretty much of a grooved game, and visualizing can definitely come into play and be employed efficiently. For example, trapshooters standing on stations 1 and 2 know that they'll never get a right-angled target, that they'll never get a target coming directly at them, and that they'll never get a perfect 90 degree deflection shot. Because of the two-hole trap machine setting so popular these days, shots from stations 1 and 2 almost invariably are left angles launched within a very narrow area. The shooter may not know the precise degree of angle the target will take, but it will be between a straightaway and a mild left angle. Consequently, a shooter can advantageously imagine a left-angle move and have his body prepared well in advance.

The reverse is true from stations 4 and 5, from which the trapshooter gets essentially right-angle targets. The only station which presents both rights and lefts in trap is Station 3, and these angles are so slight that one can succeed by visualizing the appearance of the target and keying the start of the swing with that visual stimulus.

Personally, I believe that we have so many low-scoring trapshooters because they have psyched themselves into believing that their game is terribly difficult and because they have virtually blank minds when calling for their targets. Applying some intelligence and learning to visualize can dramatically improve a trapshooter's annual average. To stand with a shouldered shotgun telling yourself, "I don't know where it's coming from and I don't know where it's going," is just plain dumb. Thus, for a trapman, concentration should mean getting the feel for a shot into a general direction.

Trapshooters who "read" trap machines are miles ahead of the game, and they can apply visualization to an even finer degree. Just knowing the trap will be pointed to the left at release is a big help in establishing the mental rehearsal for a shot in 16-yard or handicap. Of course, trap doubles are always known angles, and as such they are readily visualized. It doesn't take a "natural" athlete to run winning scores in trap for skeet doubles. All that is necessary is some visualizing to get the body flowing through a sequence from target to target; something a typical, non-athletic shotgunner can develop if he will make intelligent use of his brain in pre-playing the swing.

At present, the game of Sporting Clays is breaking upon the American scene. For a time we are bound to hear that it is much tougher than trap or skeet, as well it might be; for Sporting Clays must be shot with a low-gun starting position. Because each club can have its own stands that vary from the next club's, it will be difficult to learn one particular "groove" the way American skeet and trap shooters have done. But visualization will soon enter Sporting Clays, and scores will rise considerably.

The forte of any Sporting Clays competitor will always be a solid mount-and-swing technique that can be applied universally. Given that technique, the next step is visualizing it relative to the constantly changing challenges strung out along a Sporting course. The shots in Sporting Clays aren't pop-up surprises, of course. Each stand gives everyone in the squad the same targets from fixed traps throwing known angles. This repetitiousness lends itself to the use of visualization, for after seeing the sample targets or watching the first shooter's birds, a gunner can begin to visualize the moves he must make to handle those targets, and he can pre-play them to generate the correct coordination and timing. People who do poorly at Sporting Clays are, like low-scoring trapshooters, those who make no effort to pre-play their specific movement for a given station. They will play like hunters expecting a surprise flush, and they'll automatically do all sorts of missing due to slow starts and poke and hope moves.

There is absolutely nothing illegal or unethical about honing one's mind/body complex for optimum wingshooting results, just as there is nothing illegal or unethical about a professional golfer or an Olympic gymnast visualizing the next move. The old idea about "shooting dumb" has been disproved by modern training methods. The new shotgunner will use the wealth of information gleaned from the development of Olympians to enhance his tournament scores, his personal ability, and even his game bag.

You can't visualize afield? Yes, you can! It often seems to take forever for a wedge of geese to come over, and in that time you can visualize the shooting action before you stand up in the pit. You can imagine the long forward allowance, the accelerating swing and the positive follow-through. You can have the same images help you rehearse for doves coming into a water tank or mallards passing above the pin oaks. It isn't cheating. The NFL's place kickers visualize their technique before the ball is snapped, and NBA forwards visualize free throws before the referee hands them the ball.

Thus visualization, alias imaginal practicing, is a proven method among sports psychology experts, and shotgunners would be less than intelligent if they ignored it. By concentrated visualizing, always correlating it with muscles to "feel" the action, a shotgunner can work out a basic technique, correct or find errors, and keep the swing honed despite a lack of practice. Visualizing can also be applied on a broader, long-term scale when a shooter envisions himself in a future tournament and adjusting to a different background. Likewise, visualization can help one overcome various intimidating elements so that one's entire attention can be focused on the correct execution of a shot rather than being upset by a background, weather condition or another shooter. Finally, because it is active rather than passive practice, visualization can be a source of motivation.

One of America's early psychologists, William James, said that, "We learn to skate in the summer and to play tennis in the winter." Since there were no indoor tennis courts for winter play or indoor skating rinks for summer practice in James' heyday of the late nineteenth century, it is obvious that he was referring to the brain's role in mulling through and perfecting one's knowledge of a given athletic move. Then when the athlete returned to the field, court or rink, he or she would be a better performer, polished by mental activity. Thus, the shooter who puts his or her gun away and believes that improvement is possible only by blasting shells is dead wrong!

The trapshot who has problems with the wide right target from Station 5 often thinks that his only salvation will be locking the trap and standing on Post 5 for a full case of shells, but that's all a waste of time unless substantial mental work is invested, too. In fact, if the same shooter learned to visualize, he could learn much about handling the wide right without firing a shot! It could be done on the slow-motion replay and pre-play screen in his mind.

All this use of tapes, visualization, and imaging does not preclude the need for shooting practice, of course. The game — mental and physical — must be joined together, but one vital point must be made about application of visualization in actual shooting. Once the shooting act has started, the emphasis on visualizing must be dropped. That is the time to let the body and mind apply what has been programmed into them by tapes and visualization. There's simply no time to be systematic and thoughtful about physical technique when skeet's High 2 is streaking away or trap's wide right is disappearing. And there especially isn't time to think about minor techniques when a pair of Sporting Clays targets are whipping through the trees. That's when you go to work and let muscle memory do its job. Let the good times roll, and don't focus on minor technique points when you're on the line.

Modern sport psychology has employed new methods to extend the performances of athletes, and it will do the same for shotgunners who delve into the field. The methods employed for overcoming undue anxieties and choking in other sports will also fit the shotgun game. Many excellent books provide exceptional

SHOTGUNNING TRENDS IN TRANSITION

Sports psychology, including the technique of visualizing or imaging, has become a big factor in competitive athletics. The books on sports psychology can also help shotgunners improve their performances.

in-depth coverage of the noteworthy improvements in sports psychology.[1] Meanwhile, that tape cassette — play it again, Sam!

Chapter Notes

1. Some excellent sports psychology books include:

   Pulos, Lee, "Athletes and Self-Hypnosis," as found in Klavora, Peter and Daniel, Juri V., eds., *Coach, Athlete, and the Sport Psychologist*, Champaign, IL: Human Kinetics, 1979, p. 151.

   Bell, Dr. Keith F., *Championship Thinking*, Englewood Cliffs, NJ: Prentice-Hall, Inc., 1983.

   Dr. Bell's book presents modern trends in sports psychology which will prove interesting reading for shotgunners with a competitive spirit. Dr. Bell is a competitive swimmer and his book covers a multitude of important subjects as they relate to image practicing, motivation, confidence and anxiety handling.

   Syer, John and Connolly, Christopher, *Sporting Body — Sporting Mind*, London and New York: Cambridge University Press, 1984.

   This paperback covers the same topics as Dr. Bell's book. Shotgunners interested in improving their clay target scores would do well to read either or both books.

   Scott, Dr. Michael D. and Pelliccioni, Jr., Louis, *Don't Choke: How Athletes Can Become Winners*, Englewood Heights, NJ: Prentice-Hall, Inc., 1982.

   In a brief 125 pages, the authors blend together all sorts of psychological methods for overcoming negative approaches and anxieties that often lead to an athlete's losses. This book is especially suited to shotgunning, as skeet and trap are perfectionists' games, which (according to Scott and Pelliccioni) can cause the choking phenomenon.

   Hanson, Dr. Peter G., *The Joy of Stress*, New York and Kansas City: Andrews, McMeel & Parker, 1985.

   For shooters who feel that tournament shooting is too stressful, Hanson's book can help one learn how to utilize the energies of a stressful situation for positive rather than negative results.

   Tutko, Thomas and Tosi, Umberto, *Sports Psyching*, Los Angeles, CA: J. P. Thatcher, Inc., 1976.

   A succinct text involving self-analysis and methods of overcoming psychological barriers to improved and consistent performance.

Chapter 20

Can We Cure a Flinch with Amino Acids?

THE TARGET is up and flying, you're swinging smoothly after it, building up gun speed and getting out in front. In that split instant when everything is right, you give the mental command to shoot — but the gun doesn't go off! Every muscle fiber in your body explodes except those associated with your trigger finger; they don't move! You simply can't pull that trigger. The rest of your body, however, lunges forward to counter the anticipated recoil, and if you're a clay target shooter using a slight weight-forward stance, you practically nose-dive off the station. If you're a beginner reacting to some of your first shotgunning, you'll lower the gun and ask what's wrong.

In either case, you've flinched, my friend. Welcome to the club!

If there is such a thing as a disease in shotgunning, it is flinching. In layman's terms, it has been called a short circuit of the nervous system, but psychologists, psychiatrists and medical doctors can no doubt attach much fancier labels to it. Despite the professional terminology, however, no branch of science has yet cured a single case of flinching to perfection. Overcoming a flinch remains a challenge, and after I became a chronic flincher in the 1970s I took up that challenge seriously. Call it an obsession if you wish, but I've tried numerous methods to combat the flinch. More and more, I am reaching the conclusion that it is a chemical condition that can be treated through nutrition. But let's start at the beginning...

There are really two forms of shotgun flinching. One is the "I-can't-pull-it" flinch, which will simply be called the *trigger flinch* herein. It is the kind of flinch described in the opening paragraph of this chapter: The shooter is totally unable to pull the trigger even though he has mentally commanded the shot. The trigger flinch is a widespread affliction in trapshooting, less so in skeet, and even rarer in hunting and Sporting Clays. Hunters may make some trigger flinches without realizing it; they'll blame the gun, claiming they applied trigger pressure but it didn't go off, or believing that the safety was still on.

The second type of flinch is the *leading hand flinch*. It sometimes occurs by itself, yanking the gun down sharply. However, the leading hand flinch is also tied in with the trigger flinch, occasionally yanking the gun down when the trigger finger fails to work. A chronic flincher will commit both the trigger flinch and the leading hand flinch. The combination of both often occurs enough to make the most dedicated shotgunner think of quitting the clay target games.

For the first half of the twentieth century, it was a common belief that flinching was solely the result of too much recoil pain. Theory had it that the shotgunner's subconscious rebelled against further pain and, therefore, overrode the conscious mental command and halted the trigger pull. The standard advice from old-time shooters and writers was to rest or use a smaller gauge. The absence of pain, it was thought, would salve the abused psyche and cure the flinch. Would that it were so!

Switching to a smaller gun or taking a lengthy break from all shooting doesn't seem to negate a flinch. Both have been tried by ardent gunners to no avail. I once laid off clay target shooting for five months only to flinch on my initial round at the very first target of Station 1 in skeet. From my observations of active shotgunners, then, flinching becomes a chronic ailment. New shotgunners can't rely on the venerable advice to beat a flinch by resting or shooting a smaller bore. More advanced solutions are needed.

As sports psychology entered the scene, shooters dreamed up more reasons for flinching. Pain no longer explained it thoroughly. The psychological interpretations included greed, haste, intense desire, the fear of missing and the fear of losing. The fear of missing involved a complicated explanation. Those who proffer it as a cause of flinching argue that it is a defense mechanism, for if the body doesn't actually pull the trigger, the brain safeguards the psyche and ego from a miss. If you don't shoot, you don't miss! Unfortunately, the target sailing merrily along argues differently!

The problem with applying sports psychology to flinching is that the psychological causes can be so myriad that it would take a lifetime to ferret out *the* mental origin. While I do believe that psychological factors can contribute to a flinch or a choke, I'm personally not prepared to assign them paramount importance.

The Neurotransmitter Theory

I have long believed that flinching with a shotgun was a more sophisticated phenomenon than that covered by old-time beliefs about recoil pain and/or by pure psychological implications. Why would some shooters flinch 4 to 5 times in a round of 25 trap targets, while others went through an entire career without flinching once? Why would some have monstrous flinches with a .410? And very importantly, why does the release trigger practically (but not entirely) obliterate the flinch? There were too many questions for me to let the topic lie.

CAN WE CURE A FLINCH WITH AMINO ACIDS?

One thing that bothered me was that I could shoot almost perfectly with a release trigger, whereas I would flinch 3 to 4 times in a round of skeet if I used the same gun and loads with a pull trigger in place. For those who don't know, release triggers function just the opposite of the normal pull triggers: The shooter pulls them back as he prepares to call for his clay target, then releases it when he wishes to fire. People who haven't used release triggers immediately get the impression that they're dangerous or difficult to use, but the reverse is basically true. A tremendous number of trapshooters employ releases quite safely and effectively, and there are some skeet shooters who must also use them to avoid flinching. In a recent book, *An Insight to Sports Featuring Trapshooting* (1984), Dr. Wayne F. Martin, O.D., firmly endorsed the release trigger because of the way it lends itself to the forward continuity of scattergunning. Dr. Martin considers the pull trigger, and the physical action needed to activate it, "antagonistic" to good shotgunning technique because, "changing the direction of motion — can cause a missed target." He concludes that releasing a trigger harmonizes with all the forward emphasis of wingshooting whereas pulling a trigger goes counter to the normal flow and could produce checking of the swing and trigger timing irregularities, plus flinches. The good doctor has put a lot of time and research into sports vision, and my own experiences with release triggers parallel his writings.

My favorite clay target game is low-gun skeet, but before picking up release triggers I almost gave up the sport because I often flinched a half dozen times in each 25-target round. Whereas I once scored many perfect rounds, I was suddenly shooting around 80 percent. The fun was gone; I lived in dread of the next flinch. The I realized I could use a release trigger in low-gun skeet by applying heavy trigger-hand pressure, and I immediately returned to scores near or at the 25-straight level. But that success brought me back to the earlier question, namely, why could I suddenly shoot 100 targets with a release trigger and not flinch once, only to begin flinching repeatedly whenever I removed the release trigger and replaced the original pull-type assembly? It all seemed so crazy: same gun, same load, same skeet field — and, above all, the same trigger finger — but two entirely different performances depending upon whether I released or pulled the trigger.

The thing that bothered me most was that it was the same trigger finger in each case. Darned thing wouldn't obey the command to pull, but it would almost flawlessly obey the command to release. Of course, we all know that the human body has different muscles to perform specific tasks, and that those muscles receive their mental commands through their own individual nerves. Thus, the command to pull a shotgun trigger uses different nerves and muscles than the command to release a trigger with the same finger. The question in my mind now concentrated on what might be the reason(s) why one set of commands would malfunction while the other set proceeded smoothly.

To understand the situation, we must closely examine the human nervous system and how it transmits messages to the various muscles. We must dispense with the notion that nerves are like telephone or telegraph wires that carry messages from the source to the receiver in one straight electrical shot. It doesn't happen like that at all. Mental commands are indeed electrical waves that start in the brain, but the human nervous system is *not* comprised of continuous strands of wire. Our nerves are a series of unconnected cells with definite gaps between each cell, and the mental commands proceed like electrical waves *only* when going through the body of the cell itself. When it comes to jumping the gap from one cell to another, it relies on chemical transmission. In other words, the electrical wave which is the mental command doesn't jump the gap by itself the way an electrical charge jumps the gap of a spark plug. It crosses via a chemical action. Because of this chemical function between nerve cells, I believe we can study the gaps between nerve cells and discover a plausible explanation of flinching.

The chemicals used to carry messages from one nerve cell to another are called neurotransmitters, and they are mainly composed of amino acids, which we will discuss later. Neurotransmitters are stored in a sac on the tip of a branchlike development (axon) on the nerve cell's surface. When the electrical wave or impulse travels through the cell that tiny sac bursts and releases neurotransmitters to jump the gap (synapse) and contact a receiving branch (dendrite) on the next cell. Once the neurotransmitters have carried the message across the gap, the message again dashes through the new cell like an electrical wave until it reaches the next axon, whereupon another burst of neurotransmitters are released to relay the message farther along. Thus, the mental command to fire a shotgun goes through one's nervous system in a dash-jump, dash-jump, dash-jump manner.

Now let's relate this neurotransmitter phenomenon to flinching. Given the knowledge that mental commands on their way to the trigger finger must jump gaps between nerve cells using chemical neurotransmitters, we must ask several questions: What if a shotgunner's system lacks the appropriate neurotransmitters? What if a few nerve cells along the route can't provide such chemical assistance? And what if, during the course of 100 or 200 trap or skeet targets, some axons are depleted of the proper chemicals? After all, repeating the same action over and over again can potentially exhaust certain cells' ability to supply neurotransmitters, as varying amounts of it can be de-activated by enzymes. When a cell "runs out of gas," it can't pass on the message.

In either case, a deficiency of neurotransmitters or a lack of them means the message can't travel to the trigger finger. As noted, the message cannot jump the gap by itself; it needs the chemical burst from each cell's axon. Thus, although the mental command to pull the trigger may have been given in the brain with the correct timing to hit a target, the lack of sufficient neurotransmitters in a particular cell can bring it to a halt on its way to the trigger finger. *Bingo* — a flinch!

Thus, flinching need not be naively considered a product of pain or psychological disturbances. It may well be a matter of body chemistry.

CAN WE CURE A FLINCH WITH AMINO ACIDS?

The chemical aspect of message transmission may also explain why one can shoot almost perfectly again with a release trigger whereas he flinches mightily with a pull-type trigger on the same gun. We use different (and fewer) muscles to operate a release trigger than we do a pull trigger, which means that different (and fewer) nerves are employed. The synapse phase of the release-trigger operation may not be as depleted (chemically speaking) as that of the pull-trigger operation; therefore, the mental commands to release the trigger can be carried out perfectly by the presence of adequate neurotransmitters in the fresher release nerve/muscle combinations. Too, the fact that fewer muscles are used to release a trigger than to pull it offers less chance for malfunctioning in the synapse phases.

Can we do anything to restore the nerve cell's chemistry to ensure improved motor functioning? Nutritionists believe we can, for neurotransmitters are nothing more than the amino acids previously mentioned, and amino acids are simply forms of proteins. They are foods, not medications or nasty drugs. We normally get them from the meals we eat, but, alas, no one seems to eat the necessary "balanced diet" that nutritionists always recommend. Thus, deficiencies and imbalances exist in our bodies. If that deficiency or imbalance affects the chemistry of nerve cells, it is possible that shooting commands can be thwarted by the inability of some cells to supply the necessary tiny burst of neurotransmitters. Or cells with low supplies of neurotransmitters may be exhausted in a long, repetitious clay target event.

A key to bolstering one's nervous system to avoid flinching may well be having the proper body chemistry, namely, the correct amino acids. Accepting the fact that we don't, and probably won't, eat perfectly balanced diets, we can take amino acids safely as supplements. To date, the pair that seem important to combating flinching are glycine and taurine.

Various researchers have found that glycine helps produce the low-frequency alpha waves (as opposed to the stress-type, high-frequency beta waves) which help calm a person and keep him relaxed and fluid. Perhaps more importantly, however, it also has been learned that glycine is common to the spinal column, and that a deficiency of it results in jerky, spastic actions. In one test, a researcher treated victims of spasticity with glycine, and six out of seven showed marked improvements. Might flinchers be low on glycine? Perhaps, as scientists are convinced that it impacts our motor functions and that it tends to block abnormal motor functions.

As a personal test, I began taking glycine plus a blend of other amino acids in the spring of 1988, at which time my chronic flinching was as frustrating as ever. Because of weather conditions and various family responsibilities, I didn't get to shoot for three weeks; thus, the amino acids had a chance to build up in my body. When my godson and his younger brother had their spring break from school I took them out for some trapshooting, thinking that I would coach and pull targets rather than shoot. I also took along my Merkel over/under, as it seemed to fit

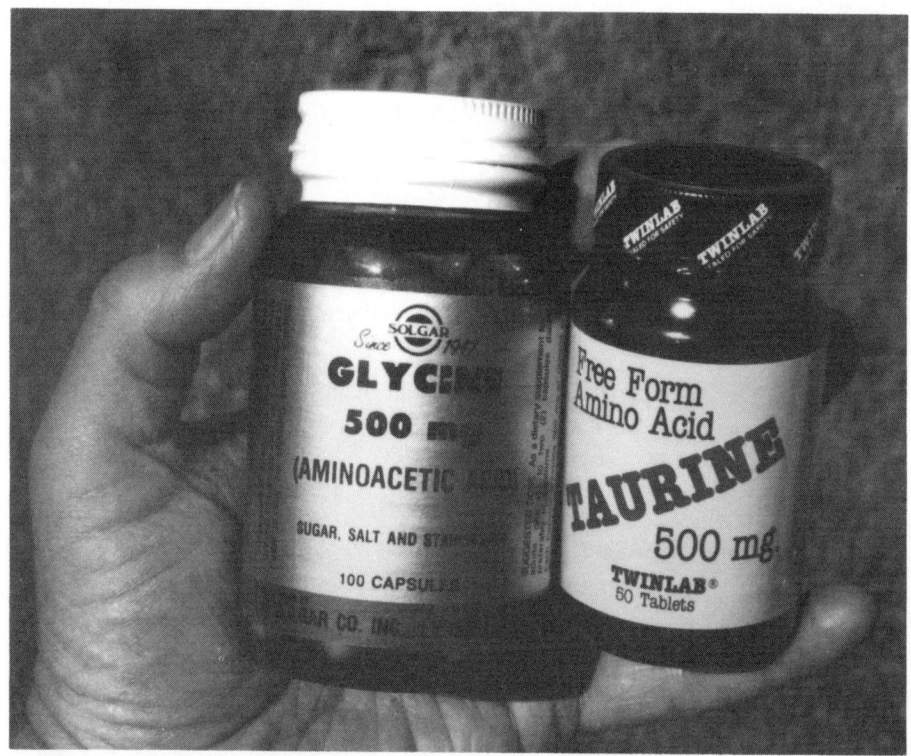

A pair of amino acids, readily available from health stores, that serve to enhance neurotransmitters in the central nervous system and combat spasticity. Other amino acids work as muscle relaxants, originators of alpha waves and inhibitors of hyper-type beta waves.

CAN WE CURE A FLINCH WITH AMINO ACIDS?

the younger boy better than the other guns we had. In the course of a morning's shooting, however, I decided to demonstrate a couple of techniques and timing points using the Merkel. Before I realized it, I had broken many targets with no thought of flinching. Everything felt so good that I got another box of shells, shot a second round and broke 25x25. I hadn't done that with a pull trigger in years. And it didn't end there...

The following week I received a consignment gun for review, and prior to working up a magazine article I fired 100 shells through it for pattern and on skeet. This included using a box of hard-kicking steel shot loads from skeet stations 3, 4 and 5. Still no flinches. I became confident that I wouldn't flinch, and the following weekend I fired 50 more shots on a simulated Sporting Clays course set up over a skeet/trap layout without flinching. A weekend later, I was still taking glycine and fired another 50 shells without a flinch in low-gun, International-style skeet, scoring 49x50 and swinging smoothly. I was as happy as a kid!

About that time I ran out of glycine and didn't replace it. I also didn't shoot for two weeks because of weather on weekends and family matters. Thus, about three weeks transpired before I got back to clay targets, and in that time I had taken no glycine. I tried a round of trap with my Merkel, got through Station 1 in good shape, but suffered a massive flinch on Station 2. The target was already settling into the grass before I got the shot away. The rest of the round was a disaster; my flinch was back, in spades. Shortly thereafter, I toured a new Sporting Clays setup and suffered another upsetting flinch on the very first stand. I felt the "yipes" while patterning, and went back to the release trigger for a brief time. The question was, of course: Was it the glycine that had eliminated my flinch for a number of weeks?

By this time, my reading into amino acids had expanded, and I started taking them again as a test. With my flinch acting up once more, this was a good time to see if it could be soothed. I took a blend of amino acids including glycine, but also added a supplement known as taurine. Basically a simple sulphur-containing compound, taurine is essential to the central nervous system, and researchers have used it successfully to combat spasticity. A main difference between taurine and glycine, however, is that taurine is found in good quantity (or at least should be) in the skeletal muscles as well as in the brain and central nervous system. (My reading indicates that taurine has been applied against seizures, such as epilepsy, with good results because it enhances neurotransmitter function. Some scientists argue that seizures occur where a person's taurine level is exceptionally low.) Thus, I tried to touch a couple of bases with glycine working in the spinal column and taurine in the skeletal muscles and central nervous system. Together, I hoped they would smooth out my motor functions.

After giving the amino acids two weeks to build up in my body, I ventured onto the trap line with a pull-triggered BT-99. I missed two birds, but didn't even come close to flinching. Was it a fluke? I went to the skeet field and broke 24x25 using the lowered gun with pull-type trigger and, once again, shot smoothly. The following day I spent 50 more shells on low-gun skeet, broke 49x50, and didn't feel a hint of a flinch. Was the flinch cured by aminos?

I gave it another week, still taking the blend with glycine and the supplemental taurine. This time, I again used the pull-triggered Model 1100 for low gun skeet, fired two rounds, and didn't draw a flinch on those 50 clays, either. The next day I fired one round of skeet and one round of trap, again going through them smoothly. As I write this chapter, I am 500 shots and counting without experiencing one flinch using pull triggers. Compared to my previous problem of flinching a minimum of 2 to 3 times per skeet or trap round, the shooting done while I was taking glycine and taurine seemed to indicate that I had at last found a partial cure. I'm extremely enthusiastic about amino acids and their potential for fighting a flinch.

The number of identified amino acids is continually growing, and research is ongoing. Besides glycine and taurine, there will undoubtedly be others to work against flinching by mitigating against stress and anxiety. They encourage the development of calming alpha waves as opposed to the upsetting beta waves and, thus, can relax the nervous system and muscles. A pair of these are tryptophan and histidine, both of which were in the blend I used in conjunction with the taurine supplement. I recommend that interested flinchers seriously study amino acid supplementation to determine the right balance for nerve/muscle relaxation. I'm sure it is partially responsible for my success in combating serial flinches per 25-target round.

In fact, there is so much to this so-called ''amino acid revolution'' that I recommend further reading for anyone before he or she follows my practice.[1] It also would be advisable to check with a professional nutritionist, because aminos are the very things they study. How do medical doctors view amino acid supplementation? The medical profession continues to be more involved with drugs, but gradually they are taking amino acids more seriously. Medical doctors, however, are seldom trained in nutrition, and most of them brush off the topic without providing any satisfaction to interested shooters.

One reason for studying amino acids is because of the complexities involved. Amino acids generally should be taken in connection with certain vitamins and minerals for optimum effectiveness. With glycine and taurine, for example, vitamins B1, B6, and B12 along with vitamin C, calcium and zinc are suggested. Carefully study which cofactors your amino acids require. Likewise, try to obtain the "free-form" aminos which are designated by the capital letter "L" (i.e., L-tryptophan). Free-form aminos are separated from the protein chains, and they are absorbed directly by the intestines without the aid of the normal digestive enzymes and acids.

The exact amino acids and their precise dosages are an individual matter, simply because each human has different chemical conditions. Each shooter may have to do some experimenting with types of amino acids and dosages. As time wears on, I seem to get perfect results by using aminos for just 2 to 3 days before I want flinch-free shooting, and the doses are not mega-sized. The point is that a shooter can't just pop any old kind of amino acid capsules and expect his particular flinch to fade away. Some personal balancing and selections are necessary. But don't worry about overdosing. Aminos are simply foods — protein. If the body doesn't need them, it excretes them like any other food or beverage. Nor do they build up into stored surpluses.

As I mentioned previously, however, it is best to study the amino acids in depth before jumping to any conclusions, as they are a sophisticated subject that is much deeper than I can detail here. For example, by themselves they are *not* carcinogens, but a few (very few) types of amino acids have been found to feed *certain* types of cancers *if* you already have that specific kind of cancer. (Hopefully, that last sentence will not be a detriment to the employment of amino acids against flinching; the aminos glycine and taurine are *not* among those few aminos which, to my knowledge, aid a cancer.)

Thus, amino acids may be the best way to battle a chronic skeet or trap flinch. Since flinching is a neurological phenomenon, the best bet is treating the nervous system chemically, for the human is a chemical animal.

Chapter Notes

1. Recommended texts follow:

    Bravermann, Dr. Eric R. and Pfieffer, Dr. Carl C., *The Healing Nutrients Within*, New Canaan, CT: Keats Publishing Inc., 1987.

    Erdmann, Dr. Robert, *The Amino Revolution*, Chicago-New York: Contemporary Books, Inc., 1987.

    Bravermann and Pfeiffer take a more analytical approach to the topic, while the Erdmann book is more casual and ebullient. The reader should approach both books with an open mind to best utilize the information offered.

Chapter 21

Changes and Refinements in Wingshooting Techniques

WHEN BARON Pierre de Coubertin successfully promoted a revival of the Olympic games in 1896, he included nearly as many shooting events as there were track events. The Baron, like many other Europeans, considered shooting a classic example of competitive sport, demanding concentration, grace, discipline, timing, steadiness and endurance. In a tournament, a shooter not only competes against others, but also measures himself or herself against perfection. To win the gold, silver or bronze is no fluke; it isn't like the twice-a-year hunter somehow managing to bag a brace of ruffed grouse in heavy cover. Olympic shooters, as well as other Olympic competitors, work on technique; their method of doing some activity in a highly skilled and efficient manner.

Perhaps because of a high school and college background in sports, especially track and field, I have always viewed shotgunning as an athletic event, be it afield or on clays. If a new method enables an Olympic shot-putter or discus-thrower to reach greater distances over former methods, and if the current bunched, hip-elevated starting style gets sprinters into their upright technique faster than the lower starting form taught in the 1920s, then isn't there room to believe that attention to and changes in details may also improve one's scattergunning? Jesse Owens was certainly a great track star and a respected gentleman, but his starting technique has been altered by modern sprinters who now run faster. In like manner, shotgun shooting techniques have changed through the years, and the new records being established indicate that they aren't all wrong.

The simple matter of gripping a shotgun, for example, has undergone changes since muzzleloaders and hammer guns were in vogue. In the past, shooters were taught a stiff, upright style, employing the shotgun like a rifle. With head held high and no shoulder lean, the shooter was instructed to aim down the barrel and pin the gun in place against his shoulder with all controlling pressure from his leading hand, which pressed the piece backward. The trigger hand did nothing more than pull the trigger; otherwise, it remained out of action, exerting no pressure whatsoever. If the shooter tracked a target, he did so by pivoting his body around his spinal axis, not by merely pushing the gun with his leading hand.

This rather static, restrained use of the hands and body has become passé with the advent of percussion ignition. As hunters took more chances at flying birds, they also began to use their hands more aggressively. That only opened another can of worms, as different opinions developed about which hand should dominate, if either, and how they should function relative to the body. Anyone who scans sporting publications of yore can come away totally confused. Some writers advocated the active use of the leading hand while minimizing the trigger hand's role; others recommended that the leading hand should do nothing more than elevate the gun while the trigger hand dominated because of its proximity to the body and its pivot. And finally, for much shotgunning, the twentieth century school of thought advocates the smooth coordinated use of both hands rather than allowing either to dominate.

Which is correct? Among astute field gunners, Olympic skeet shooters, and Sporting Clays experts, the coordinated use of both hands has become the accepted technique. In some clay target situations, however, where the shooter starts with a pre-mounted gun, such as American trapshooting and skeet, some room remains for the employment of a strong trigger hand with less emphasis on an active leading hand. Suffice it to say, however, that the aggressive, independent leading hand plays no major role in modern shotgunning methodology; its tendency to push or pull the gun away from the master eye is a classic fault, as the body seldom pivots as rapidly as an impetuous leading hand can yank, punch, poke or slash.

The British Churchill Technique

When side-by-sides were discussed in Chapter 2, I proposed that the horizontal double deserved another day stateside because American hunters didn't know how to use them the first time around. Much early American shotgunning reflected rifle shooting: Hunters aimed their guns rather than pointing them, they stood erect, the guns had exceedingly crooked stocks, and the trigger hand didn't play a coordinating role. If one carefully breaks down the self-taught style of most American bird hunters, including that of many today, he will note that it is a slow, jerky, two-part move with 1) the gun first being brought solidly to the shoulder and the head wiggled into place before 2) the swing is started after the flying mark. Watch closely on public hunting grounds, shooting preserves and firing lines around goose refuges as weekend hunters stab at birds. You'll invariably spot the two-part movement if you have any sort of eye for athletic performance. You'll also spot numerous misses as the American two-part move is horribly ineffective. (A common complaint and miscue by hunters using the jerky two-part move which brings the gun immediately to the shoulder, is that the butt gets hung up in their armpits. In athletics, this is comparable to a sprinter clumsily tripping over his starting block.)

CHANGES AND REFINEMENTS IN WINGSHOOTING TECHNIQUES

The self-taught American shotgunner normally uses a jerky two-part mount which begins with the gun being brought to the shoulder before...

SHOTGUNNING TRENDS IN TRANSITION

...the head is somehow scrunched down on the comb. This minimizes the application of eye-hand coordination and tends to leave the hunter with a static gun.

CHANGES AND REFINEMENTS IN WINGSHOOTING TECHNIQUES

The American penchant for first shouldering the gun and then bringing the face to the comb and swinging on the bird is a study in putting last things first. It spoils the assist that natural eye-hand coordination can contribute, and it fails to utilize gun/body momentum for swing smoothness and positive follow-throughs. To a large degree, the two-part movement is why so many American hunters and shotgun writers emphasize the fast-swing, alias the swing-through system of leading. This method begins with the gun behind the target and finds it racing through. The shot is delivered as the muzzle passes the mark. With the slow and awkward two-part movement, America's self-taught hunters invariably find themselves coming up behind the bird and trying to catch up!

The technique that developed vis-à-vis the classic British game gun is smoother, faster and far more efficient than the Yankee two-part debacle. It is also unknown to most stateside hunters although Bob Nichols tried to publicize it in *The Shotgunner*. Unfortunately, he renamed the footwork part of it his "minimove" method, but either Americans didn't read Nichols or weren't ready for a more sophisticated wing-gunning style. In any case, the closest that any American wingshooting theory came to the British method — which is also referred to as the Churchill method because of the way Robert Churchill's writings emphasized it — was advanced by Dr. W. F. Carver, one of America's first truly great wingshots.[1]

The British side-by-side game gun was devised to be the least amount of gun possible so that eye-hand coordination and movement weren't damped. As I detailed in both editions of *The Double Shotgun*, the form of true game guns jibes with their function of working naturally and responsively to the equalized hand action of eye-hand coordination. Rather than being comprised of two distinct parts like the American mount-first, swing-second scramble, the British/Churchill technique combines everything — point, mount, swing, forward allowance and trigger pull — into one fell swoop.

To visualize the British/Churchill method in action, we must make three assumptions: first, that the gun is started from a lowered position; secondly, that the shooter follows the advice in Chapter 18 and focuses sharply on the target at all times; and, thirdly, that the shooter knows enough to point the gun, *not* aim it by attempting to align the front bead with a matted receiver top or a rib.

With the eyes focused on the target, the gun is brought up from its lowered position by a controlled forward thrust of both hands working in tandem. The leading hand goes to the spot where the eyes are focused and zooms with the target while the trigger hand coordinates. This controlled thrust not only builds gun momentum, but it accurately aligns the bores with the eyes *and* brings the butt well forward to escape the armpit.

Now, here's the vital point: As the hands push the gun out toward the target and raise it to eye level, they and the shooter's body should already be swinging the gun in its arc which carries the muzzles to and through the target and into the lead (which the British term "overthrow"). In other words, the gun isn't solidly shouldered before it starts swinging; the swing begins and is nearly completed during the mounting dynamic as the hands flow in coordination with the eyes. Stated bluntly, the mounting move *is also* the swing. As the gun rises and comes near the shooter's shouldering location in the British style, the body should also be pivoting with the target.

The first point of gun-to-body contact in the British/Churchill method is at the cheekbone, not the shoulder. The comb meets the cheekbone to ensure quick and accurate eye-muzzle-target alignment. The shooter's on-side eye is, in reality, the shotgun's rear sight. If it isn't centered squarely atop the comb, inaccuracies inevitably will occur. However, this type of alignment does *not* mean one should sneak a quick peek at the gun's upper surface or bead; the British/Churchill method assumes a well-fitted shotgun, and getting its comb properly planted under the on-side eye should assure automatic alignment. Thus far, then, we have a bird a-wing and a shooter with both hands working equally to bring the shotgun to the cheekbone as the body pivots and the eyes remain sharply focused on the speeding gun.

The finale of the British/Churchill mounting method occurs when the butt makes contact with the shouldering hollow after first having slid under the cheekbone. The shouldering hollow is that place between the rounded shoulder (deltoid) and the collarbone where a flat spot develops when the trigger arm's elbow is elevated. Placing the butt on the rounded shoulder or well out on the deltoid or biceps, as so many Americans do, is a mistake because it forces one to strain first for eye-to-comb contact and secondly to retain it. Some trapshooters get away with mounting the gun too far out, but they enjoy the luxury of time to get perfectly set before calling the target, not to mention the fact that modern trap throws very shallow, outgoing angles that don't necessitate the wide lateral swings that live game, skeet and Sporting Clays do.

The gun is finally shouldered by a slight forward roll of the shoulders to contact the butt. This need not be a distant forward roll or movement of one's shoulder, as the gun's thrust should be moderate rather than exaggerated (as is likely in photos of the thrust-out system). Thus, one not only brings the gun to his face, but also brings his shoulder to the butt. This whole process sounds complicated, but it won't be if the shooter becomes familiar with it through dry-firing.

Now comes the part that shocks American hunters: The British/Churchill method teaches — indeed, preaches — an *immediate* trigger pull upon butt-to-shoulder contact! It assumes that the outward thrust, combined with the body pivot, generates enough gun/body accuracy and momentum to produce hit-scoring leads while the trigger pull is being commanded and executed. If the shooter delays his trigger pull to admire his lead, or if he mistakenly tries to aim the shot, he will lose the advantage of built-up gun/body momentum and coordination. British call this slowing of the swing "checking," and it invariably produces a miss.

CHANGES AND REFINEMENTS IN WINGSHOOTING TECHNIQUES

A far more efficient way to utilize eye-hand coordination for fast, accurate shotgun pointing is to extend the hands slightly toward the target as the gun comes up.

SHOTGUNNING TRENDS IN TRANSITION

Bring the comb to the face directly under the eye while keeping one's eyes always focused on the target and then . . .

CHANGES AND REFINEMENTS IN WINGSHOOTING TECHNIQUES

...complete the mounting action by rolling the shoulder into the butt while the body continues the swing which started when the eyes first saw the target and the hands began bringing up the gun. Given this gun/body stance, the first shot should be fired as soon as shoulder/gun contact occurs.

SHOTGUNNING TRENDS IN TRANSITION

The British/Churchill method, therefore, is faster and smoother than the ridiculous two-part system that most Americans teach themselves, because it combines practically everything in one compact move: Alignment is established by the hands working in unison with each other, the eyes and the body; the body pivot is started and in full swing while the gun is coming up; the forward allowance is generated as the gun and body pivot; and the shot is fired crisply just as the butt slides home while the pivot and swing continue. Only the follow-through comes after the gun has been fully mounted. If all other aspects of the swing are correct, the follow-through should be automatic (even with a relatively lightweight gun) since the body's pivot also becomes a continuing energy force.

The British/Churchill method need not be limited to close-in upland chances, of course. It also works nicely on those "tall" pheasants shot on British and European drives, and that sort of gunning closely resembles American duck and dove shooting. I have used the method with pumpguns and autoloaders on high geese and ducks with excellent results. That success apparently is due to the momentum built into the gun as it starts swinging from a lowered position and helps set off those long leads needed at 50 to 65 yards. However, one point must be made about applying the British/Churchill method to ultra-long-range wingshooting: Few hunters can generate enough swing speed to set off those longer leads unless they delay the trigger pull slightly and let some "daylight" show between the sharply seen bird and the out-of-focus muzzles. To bring this sort of shot off cleanly, one must consciously maintain the swing speed and body pivot, of course. A lightweight gun that dies and/or a shotgunner who doesn't continue pivoting will contribute to misses well behind the high bird regardless of how much daylight is seen.

The British/Churchill method is very appropriate in Sporting Clays and low-gun skeet. Sporting Clays participants who use their self-taught, two-part method always find themselves pathetically far behind the clays. One of the funniest things in shotgunning is watching a macho, know-it-all hunter work his first round of Sporting who, after having bragged about his 70-yard duck kills and 60-yard pheasants, bumbles through a 15x50 score because his gun handling routine is antiquated. Moreover, with International skeet clays leaving the houses at roughly 100 mph, there's no time to emphasize butt-to-shoulder contact before launching into a swing; the gun must be started through the target as it comes up and before it reaches the shoulder.

Before stateside shotgunners can improve their scores, then, they must honestly admit that their self-taught, two-part shotgun struggles are far from perfect. They have to forget those occasional lucky shots and make intelligent assessments on the basis of their myriad misses (which most hunters seem to forget).

Shotgunning isn't something everyone does well because he has been in the Army or because he has good eye-hand coordination with a pool cue. There is a definite technique to wingshooting, just as there is to any sport. To ignore advanced technique is to doom oneself to little more than mediocrity. Having top-drawer equipment isn't enough. You won't hit 60 home runs in the big leagues just because you have one of Babe Ruth's bats! Thus, it will require practice to learn the British/Churchill method of shotgun handling, but the practice will pay off in muscle memory so that a hunter can snap into action efficiently with speed, alignment, pivot and smoothness when game breaks cover unexpectedly or doves pass like arrows overhead. As Bob Nichols observed back in 1949, "The British have something to teach us about shooting on the wing, if only we are not too stubborn to learn." Although the British/Churchill method certainly isn't new, I haven't found anything better for compact, fast-action shotgun pointing.

Trap and Skeet Techniques

At first glance, it appears that trapshooting technique hasn't changed much, if at all, since midcentury. Shooters still stand relatively erect, their feet reasonably close together, and they take the clays on the rise. But if one looks closely, subtle alterations along with different coaching instructions are apparent.

One change in trapshooting technique focuses on footwork and leg drive. Today, with trap angles reduced by the universal acceptance of two-hole trap machine settings, most coaches teach their students and/or write their columns with an emphasis on pivoting *only* from the waist! They totally reject any footwork or leg drive. One widely traveled instructor goes so far as to have his students shoot trap while sitting on chairs, thus eliminating any assistance from the legs. In my humble opinion, such coaches are this generation's answer to a past generation's "Wrong Way" Corrigan! Besides, pivoting only from the waist seems to hinder modern shooters more than it helps them. Even with reduced target angles in trapshooting, many gunners can't swing around efficiently and/or consistently on the wider angles when their feet and legs are isolated as if they were trapped in concrete.

Before the 1970s, it was common to see the pivot-and-drive method used for all shotgun shooting. The method was discussed and illustrated in a classic booklet (now a collector's item), *Handbook on Shotgun Shooting*, as published by the Sporting Arms and Ammunition Manufacturers' Institute (SAAMI). To my knowledge, this booklet was last published in 1956. However, the same approach is outlined in *Skeet and How to Shoot It* by our old friend, Bob Nichols.

As long as we have legs, why not use them to good advantage? The pivot-and-drive technique does just that. As the SAAMI handbook pointed out, "The lower part of the body, from feet up to and including the hips, regulates lateral movement. The upper part of the body controls vertical movement." Although some lateral movement can be done from the waist up, it often proves insufficient for many trapshooters on the wider targets. To score better on the rights and lefts, therefore, trapshooters need help in obtaining more effective and efficient lateral movement than the pivot-from-the-waist-only technique provides. The pivot-and-drive method works to spin the shooter as follows:

SHOTGUNNING TRENDS IN TRANSITION

Although many trapshooting coaches today advocate swinging from the waist, the author believes that more shooters would do better if they flexed their leading knee somewhat and employed the old pivot-and-drive method for taking the wider trap angles, as illustrated by this father and son team.

CHANGES AND REFINEMENTS IN WINGSHOOTING TECHNIQUES

Assume that a right-handed shooter is at Station 5 of a trap line. His leading foot/leg tandem becomes the pivot point, and his leading knee is flexed slightly to permit rotation. This leading foot/leg also carries a slight majority of the body's weight, although exactly how much can be decided by the individual shooter. The important point is that it must bear a little more than the half-weight. When the shooter swings on a target, which we'll say is the wide right, his body will pivot on this leading limb.

How is the pivot energized? That's where the rear foot comes in. Using pressure from the ball of that rear foot, the trapshooter pushes his body around the pivot point to keep his shoulders square to the target. It's easily done, almost like a dance step, and it can be just as graceful if one practices it and muscle memory becomes established. The importance of keeping the shoulders square to the trap target, of course, is to make it easy to retain optimum eye-to-comb contact for alignment. If the shoulders don't turn with the hands and the gun, the eye will be left behind as the gun is pushed or pulled out of alignment.

Many skeet shooters already use the pivot-and-drive technique, employing an obviously wider foot placement to effect the drive power of the rear leg. This is frequently called a "straddle stance" by onlookers and is criticized by trapmen who, for whatever reasons, believe their upright postures are the only way to shoot. But if one studies the scores of many critical trapshooters, it becomes evident that their technique could use a bit of sharpening, too. So don't snicker at the pivot-and-drive technique in trap. People who can't get around perfectly on the wide rights and lefts will discover that it gets them onto those sharp angles very efficiently. A mere push with the ball of the rear foot sends the body around the leading leg, practically forcing the shoulders to remain properly square to the line of flight and directly behind the moving gun. It's a position that pivoting from the waist won't accomplish for everyone.

A trapshooter who is bungling along with low scores by swinging only from the waist, however, will find his scores jumping dramatically when he begins utilizing that part of his body which has the most influence on lateral movement — the lower half. New guns, factory loads, custom stocks, overbored barrels, chokes regulated for a certain pattern — nothing will help the trapshooter as much as a positive shoulder turn in the direction of the emerging target.

One of the most radical stances of all time in shotgunning has popped up in skeet. That's International skeet, to be precise, but it may well invade American-style skeet because it has been winning so consistently in world class competition.

This radical stance was introduced by Matt Dryke, 1984 Olympic gold medalist who has accumulated a record number of perfect 200s in the tough international discipline. No one else has done what Dryke has in low-gun skeet, and now that some of his American teammates have switched to his stance and style, they're winning, too.

The radical skeet stance in question is a veritable squat, closely resembling the way a big league catcher might pose behind home plate while waiting to catch the pitch and throw to second base. The feet are spread, the knees acutely bent, and the thighs almost parallel with the ground. The accompanying photo tells the story better than words can describe.

Why assume such a squatting position? The main theory is that it stabilizes the shooter during his fast gun handling and swing after those 100 mph targets. With the body centered between the feet, there is less chance for sway than there is in a more upright posture. The inside edges of one's feet can also be used for leverage when the pivot-and-drive mechanism is used on the major lateral swings.

The British will never endorse the American squat-stance, of course, because it is totally foreign to their additional thrust-out method involving a graceful upright attitude. But arguing with success has always been difficult, and in the case of Olympic skeet Dryke has more than proved his point.

Long-Range Wing-Gunning

Americans do more long-range wingshooting each season as waterfowling becomes concentrated around refuge systems. Gunners lie in wait along the fringes waiting for feeding or returning flights, whereupon they rise up from the marsh grasses or cattails and let drive with three quick shots, all of which normally miss. I have personally seen hunters blast away two boxes of shells in a morning and not cut one feather even though many of the birds were actually within range of steel No. 1s and BBs. In the days before steel shot became mandatory, I spent an afternoon doing photography on a farm near Wisconsin's Horicon Marsh where nearly 200,000 geese were congregated. One hunter burned up 36 two-ounce loads in his 10-gauge Magnum before he finally wing-broke a honker. He wasn't skybusting, either. The birds had mainly been in range. Like so many other modern hunters, he simply couldn't shoot a shotgun; he had absolutely no idea about long-range techniques and swing dynamics.

During the last 25 seasons or so, I've hunkered down behind goose and duck hunters who failed miserably on long-range shots, and in each case I've noted a total absence of swing speed. The scenario was almost always the same:

The birds came over, high, and therefore appeared slower than they actually were. The hunters hid until the birds were practically overhead (their first mistake). They then arose, having to shoot almost vertically. Instead of swinging aggressively with either the sustained lead or fast-swing method, they merely pointed the gun somewhere ahead of the big birds and started yanking the trigger. When nothing fell, they slowly lowered their guns and said, "Must have been too high; I sure was leading 'em."

Leading, hell! What they called a "lead" was nothing more than a poked or aimed shot with a practically static gun. Even when the hunters claimed to be

CHANGES AND REFINEMENTS IN WINGSHOOTING TECHNIQUES

A cover photo on the International Shooting Union's official magazine, the *UIT Journal International*, shows Olympic and Pan American gold medalist Matt Dryke in the "squat" stance he developed for International skeet. The widely spread feet and low center of balance provide stability, and the shooter can use the inside edges of his feet for pivoting leverage.

SHOTGUNNING TRENDS IN TRANSITION

leading by 15 feet, their wads and shot strings churned air well behind the target bird which was cruising deceptively fast. It all looked too easy. They thought they could squint down the rib and fold one like they shoot beer cans off a fence post. More importantly, many such hunters apparently know absolutely nothing about the athletics of shotgun swinging; they are sheer herky-jerky shotgun drivers.

The most vital element in long-range wing-gunning is gun speed. Birds at long range only look slow. Indeed, if one stands in an airport and watches a Boeing 747 land well out on the runway, it looks as if that monster is floating gently to earth. If one stood alongside that runway, however, he'd realize that the 747 has considerable air speed as it whistles past. So, too, with high birds; they must move right along or they would stall and fall. Thus, the shotgun must swing aggressively ahead of a bird and continue into a positive, equally crisp follow-through. If at any point the hunter slows his swing, the bird will catch up to the muzzle quickly and negate whatever forward allowance has been generated.

Very few hunters can apply the sustained lead in its purity on long-range targets. Their swing is too slow relative to the target's speed, and there is an almost universal tendency for them to stop or slow at trigger pull, thereby losing some or all of the forward allowance. Likewise, most typical hunters have difficulty setting off the 12 to 20-foot leads using the sustained lead method because of the visual gap between target and muzzle blur. They don't feel comfortable unless the target is riding the front bead like a bullseye rides a rifle's front blade; consequently, they check to ensure precise alignment and lose all semblance of a true, aggressive swing.

The fast swing or swing-through method, which teaches that the gun should start behind the bird and swing through it with the trigger being tapped as the muzzle passes the bird, also fails most hunters when used in its purity. Few hunters, if any, can swing fast enough to develop a 12 to 20-foot lead while the trigger is being pulled and the load's lock/barrel times take place. It is my feeling, however, that most hunters will be more successful if they start their swings on long-range targets by coming from behind, since that provides initial alignment with the target and the need to swing rapidly. Once that swing speed is produced, it can be utilized in a method I've termed the "extended fast swing."

Essentially, the extended fast swing is the basic swing-through method with a delayed trigger pull that lets the gun speed up and move further ahead of the target before the shot is fired. The exact amount of delay will depend upon each hunter's swing speed and trigger timing, of course. It is interesting, however, to note how universally well hunters seem to do when they let three to four feet of daylight appear before pulling the trigger while stroking crisply ahead of the target and continuing into an overthrow and a follow-through. Hunters who know their swing is the slow, tracking type may need twice as much daylight. Personally, I would suggest that hunters who have a poor birds-to-shells ratio on long-range shots not only try the extended fast swing method, but also get in some dry-firing practice to enhance coordination at a higher rate of swing speed. The truly good shots almost always admit that they don't know how far they're leading distant birds because they're swinging too fast. On the other hand, bum wingshots can tell you exactly how much they led a target when they missed, since their guns track at a hesitant, pedestrian rate.

The extended fast swing isn't really new, of course. Even before World War II, Nash Buckingham was writing about a variant of it. Buckingham advocated selecting a spot ahead of the bird and swinging through it rather than the primary target to get that extra forward allowance. That may have worked for Buckingham, but I would sooner follow the advice to keep my eyes sharply on the target rather than looking ahead of it.

Whatever method a shotgunner uses for his long-range wing-gunning, however, he is advised to get that piece moving as the birds approach instead of waiting for them to get directly overhead. Time and distance are needed to build gun speed and momentum, and neither is available when the gun is merely poked vertically at overhead targets. In other words, don't lie in wait until the birds are directly atop the blind as so many hunters do. Take them coming or passing with a longer, speed-building swing. Moreover, don't stop the first swing to admire the forward allowance or to observe the results of the shot. Keep swinging through the recoil, never slowing. If any change is made, let it be to the faster side. Most misses are behind the target, and continuing into the second shot with added swing speed often scores even though inexperienced hunters may initially believe the second shot was recklessly thrown. It is the gun speed that scores. Many hunters are their own worst enemies because they have never learned to handle a smoothbore with smooth, swift, graceful and athletic technique.

How does one develop a faster swing? Back off an additional 10 yards from stations 3, 4 and 5 on any skeet field and practice. That's about a 30-yard shot, and the forward allowances for it are significantly greater than the $3\frac{1}{2}$ to four-footers normal from said stations. Unfortunately, few hunters employ skeet practice, which is clearly indicated by their shooting performance.

Hunters who do choose to hone their skills will realize that the name of the game is technique, and technique comes from an in-depth study of wingshooting's mental and physical requirements. The most modern guns and loads won't help a hunter one bit unless he or she learns how to make good, solid, coordinated swings based on sound fundamental technique rather than dumb luck. The place to learn is the skeet field. Today, many would advocate Sporting Clays as the game for hunting practice, but skeet is a far better training ground for those who must still grapple with fundamentals.

Chapter Notes

1. As Charles Askins Sr., summarized in *The American Shotgun* (1910), "Shooting a shotgun in the Carver fashion, in its primary principle, is merely training the two hands to point at the exact spot at which the eyes are looking or the brain directs, without any lost motion or focus upon sights."

    Some authorities propose that Carver's method evolved out of the eye-hand coordination employed by frontier gunfighters who thrust from the hip, but one is inclined to wonder how much a well-traveled and astute shooter like Carver was influenced by the evolving British method to which he was obviously exposed.

Chapter 22

New Traditions: The Changing Nature of Hunting and Gunmaking

IT WAS A grassy, vine-entwined fence that separated the woodlot from the cornfield. A bit to the west the land dropped off sharply and angled down to a long cattail swale that curved like a big question mark around another cornfield. If you headed north from the top of the question mark, you would climb through a hillside thorn apple thicket before emerging into a broad, weedy field where pheasants nested in the spring. There were normally some Hungarian partridge around, too, plus ubiquitous cottontails and a few fox squirrels in the woodlot.

All of that was within a 10-minute walk of my home when I began hunting, and it was traditional for the kids thereabouts to cut their hunting teeth in those covers. I bagged some of my first ringnecks there; blooded my spanking new 20-gauge pump along the fence when a flock of Hungarians popped from the frost-speckled headland of the cornfield; and tumbled any number of cottontails. In the summer, I called in more than a few crows, taking them as they skimmed the woodlot.

The best part of it was, of course, that nobody complained about trespassing, or about hunting, or about kids with shotguns. It was a long-established tradition. The fence line was forever.

Or so it seemed, for all of that preceded post-World War II "progress" and the population explosion that changed the world. The fence row is gone now, replaced by a four-lane bypass that swings around an ever-expanding city. Nobody ever plants corn in the fields anymore. In fact, the fields are mainly housing developments. The spot where I dropped those first Hungarian partridge with my then-new 20 gauge is now somebody's neatly furnished dining room. And the weed-grown field where pheasants used to court and nest is now a shopping mall with its black-topped parking lot covering a full city block. There probably hasn't been a pheasant or partridge hatch in the area for over five years, and what cottontails remain live under the hedges of the houses. The crows and starlings have multiplied like crazy, but I'd have some sheriff's deputies or the city police down on me posthaste if I let go with two *caws* from a crow call thereabouts.

SHOTGUNNING TRENDS IN TRANSITION

The old traditions have died. Their demise was joined by the convenience that children and their parents had of free hunting near home, of wandering the fields, of running a dog, of just plain being outdoors and operating in a hunting mode. Oh, free public hunting isn't totally dead, of course, but the signs point toward that direction and the prognosis isn't favorable. In some states, especially those on the East Coast and Texas, land access is extremely limited; free public hunting there is non-existent. In other areas, state governments have established public hunting grounds, but in reality those public places are nothing but competitive free-for-alls with gangs of hunters crisscrossing and spraying shot wildly. There can be no doubt that, with the shrinkage of hunting space without a similar decline of hunters, the trend will be toward controlled hunting on state and federal lands for many species.

At one point or another, hunters will abandon the sport. Already, with small game bags and limited excitement, the number of hunters has not been increasing. Stateside gunmakers agree that they no longer have an expanding market, and their marketing strategy has changed: Instead of making one or two basic models for universal hunting, they are designing specialty models to fit individual niches. They hope to sell more of these specialized sporting arms to those hunters who remain active and become more sophisticated about matching equipment to challenges. But fewer hunters don't solve the problem of available land.

Nor does it solve the problem of low game bird populations in those areas where agricultural chemicals have wiped out native birds, and where industrial pollutants have been another contributing factor to poor nesting and/or negative carryover. When agricultural chemicals kill the insects and weeds which young birds depend upon for early protein, there is little hope for natural reproduction. Indeed, agricultural chemicals may not poison mature birds directly, but indirectly they destroy the necessary food chain. Finally, the introduction of pen-raised pheasants into many areas has probably weakened local strains and left them vulnerable to winter and predation. If pheasants are to make a comeback in the Midwest, they will have to be of a hardier strain, and they will have to be kept free of potentially weakening interlopers.

But despite the loss of land area, and despite not having any native pheasant populations to speak of, the enthusiastic hunters in my area have been bagging more pheasants, mallards and quail than they did in the good ol' days. New traditions are developing. In this case, they are called hunting preserves. These outdoor institutions are correctly named, of course: A hunting preserve's role is to preserve hunting. Without them, many geographical areas of our nation would be without an outlet for the hunting and wingshooting urge. There would be no places for fathers to instruct kids, to enjoy their growing up, their companionship. There would be no scenes of pointers locking up or of black Labs springing eagerly to the retrieve. There would be no laughs after misses, no congratulations after hits, no spectacular shots. Beginners would have a difficult time finding the thrills

NEW TRADITIONS: THE CHANGING NATURE OF HUNTING AND GUNMAKING

and challenges of the hunt and the shot. And the peaceful contentment of smelling gun smoke drifting on the still air of a snappy morning would be lost to eternity. Thus, the hunting preserve has become an established part of American hunting, and it will undoubtedly become more vital as added lands are lost to agricultural and commercial exploitation.

Predation is another problem for the modern hunter. At one point in *The Shotgunner*, Bob Nichols tells of spending a September day gunning migrating hawks from a blind. Throughout most of the 1940s and 1950s the ranking outdoor magazines promoted crow shooting and fox hunting. Since that time, however, laws have been enacted to protect predators. Schoolchildren are taught that predators aren't bad, that they take very few game birds and rabbits, and that they feed mainly on field mice. Perhaps some species are heavy feeders on mice and other vermin, but many species of hawks and owls feed on mice only when game isn't available. Watch an area where pheasants are planted by the state prior to opening day, and you'll see hawks congregate.

In the days of Aldo Leopold, it was fashionable to believe that game could hold its own if it were given adequate habitat; however, habitat has been continually reduced, and a high population of predators now zeros in on increasingly smaller coverts with devastating results.

Observations made by the Wisconsin Department of Natural Resources proved that, in an experimental area, over 60 percent of the game (pheasants) was killed by avian and mammalian predators in a two-year period. Areas that I watch closely have had most of their game killed in the spring by owls and foxes foraging for their young. Thus, we now have an abundance of legally protected predators. (This parallels the problem of human criminals having more rights than the victims.) Departments of Natural Resources in many states recognize this loss to predation, but are faced with the problem of trying to reverse the popular dictum that hawks, owls and foxes aren't "bad." Until predation is brought into line with game supplies and land area, resources that could contribute to sport and the national economy continue to be lost. Instead of protecting the nest-robbing crow, the international treaty covering migratory birds should place a price on its black head!

In days past, when I was just beginning to roam that vine-entwined fence row, the commercial hunting preserve wasn't held in very high esteem. Hunters of the 1920s, 1930s and 1940s wouldn't hear of paying to hunt birds. They likened that to something unethical. Their feelings were understandable because those generations equated hunting with the lingering frontier traditions where it was a cheap way to feed one's family. But history tells us that frontiers don't last forever. Observe, for instance, the formerly great land masses of Africa and South America where environmental and political confusion now exists. Indeed, those people who think solely in terms of meat hunting, of making a hunting license "pay for itself," are disappearing from the sport.

SHOTGUNNING TRENDS IN TRANSITION

Those who remain in hunting and wingshooting gradually are revamping their attitudes and understand that today's and tomorrow's bird hunting and wing-gunning have become costly sports and are no longer cheap or easy meat procurement practices. If an individual doesn't like that, he is free to sell his gun and leave the sport; the world will not turn back time for him. Once hunting is based on pure sporting (rather than on a nonsensical "harvest" basis), it can again be productive, action-packed and thrilling. The main point is that today good wingshooting costs money. That may offend some people, but is there any sport today that *doesn't* cost money — often much more than clay target shooting and commercial preserve hunting? Bowling isn't free, nor is golf, tennis or racquetball. Set on the same plane, bird hunting will have a bright, continuing future, but hunters must learn to pay their way. They cannot expect to hunt freely on someone else's land and kill birds at no or low cost.

If any nation epitomizes the changes that can occur when people adjust to the cost of shotgunning, it is England. In many respects, this island race is experiencing a tremendous explosion in the shotgun sports, from bird hunts on smaller farms to Sporting Clays. The surge is documented in the 1988 *Gun Digest* by Sidney DuBroff's "Revolution in Britain."

The same phenomenon could easily happen in the United States. Hunting and shooting are far from dead stateside despite incursions by land developers, highway commissions and threats from animal rights, anti-hunting and anti-gun groups. The British have always had somewhat more restrictive firearms legislation and far less available land then Americans, but that hasn't kept them from enjoying their Glorious Twelfth or from building over 500 Sporting Clays courses! When sportsmen are willing to pay for their games, amazing things happen.

The important point is that the current generation of British sportsmen apparently think shooting and hunting are worth the price; they're willing to pay. Indeed, once that mental/financial block is overcome, any nation's shooting sports will expand again. That could happen when America's farmers quit complaining and offer good, controlled hunting rather than threatening to call the sheriff on trespassers. But before that occurs, hunters must learn that land and game have value. The main problem in the U.S. will be keeping the prices within reason.

Trends in Gunmaking

It is interesting to note that when hunting shifts from free public access to a fee structure (be it land-use payments, per bird pricing or club membership), it can also impact shotgun selection and marketing. Obviously, these changes force new gunmaking trends. If the situation can be generalized, it would indicate that higher quality guns are in greater demand and that hunters have become more sophisticated and want specialized equipment for each phase of their wing-gunning. At the root of these market forces is the fact that people who can still afford pay-as-you-go bird hunting and clay target shooting are in advanced income levels, have higher educations and are willing to pay for quality.

NEW TRADITIONS: THE CHANGING NATURE OF HUNTING AND GUNMAKING

During the period when I was interested in competitive skeet shooting I attended a tournament in Ohio where I met a man who ran a small gun shop. There was no way he could have made a living from that store, he maintained, because nobody bought standard field-grade guns anymore due to the decline in free public hunting thereabouts. He observed, however, that most of his gun sales were in the fancier grades. His theory was that few people entered hunting when game was scarce, and that his customers were dedicated people who hunted commercial preserves and took a sophisticated approach to their sport. Hunters from the middle and upper income groups didn't mind paying for advanced equipment of their sport's other expenses. It's comparable to buying a Cadillac when a battered Volkswagen will also get one across town — some sportsmen simply appreciate higher quality, be it in the form of a gun or a day afield. They will support the market of the future.

Tomorrow's gun market will become one of high-quality pieces and specialized "niche" guns. Gun owners are less likely to have one all-around shotgun in the corner. They are more likely to be multiple-gun owners with advanced grades designed and built especially for each type of shooting. Gunmakers realize that their market is no longer expanding and that they will not find large numbers of people entering the sport; consequently, their marketing strategy is not pointed toward broad sales of basic models as it was prior to 1970 to 1975. Instead, they now concentrate on selling more than one gun to each sportsman to make up for the loss of overall expansion. This strategy demands specialty items — upland guns, waterfowl models, advanced grades, Sporting Clays designs, and new concepts in skeet and trap guns — which appeal to the sophisticated gunner. Luckily, current technology can handle the new marketing strategy. Computers and robotics are revolutionizing gunmaking, and companies can now realize profits on shorter runs of variations.

Modern technology has taken gunmaking to the seemingly incongruous state of making shotguns faster *and* better. Normally, a traditionalist would equate speed with mistakes and less quality, but that's changing. The Japanese actually showed the sporting world how to combine technological production advances with fine workmanship to produce guns which, inside and out, are excellent examples within their price ranges.

There are, however, some operations that computers and robots can't do that remain exceedingly important to shotgun quality: They don't conjure up the initial design concepts; they don't punch in their own figures; and they don't perform the final assembly and finishing. Those are human tasks, and savvy designers teamed with careful assemblers and finishers, working with precisely made parts can indeed fashion current shotguns which are more than a match for the older production-line guns of the postwar period of the mid-1960s to the early 1980s.

This was the time when many American gunmakers had financial difficulties as they began to bump heads with the Japanese. Outfits like Winchester (Olin), Harrington & Richardson, Ithaca and High Standard all saw their ledgers covered

SHOTGUNNING TRENDS IN TRANSITION

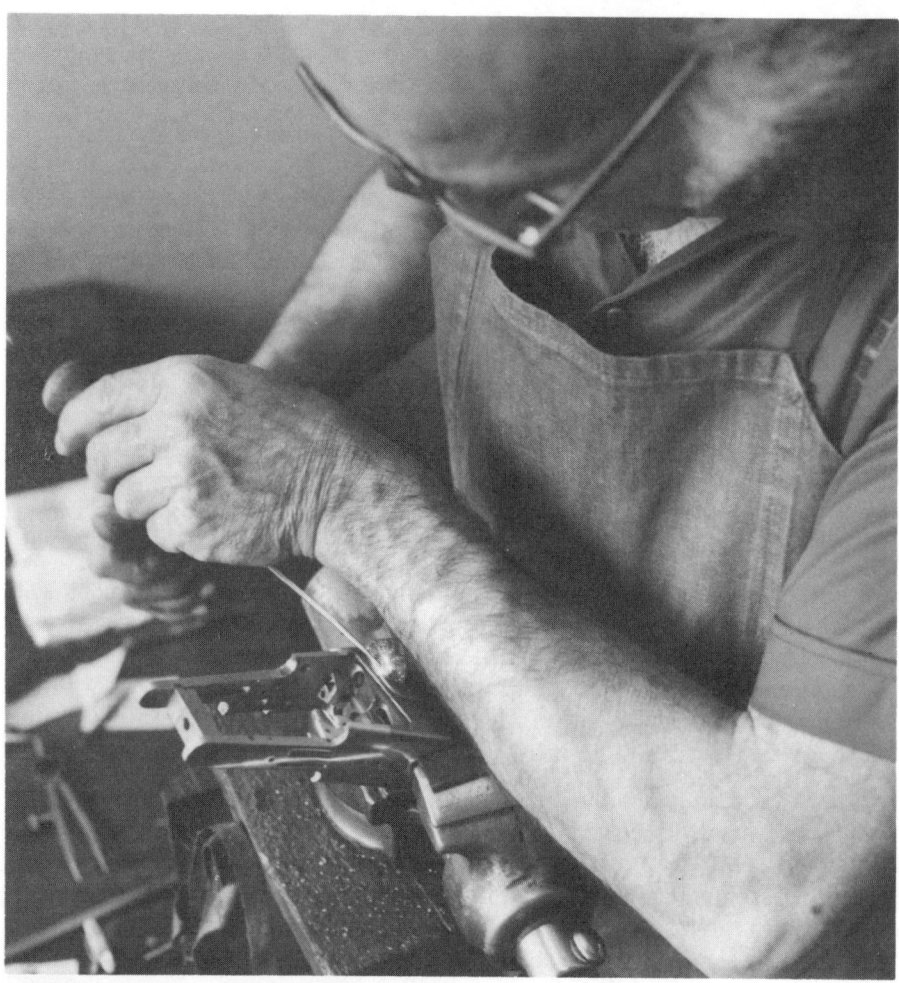

Because the changing nature of hunting will gradually eliminate the meat hunters who want cheap guns, the author believes that the market for high-quality shotguns will increase as those who can still afford to hunt and shoot will seek out advanced gun dynamics and artistry.

NEW TRADITIONS: THE CHANGING NATURE OF HUNTING AND GUNMAKING

Believe it or not, this is the heart and soul of a modern gun shop. It's the computer deck of Remington's new Flexible Machining System, which not only reduces machining time but improves precision.

with red ink because they stuck with older manufacturing methods in a dwindling and competitive market.

Meanwhile, guns like the Japanese-built SKBs, Winchester 101s and some Brownings continued to attract attention. In general, the Japanese weren't only doing it cheaper, they were doing it better! Guns like the higher grades of the Citori, the B-SS Sidelock, the Winchester models 101 and 23 (which have recently become the property of a new firm, Classic Doubles International) and the Miroku, were of considerable quality. To a sharp shotgunner, quality is still the name of the game. American gunmakers who tried to hold their prices by cheapening their pieces lost their followings. Thus, the 1960s, 1970s and some of the 1980s may well have been considered the "Dark Ages" for American gunmaking.

Stateside gunmaking isn't out of the financial woods yet, but manufacturers have begun to understand their current market and, to a degree, are utilizing the newest technologies. Remington has joined the battle with foreign gunmakers by installing a $10 million computerized machining line which, serviced by a robot, expedites the precision cutting of shotgun receivers. Developed by Cincinnati Milacron and known as the Flexible Machining System (FMS), this setup hastens gun production without sacrificing one iota of precision. In fact, precision is enhanced. Whereas it once took Remington roughly 16 hours to machine a Model 870 receiver as it passed through the various milling machines, the FMS layout does it in just five hours. Moreover, the Coordinated Measuring Machine, which checks the finished product's dimensions after cutting, measures to .0002 inch! It will be interesting to see what Remington can do with their gun line if they apply the FMS to their new over/under or, say, to a lower-priced version of their born-again Parker side-by-side.

Computers are now vital to gun designers. They not only speed up gun design, but reduce the time it takes to design all the tooling needed for production. A rough guesstimate indicates that such computerized assistance shaves at least 40 percent from design times, which saves a gunmaker money and gets the new concept into production much faster to serve a special demand.

I see no stigma attached to the use of modern technologies in shotgun making. The important thing is the quality of the final product. The idea that guns *must* be completely hand-made is faulty. Such pieces are definitely works of art, one-of-a-kind examples of the handcraftsman's skills. We will continue to cherish them, thrill to them, wish we had enough money to buy more of them (or even one of them), but components cut by a machine can be just as accurate, if not more so. A machine can repeat its precision — a human can't.

Thus, the nature of modern gunmaking is changing, but not away from skills and quality as it was in the 1960s and 1970s. The current trend is returning to skills and greater quality, although they may not be the same skills which produce that quality. In today's successful company, computer experts dominate, not

This cross-shaped device can measure to .0002-inch. Shown here, it is checking a freshly machined Remington 870 receiver.

file-wielding roughers and finishers. And I don't mind one bit if the resulting gun is responsive, looks nice, strokes the high goose from the October sky, and swings smoothly through a 25-straight.

But I would still like to own a handmade Purdey, Powell or Holland & Holland — and I'd like just one more chance to hunt that grassy, vine-entwined fence that separated the woodlot from the cornfield, then dropped down to the long cattail swale that curved like a big question mark around another cornfield! Just one more chance.